G present simple and continuous, action and non-action verbs
V food and cooking
P short and long vowel sounds

Do you drink a lot of coffee?

Yes, but I'm trying to cut down at the moment.

1A Mood food

1 VOCABULARY food and cooking

a Do the quiz in pairs.

FOOD QUIZ

Can you think of...?

ONE red fruit, **ONE** yellow fruit, **ONE** green fruit

TWO kinds of food that some people are allergic to

THREE kinds of food that come from milk

FOUR vegetables that you can put in a salad

FIVE containers that you can buy food in

SIX things that people sometimes have for breakfast

b ➤ **p.152 Vocabulary Bank** *Food and cooking.*

c (**1 4**》) Listen to these common adjectives to describe food. Do you know what they mean? Then say one kind of food which we often use with each adjective.

| fresh | frozen | low-fat | raw | spicy | takeaway | tinned |

2 PRONUNCIATION short and long vowel sounds

a Look at the eight sound pictures. What are the words and sounds? What part of the symbol tells you that a sound is long?

1		squid chicken spicy grilled	5		sausages roast chocolate box
2		beef steamed beans breakfast	6		raw fork boiled salt
3	æ	prawns salmon lamb cabbage	7		cook sugar mushrooms food
4		margarine carton jar warm	8	uː	cucumber beetroot fruit duck

b Look at the words in each list. Cross out the word which *doesn't* have the sound in the sound picture.

c (**1 5**》) Listen and check.

d ➤ **p.166 Sound Bank.** Look at the typical spellings of the sounds in **a**.

3 LISTENING & SPEAKING

FOOD & EATING

1 Is there any food or drink that you couldn't live without? How often do you eat / drink it?

2 Do you ever have
   a ready-made food?
   b takeaway food? What kind?

3 What's your favourite
   a fruit?
   b vegetable?
   Are there any that you really don't like?

4 When you eat out do you normally order meat, fish, or vegetarian?

5 What food do you usually eat
   a when you're feeling a bit down?
   b before doing sport or exercise?
   c before you have an exam or some important work to do?

a (**1 6**》) Listen to five people talking. Each person is answering one of the questions in *Food & Eating* above. Match each speaker with a question.

4	Speaker A		Speaker D
	Speaker B		Speaker E
	Speaker C		

b Listen again and make notes about their answers. Compare with a partner.

c Ask and answer the questions with a partner. What do you have in common?

4

Christina Latham-Koenig
Clive Oxenden

ENGLISH FILE

Intermediate Student's Book

Paul Seligson and Clive Oxenden are the original co-authors of
English File 1 and *English File 2*

OXFORD
UNIVERSITY PRESS

Contents

4 READING

a Are the foods in the list **carbohydrates** or **proteins**? With a partner, think of four more kinds of food for each category.

cake   chicken   pasta   salmon

b With a partner, answer the questions below with either **carbohydrates** or **proteins**.

What kind of food do you think it is better to eat…?
- for lunch if you have an important exam or meeting
- for breakfast
- for your evening meal
- if you are feeling stressed

c Look at the title of the article. What do you think it means? Read the article once to find out, and to check your answers to **b**.

d Read the article again. Then with a partner, say in your own words why the following people are mentioned. Give as much information as you can.

1 Dr Paul Clayton
2 people on diets
3 schoolchildren
4 Paul and Terry
5 nightclub owners in Bournemouth

e Find adjectives in the article for the verbs and nouns in the list. What's the difference between the two adjectives made from *stress*?

stress (*noun*) (x2)   relax (*verb*)   wake (*verb*)
sleep (*verb*)   power (*noun*)   violence (*noun*)
oil (*noun*)

f Ask and answer the questions with a partner.

1 What time of day do you normally eat protein and carbohydrates? How do they make you feel?
2 How often do you eat chocolate? Does it make you feel happier?
3 After reading the article, is there anything you would change about your eating habits?

Mood food

We live in a stressful world, and daily life can sometimes make us feel tired, stressed, or depressed. Some people go to the doctor's for help, others try alternative therapies, but the place to find a cure could be somewhere completely different: in the kitchen.

Dr **Paul Clayton**, a food expert from Middlesex University, says 'The brain is affected by what you eat and drink, just like every other part of your body. Certain types of food contain substances which affect how you think and feel.'

For example, food which is high in carbohydrates can make us feel more relaxed. It also makes us feel happy. Research has shown that people on diets often begin to feel a little depressed after two weeks because they are eating fewer carbohydrates.

On the other hand, food which is rich in protein makes us feel awake and focused. Research has shown that schoolchildren who eat a high-protein breakfast often do better at school than children whose breakfast is lower in protein. Also, eating the right kind of meal at lunchtime can make a difference if you have an exam in the afternoon or a business meeting where you need to make some quick decisions. In an experiment for a BBC TV programme two chess players, both former British champions, had different meals before playing each other. Paul had a plate of prosciutto and salad (full of protein from the red meat), and his opponent Terry had pasta with a creamy sauce (full of carbohydrate). In the chess match Terry felt sleepy, and took much longer than Paul to make decisions about what moves to make. The experiment was repeated several times with the same result.

Another powerful mood food could become a secret weapon in the fight against crime. In Bournemouth in the south of England, where late-night violence can be a problem, some nightclub owners have come up with a solution. They give their clients free chocolate at the end of the night. The results have been dramatic, with a 60% reduction in violent incidents.

Why does chocolate make people less aggressive? First, it causes the brain to release feel-good chemicals called endorphins. It also contains a lot of sugar, which gives you energy, and can help stop late-night tiredness turning into aggression. These two things, together with a delicious taste, make chocolate a powerful mood changer.

Mood food – what the experts say
- Blueberries and cocoa can raise concentration levels for up to five hours.
- Food that is high in protein helps your brain to work more efficiently.
- For relaxation and to sleep better, eat carbohydrates.
- Dark green vegetables (e.g. cabbage and spinach) and oily fish (e.g. salmon) eaten regularly can help to fight depression.

Adapted from a British newspaper

5 LISTENING & SPEAKING

a Ask and answer the questions with a partner.

RESTAURANTS

1 How often do you eat out?
2 What's your favourite...?
   a kind of food (French, Italian, etc.)
   b restaurant dish
3 How important are these things to you in a restaurant? Number them 1–4 (1 = the most important).
   ☐ the food
   ☐ the service
   ☐ the atmosphere
   ☐ the price
4 Have you ever tried English food? What did you think of it?

b **1 7))** Read the text about Steve Anderson. Then listen to **Part 1** of an interview with him, and number the photos in the order he mentions them.

c Listen again. Why does he mention each thing?

d **1 8))** Now listen to **Part 2** and answer the questions.

1 What does he say is the best and worst thing about running a restaurant?
2 What's the main difference between British and Spanish customers?
3 What kind of customers does he find difficult?
4 How does he think eating habits in Spain are changing?

e What about you? Answer the questions with a partner.

1 What was your favourite food when you were a child?
2 Is there anything that you like / don't like cooking?
3 In your country, when people eat out would they normally tell the chef what they really think about the food?
4 Do you know anyone who is a 'difficult customer' in restaurants?

A

STEVE ANDERSON has always had a passion for food. He was first taught to cook by his mother, who is half Burmese. After studying physics at university, he got a holiday job helping on a cookery course in Italy, where he met several famous chefs. One of them, Alastair Little, later employed him as a trainee chef. Two years later he moved to Valencia in Spain and opened a restaurant, *Seu Xerea*, now one of the most popular restaurants in town.

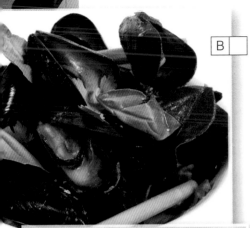

B

C

D

E

F

6 GRAMMAR
present simple and continuous, action and non-action verbs

a **1 9))** Listen again to some of the things Steve said. *Circle* the form of the verb he uses.

1 This week for example *I cook | I'm cooking* nearly every day. We *usually close | are usually closing* on Sundays and Mondays, but this Monday is a public holiday.

2 The British always *say | are saying* that everything is lovely.

3 Actually, I think *I prefer | I am preferring* that honesty, because it helps us to know what people like.

4 Unfortunately, I think *they get | they're getting* worse. People *eat | are eating* more unhealthily.

b With a partner, say why you think he has chosen each form.

c ► **p.132 Grammar Bank 1A.** Learn more about the present simple and the present continuous, and practise them.

d Make questions to ask your partner with the present simple or continuous. Ask for more information.

On a typical day
- What / usually have for breakfast?
- / drink Coke or fizzy drinks? How many glasses / drink a day?
- Where / usually have lunch?
- What / usually have for lunch during the week?
- / ever cook? What / make?
- / prefer eating at home or eating out?

At the moment / nowadays
- / need to buy any food today?
- / want anything to eat right now? What?
- / take vitamins or food supplements at the moment?
- / try to cut down on anything at the moment?
- / the diet in your country / get better or worse?

7 SPEAKING

WHAT DO YOU THINK?

1 Men are better cooks than women.
2 Both boys and girls should learn to cook at school.
3 Cheap restaurants usually serve bad food.
4 On a night out with friends, where and what you eat isn't important.
5 Not all fast food is unhealthy.
6 Every country thinks that their cuisine is the best in the world.

a **1 13))** Listen to two people discussing sentence 1. Who do you agree with more, the man or the woman? Why?

b **1 14))** Listen to the phrases in the **Useful language** box. Copy the intonation.

> **O Useful language: Giving your opinion (1)**
> I agree.   I'm not sure.   For example...
> I don't agree.   (I think) it depends.   In my opinion...

c In small groups, say what you think about sentences 2–6. Try to use the **Useful language** phrases.

G future forms: present continuous, *going to, will / won't*
V family, adjectives of personality
P sentence stress, word stress, adjective endings

Are you seeing your grandparents this weekend?

No, I'm going to stay at home. I'll probably see them next weekend.

1B Family life

1 VOCABULARY & SPEAKING
family

a Look at some photos showing family members. What's happening in each one? What do you think the relationship is between the people?

b With a partner, explain the difference between each pair.

1 a father and a parent
2 a mother and a stepmother
3 a brother and a brother-in-law
4 a grandfather and a great-grandfather
5 a nephew and a niece
6 a child and an only child
7 your immediate family and your extended family

c The BBC recently did a survey of 21st-century families in the UK. Read *Changing – for the better?* and try to guess what the missing percentages are. Choose from the list.

| 17% | 26% | 60% | 75% | 85% |

d (1 15)) Listen and check. Do any of the statistics surprise you? Which ones do you think would be very different if the survey was carried out in your country?

e Work in small groups. Say what you think and give reasons.

> ### Do you think that...?
> - families should have a meal together every day
> - children should leave home as soon as they can afford to
> - parents should charge their children rent if they live at home and have a job
> - parents should be 'friends' with their children on social networking sites, e.g. *Facebook*
> - elderly parents should live with their children when they are too old to live alone

> 🔍 **Useful language:**
> **Giving your opinion (2)**
> We often use *should* + verb to say what we think is the right thing or a good thing (to do), e.g.
> *I think families **should have** dinner together every day because...*
> *I don't think parents **should be** friends with their children on Facebook because...*

Changing – for the better?

Family life is changing in the UK – but not in the way we might think. When the BBC did a survey of families in Britain, they expected to find that family relationships were suffering because of the decline in traditional family structures.

However, some of the results were quite surprising...

58% of men and **39%** of women aged 20–24 still live at home with their parents.

1 _____ think that it is right for parents to charge rent to children over 25 who have a job and are living at home.

30% use the internet at least once a week to contact their families.

On average, adults live **130** kilometres from their parents.

2 GRAMMAR future forms

a (1 16)) Listen to three dialogues between different family members. Who is talking to who (e.g. brother to sister)? What are they talking about?

b Listen again and match two sentences with each dialogue (1–3).

A ☐ Shall I make you a cup of tea?
B ☐ You'll drive too fast.
C ☐ I'm not going to go to university yet.
D ☐ I'm staying the night there.
E ☐ I'll drive really slowly.
F ☐ It's going to be cold tonight.

c With a partner, decide which sentence (A–F) is...

☐ a plan or intention   ☐☐ a prediction   ☐ an offer
☐ an arrangement   ☐ a promise

d ➤ p.133 Grammar Bank 1B. Learn more about future forms and practise them.

3 PRONUNCIATION sentence stress

> 🔍 **Sentence stress**
> An important aspect of speaking English is stressing the words in a sentence which carry the information, and not stressing the other ones. This will help you to communicate better and to speak with good rhythm.

a (1 21)) Listen to the rhythm in these three dialogues.

> 1 A Are you **coming home** for **dinner tonight**?
>   B **No.** I'm **going out** with my **friends.**
> 2 A **What** are you **going** to **do** in the **summer**?
>   B We're **going** to **rent** a **house** with my **sister** and her **husband.**
> 3 A Do you **think** they'll **have children soon**?
>   B I **don't think** so. **Not** for a **few years anyway.**

b Practise them with a partner. Copy the rhythm.

c Ask and answer the questions below. Give as much information as possible.

ARE YOU...?
• having dinner with your family tonight
• or is anyone in your family getting married soon
• doing something with a family member this week
• visiting a relative this weekend

ARE YOU GOING TO...?
• have a new nephew or niece soon
• have a big family get-together soon
• go on holiday with your family this year
• buy a present for a member of your family this month

DO YOU THINK...?
• the number of people getting divorced will go up or down in the future
• the birth rate will go up or down in your country
• anyone in your family will live to be 90 or more
• you will move away from (or back to) the area where your family live

4 (1 22)) SONG Our House ♫

95% of people say that they have a close family.

2 _____ of people have a meal with their immediate family every day.

3 _____ say that their families never argue.

4 _____ have family members who they don't speak to any more.

5 _____ think that families should look after grandparents.

 75% of people are happiest with their families.

 17% are happiest with friends.

5 READING

a Which do you think has more advantages, being an only child, or having brothers and sisters? Why?

b Work in pairs. **A** read *The younger brother*, **B** read *The only child*.

c Tell your partner about 1 and 2 below. Whose childhood sounds happier?

   1 other family members who are mentioned

   2 how the writer's experience as a child affects him / her now

d Look at the highlighted words in the two texts. Try to work out their meaning from the context. Then match them with definitions 1–12.

  1 _____ *adj* ill

  2 _____ it's no surprise that

  3 _____ *noun* competition between two people

  4 _____ *noun* the time when you were a child

  5 _____ *noun* a meeting of people, e.g. family

  6 _____ *noun* people who are fully grown

  7 _____ *adj* knowing about or being conscious of sth

  8 _____ *noun* a school where children can live during the year

  9 _____ *verb* think that sb or sth is important

  10 _____ *verb* divided sth between two or more people

  11 _____ *verb* try to hurt sb else

  12 _____ *noun* a group of friends

> 🔍 **each other**
> *When brothers and sisters get older they value **each other** more.*
> Use *each other* to talk about an action between two people or groups of people, e.g. *I don't get on very well with my dad – we don't understand **each other**.*

e Talk to a partner. Do you have brothers and sisters, or are you an only child? Do you feel positive or negative about it?

Younger brother **or** only child?
HOW WAS IT FOR YOU?

THE YOUNGER BROTHER
NOVELIST TIM LOTT

Rivalry between brothers is normal, but there was a special reason for the tension between us. I was very ill when I was born, and spent three months in hospital with my mother. My brother did not see her at all during that time, as he went to stay with an aunt. When our mother returned home, it was with a sick newborn baby who took all the attention. No wonder he hated me (although if you ask Jeff, he will say that he didn't – we remember things differently).

My brother and I were completely different. We shared the same bedroom, but he was tidy, and I was really untidy. He was responsible, I was rebellious. He was sensible, I was emotional. I haven't got any positive memories of our childhood together, though there must have been good moments. Jeff says we used to play Cowboys and Indians but I only remember him trying to suffocate me under the bedcovers.

My relationship with Jeff has influenced my attitude towards my own four daughters. If the girls fight, I always think that the younger child is innocent. But the good news about brothers and sisters is that when they get older, they value each other more. Jeff is now one of my best friends, and I like and admire him greatly. For better or for worse, we share a whole history. It is the longest relationship in my life.

THE ONLY CHILD
JOURNALIST SARAH LEE

I went to boarding school when I was seven, and the hardest thing I found was making friends. Because I was an only child, I just didn't know how to do it. The thing is that when you're an only child you spend a lot of your time with adults and you're often the only child in a gathering of adults. Your parents go on living more or less the way they have always lived, only now you are there too.

I found being an only child interesting because it gave me a view of the world of adults that children in a big family might not get. And I know it has, at least partly, made me the kind of person I am – I never like being one of a group, for example. If I have to be in a group, I will always try to go off and do something on my own, or be with just one other person – I'm not comfortable with being one of a gang.

My parents are divorced now and my mother lives in the US and my father in the UK. I feel very responsible for them – I feel responsible for their happiness. I'm the closest relative in the world to each of them, and I am very aware of that.

Adapted from a British newspaper

6 VOCABULARY
adjectives of personality

a Without looking back at *The younger brother* text, can you remember who was *tidy, responsible, and sensible* and who was *untidy, rebellious, and emotional*? Do you know what the adjectives mean? Would you use any of them to describe yourself?

b ➤ **p.153 Vocabulary Bank** *Personality.*

c Write down the first three adjectives of personality that come into your head. Don't show them to your partner. Now go to ➤ **Communication** *Personality p.104.*

7 PRONUNCIATION
word stress, adjective endings

a **1 26**)) Underline the stressed syllable in these multi-syllable adjectives. Listen and check.

1 jea|lous an|xious am|bi|tious
   ge|ne|rous re|be|llious

2 so|cia|ble re|li|a|ble

3 re|spon|si|ble sen|si|ble

4 com|pe|ti|tive tal|ka|tive
   a|ggre|ssive sen|si|tive

5 un|friend|ly in|se|cure
   im|pa|tient i|mma|ture

b Listen again and answer the questions.

1 Is **-ous** pronounced /aʊs/ or /əs/?
2 Is **-able** pronounced /əbl/ or /eɪbl/?
3 Is **-ible** pronounced /əbl/ or /ɪbl/?
4 Is **-ive** pronounced /əv/ or /ɪv/?
5 Are **-ous** | **-able** | **-ible** | **-ive** stressed?
6 Are **un-** | **in-** | **im-** stressed?

8 LISTENING & SPEAKING

a What's your position in the family? Are you the oldest child, a middle child, the youngest child, or an only child?

b **1 27**)) Look at the cover of Linda Blair's book. Now listen to a journalist talking about it on a radio programme. Complete the chart by writing four more adjectives of personality in each column.

Oldest children	Middle children	Youngest children	Only children
sensible	relaxed	outgoing	self-confident

c Compare with a partner. Then listen to the four sections one by one. Check your answers. What reasons or examples does the journalist give?

d Look at the completed chart above. In pairs, say…

...if you think it is true for **you** – and if not, why not?

...if you think it is true for **other people** you know (your brothers and sisters, friends, etc.)

9 WRITING

➤ **p.113 Writing** *A description of a person.* Write a description of a friend you know well.

1 ◼◄ INTRODUCTION
VIDEO

a Look at the photos. Describe Jenny and Rob.

b (1 28)) Watch or listen to Jenny and Rob talking. Complete the gaps.

Jenny Zielinski and Rob Walker work for a ¹_____ called *New York24seven*. She's American and he's ²_____. Rob came to New York a few ³_____ ago. He had met Jenny when she went to ⁴_____ on a work trip. They got on very well, and he was offered a job for a month in ⁵_____. Later he was offered a ⁶_____ job. Jenny helped Rob ⁷_____ an apartment, and they are enjoying life in the USA, although Rob misses his friends and ⁸_____.

> 🔍 **British and American English**
> *apartment* = American English
> *flat* = British English

2 ◼◄ REACTING TO WHAT PEOPLE SAY
VIDEO

a (1 29)) Watch or listen to Jenny introducing Rob to her parents. What bad news does Rob have for Jenny? What good news does Jenny have for her parents?

> 🔍 **British and American English**
> *mom* = American English
> *mum* = British English

b Watch or listen again and mark the sentences **T** (true) or **F** (false). Correct the **F** sentences.
   1 Rob left the chocolates at the office.
   2 Rob's desk is usually very tidy.
   3 It's the second time that Rob has met Jenny's parents.
   4 Sally has prepared a big dinner.
   5 Jenny's new job is Managing Director.
   6 Jenny is going to be Rob's manager.

c (1 30)) Look at some extracts from the conversation. Can you remember any of the missing words? Watch or listen and check.

1 **Jenny** Don't forget the chocolates.
   Rob   OK. Oh _____!
   Jenny I don't _____ it. Don't tell me you forgot them?
   Rob   I think they're still on my desk.
   Jenny _____ kidding.

2 **Jenny** Mom, I'm really sorry – we bought you some chocolates, but we left them at the office.
   Sally What a _____. _____ mind.

3 **Jenny** But I also have some good news.
   Sally _____? What's that?

4 **Sally** So you've got a promotion? _____ fantastic!
   Harry That's great _____!

5 **Sally** Let's go and have dinner.
   Jenny What a _____ idea!

d (1 31)) Watch or listen and repeat the phrases in the chart below. Copy the rhythm and intonation.

REACTING TO WHAT PEOPLE SAY

What you say when you hear...	
something surprising	You're kidding. I don't believe it.
something interesting	Really?
some good news	How fantastic! That's great news! What a great idea!
some bad news	Oh no! What a pity. Never mind.

> 🔍 *How* + adjective, *What* + noun
> We often use *How* + adjective or *What* + noun to respond to what people say.
> *How interesting! How awful! How amazing!*
> *What a pity! What a good idea! What terrible news!*

e Practise the dialogues in **c** with a partner.

f 👥 ➤ **Communication** *How awful! How fantastic!* **A** *p.104* **B** *p.109.*

3 📹 HARRY FINDS OUT MORE ABOUT ROB
VIDEO

a (1 32)) Watch or listen to the after dinner conversation. Does the evening end well or badly?

b Watch or listen again and answer the questions.
1 What university did Jenny go to?
2 Is Harry impressed by Rob's job? Why (not)?
3 What does Harry like doing in his free time?
4 Who are most of the photos in the dining room of?
5 Who are Miles Davis, John Coltrane, and Wynton Marsalis?
6 What surprises Harry about Rob?

c Look at the **Social English phrases**. Can you remember any of the missing words?

Social English phrases	
Harry	How do you _____ your career?
Rob	Not _____. I'm more of a writer.
Rob	Oh, you know, interviews, reviews, _____ like that...
Rob	I _____, I like photography.
Harry	That's _____ most of them are of Jenny.
Harry	How _____!
Rob	Well, he's a really nice _____.
Harry	Go _____, son!

d (1 33)) Watch or listen and complete the phrases.

e Watch or listen again and repeat the phrases. How do you say them in your language?

> 👤 **Can you...?**
> ☐ react to good news, bad news, unexpected news, and interesting news
> ☐ introduce yourself and other people
> ☐ use phrases which give you time to think, e.g. *you know, I mean*, etc.

G present perfect and past simple
V money
P the letter *o*

Have you paid the phone bill yet?

Yes, I paid it yesterday.

2A Spend or save?

1 VOCABULARY money

a (1 34))) Listen to a song about money. Complete the gaps with phrases A–G.

A a material world
B comes with a fee
C foot the bill
D for free
E paper or plastic
F shopping sprees
G with money

b Listen again and read the lyrics. Which phrase (A–G) means…?

1 _____ rich
2 _____ cash or credit cards
3 _____ you have to pay for it
4 _____ pay the bill
5 _____ that you don't have to pay for
6 _____ buying a lot of things at one time
7 _____ a consumer society

c What do you think the song is saying? Do you think it is…?

• very cynical
• sad, but sometimes true
• offensive to women (and men)

d ➤ p.154 **Vocabulary Bank** *Money*.

Girls & Boys

Educated, ¹_____
He's well-dressed
Not funny
And not much to say in
Most conversations
But he'll ²_____ in
All situations
'Cause he pays for everything

Girls don't like boys, girls like cars and money
Boys will laugh at girls when they're not funny

³ _____
Don't matter
She'll have it
Vacations
And ⁴_____
These are a few
Of her favourite things
She'll get what she wants
If she's willing to please
His type of girl
Always ⁵_____
Hey, now, there's nothing ⁶_____

Girls don't like boys, girls like cars and money
Boys will laugh at girls when they're not funny
And these girls like these boys like these boys like these girls
The girls with the bodies like boys with Ferraris
Girls don't like boys, girls like cars and money

All of these boys, yeah get all of these girls
Losing their souls in ⁷_____

2 PRONUNCIATION the letter o

a Can you remember which word rhymes with *money* in the song *Girls & Boys*?

b Look at some more words with the letter *o*. Put them in the correct column.

clothes	cost	dollar	done	honest	loan	money	note
nothing	owe	shopping	some	sold	won	worry	

c (1 38)) Listen and check.

d Look at some words with the letters *or*. How is *or* normally pronounced when it's stressed? Which two are different?

afford	order	worth	organized	mortgage	store	work

e (1 39)) Listen and check.

f Practise saying these sentences.

Let's go shopping for clothes.
Can I borrow some money?
He won a million dollars.
They can't afford to pay the mortgage.
I work in a store.
I've done nothing wrong.

3 READING & SPEAKING

a Read the questionnaire and choose your answers.

b Compare your answers with a partner. Say why.

c ➤ **Communication** *Spender or saver? p.104*. Find out if you are a spender or a saver.

4 LISTENING

a (1 40)) Listen to six people answering the question *Are you a spender or a saver?* How many are savers?

b Listen again and match speakers 1–6 with A–F. Who…?

A ☐ always has money in the bank
B ☐ often ends up with no money
C ☐ thinks he / she is careful with money, but not mean
D ☐ enjoys spending money on his / her hobby
E ☐ can save money if he / she needs to
F ☐ prefers to live now than worry about the future

ARE YOU A **SPENDER** OR A **SAVER**?

1 **You go shopping and you see something very expensive that you really want, but can't afford. You…**

  a buy it with your credit card. You can worry about the bill next month.
  b already have some money in the bank and plan to save for a couple of weeks and then buy the thing you want.
  c borrow the money and agree to pay back a small amount every week.

2 **You get £100 for your birthday. You…**

  a spend some of it and save some.
  b go straight to a shopping centre and spend it all.
  c put all of it in your bank account until you know what you want to spend it on.

3 **Do you always know how much money you have, how much money you have spent, and on what?**

  a Yes. I'm very organized and know exactly what I have and what I've spent.
  b No. I haven't got a clue. When I have money I usually just spend it.
  c I usually have a rough idea about what I spend my money on.

4 **You've borrowed some money from a friend, but you don't think that you'll be able to pay it back by the time you promised to. You…**

  a don't worry about it. Hopefully your friend will forget about it too!
  b work out how much money you have and how much you owe. You speak to your friend and explain the situation and offer to pay the money back in small instalments.
  c speak to your friend and promise that you'll pay him / her back, but it might take a bit longer than you first thought.

5 **You have a friend who often borrows money from you and never pays it back. He / she wants to borrow £50. You…**

  a lend him / her the money. You can afford it and it doesn't matter if you don't get it back.
  b say no; he / she owes you too much already.
  c lend the money, but explain that it is the last time, until he / she has paid back this loan.

5 GRAMMAR present perfect and past simple

a Read the conversation. What are they arguing about?

b (1 41)) Read the conversation again and put the verbs in the present perfect or the past simple. Then listen and check.

David I ¹*haven't seen* (see) those shoes before. Are they new?
Kate Yes. I ² _____ (just buy) them. Do you like them?
D They're OK. How much ³ _____ they _____ (cost)?
K Oh, not much. They ⁴ _____ (be) a bargain. Under £100.
D You mean £99.99. That isn't cheap for a pair of shoes. Anyway, we can't afford to buy new clothes at the moment.
K Why not?
D ⁵ _____ you _____ (see) this?
K No. What is it?
D The phone bill. It ⁶ _____ (arrive) this morning. And we ⁷ _____ (not pay) the electricity bill yet.
K Well, what about the iPad you ⁸ _____ (buy) last week?
D What about it?
K You ⁹ _____ (not need) a new one. The old one ¹⁰ _____ (work) perfectly well.
D But I ¹¹ _____ (need) the new model.
K Well, I ¹² _____ (need) some new shoes.

c Do we use the present perfect (**PP**) or past simple (**PS**)...?

1 for a completed action in the past _____
2 for recent actions when we don't ask / say exactly when _____
3 in sentences with *just*, *yet*, and *already* _____

d ➤ p.134 Grammar Bank 2A. Learn more about the present perfect and past simple, and practise them.

e In pairs, interview each other with the questions. Ask for more information.

HAVE YOU EVER...?

- bought or sold something on eBay or a similar site
- lost a credit card or your wallet
- saved for something for a long time

What?

- wasted money on something you've never used

- won any money (e.g. in a lottery)
- lent money to someone who didn't pay you back

When?

- bought something online and then discovered that it was a scam
- been charged too much in a restaurant

How much?

What happened?

Have you ever bought or sold something on eBay?
Yes, I sold my old computer.

Who did you sell it to? How much did you sell it for?

6 READING & SPEAKING

a In pairs, answer the questions. Give as much information as you can.

1 Think of two people you know personally or have heard of who are very rich. Did they…?
 a earn their money (how?)
 b inherit their money (who from?)
 c win it (how?)

2 If they earned their money, was it because…?
 a they were very lucky
 b they worked very hard
 c they had a special talent

b Now read an article about a millionaire. How did he become so rich? Why is his success surprising? How did he make his daughter proud of him?

c Now read the article again and number the events in the order in which they happened.

A ☐ He became a millionaire again.
B ☐ He learnt to read and write.
C ☐ He lost all his money.
D ☐ 1 He sold old clothes in the market.
E ☐ He opened a department store.
F ☐ He won an important prize.
G ☐ He opened a small clothes shop.
H ☐ He became a millionaire.
I ☐ He sold clothes in the market again.
J ☐ He wrote his autobiography.
K ☐ His shop was on the front page of a newspaper.

d What do you think you can learn from Jeff's story?

e Look at the highlighted words and phrases related to money and business. With a partner, try to work out the meaning from the context.

f Complete the questions with one of the highlighted words and phrases. Then ask and answer the questions with a partner.

1 When was the last *recession* in your country? How long did it last (has it lasted)?

2 Do you know anybody who works as a _____? What does he (she) sell? Does he (she) enjoy his (her) job?

3 If you were completely _____, who would you ask to lend you some money?

4 Have you ever bought something the first day it _____? What?

5 Do you know anybody who has _____ on their own? Is it successful?

THE MILLIONAIRE WITH A SECRET

Jeff Pearce was a successful businessman – but he had a secret: he couldn't read or write.

His name is not really Jeff. His mother changed it because he could never spell his real name, James, and she thought Jeff was easier.

Pearce was born in Liverpool in the 1950s, in a very poor family. At school, all the teachers thought he was stupid because he couldn't learn to read or write – at that time, not many people knew about dyslexia. But there was something that he was good at: selling things. Pearce's first experience as a salesman was when he was a boy, and he and his mother used to go door-to-door asking for old clothes that they could sell in the market. He instinctively knew what people wanted, and it soon seemed that he could make money from anything. His mother always believed in him and told him that one day he would be successful and famous.

In 1983, when he already owned a small boutique, he decided to invest £750 in leather trousers, and to sell them very cheaply in his shop. 'It was a bit of a gamble, to tell you the truth,' he says. But Liverpool loved it, and there were photos of shoppers sleeping in the street outside his boutique on the front page of the local newspaper. The first day the trousers went on sale, the shop took £25,000. Jeff became a millionaire, but later he lost most of his money in the recession of the Nineties. He was almost 40, and he was broke again. He even had to go back to selling clothes in the market. But he never gave up, and soon he set up a new business, a department store, called *Jeff's*, which again made him a millionaire.

However, success didn't mean anything to Jeff because he still couldn't read or write. Even his two daughters did not realize that their father couldn't read. When one of them asked him to read her a bedtime story he went downstairs and cried because he felt so ashamed. At work he calculated figures in his head, while his wife Gina wrote all the cheques and read contracts.

In 1992 Pearce was awarded a Businessman of the Year prize for the best clothes store in Liverpool. It was at this moment that he told his friends and colleagues the truth, and decided to write a book about his experience. But first he had to learn to read and write. He went to evening classes, and employed a private teacher, but he found it very difficult because of his dyslexia. Finally, with the help of a ghost-writer*, his autobiography, *A Pocketful of Holes and Dreams*, was published, and became a best-seller. Recently, he was woken in the middle of the night by someone knocking on his front door. It was his daughter to whom he hadn't been able to read a bedtime story all those years earlier. She had come to tell him that she had just read his book. 'Dad, I'm so proud of you,' she said – and burst into tears in his arms.

*a **ghost-writer** is somebody who writes a book for another person

Adapted from The Times

G present perfect + *for* / *since*, present perfect continuous
V strong adjectives: *exhausted, amazed,* etc.
P sentence stress, stress on strong adjectives

How long have you been working here?

For a long time! Since 2001.

2B Changing lives

1 LISTENING

a Look at the photos. Where do you think they were taken? What can you see in each photo?

b (1 45》) You are going to listen to an interview with Jane, talking about a trip she made in 2008. Listen to **Part 1**. Where did she go? What did she decide to do after the trip?

c Listen again. What does Jane say about:

1 her normal job
2 the holiday to Uganda
3 what happened when the lorry broke down
4 the condition of the school
5 the children
6 what the headmaster asked her for

d (1 46》) Now listen to **Part 2**. Correct the wrong information in these sentences.

1 Jane's son chose the name *Adelante África,* which means 'Go forward, Africa' in Spanish.
2 The new school opened in 2012.
3 Today the school has 75 children.
4 *Adelante África* has also been trying to improve the children's English.
5 They are building a home for the teachers.
6 Two of Jane's children have been helping in Uganda.
7 Jane says the school has changed children's lives because it has given them an education.
8 Jane thinks that she gives more than she gets.
9 The website has a video Jane's daughter took of her teaching the children.

e Compare your answers with a partner. Then listen again to check.

f Do you know anybody like Jane who does a lot of work for a charity? What do they do?

2 GRAMMAR present perfect + *for* / *since*, present perfect continuous

a Match the questions and answers.

1 How long has Jane been a writer? _____
2 How long has *Adelante África* had a website? _____
3 How long has she been working for *Adelante África*?

_____

A Since 2008.
B For about 22 years.
C For four years.

b Answer with a partner.

1 Are the three questions and answers in **a** about…?
   a a period of time in the past
   b a period of time from the past until now
   c a period of time in the present
2 What's the difference in form between the first two questions and question 3?

c ➤ **p.135 Grammar Bank 2B.** Learn more about the present perfect with *for* / *since* and the present perfect continuous, and practise them.

3 PRONUNCIATION sentence stress

a (1 49)) Listen once and try to write down the stressed words in the large pink rectangles.

1 *How*   *long*   *learning*
  French   ?

2

   .

3   ?

4   .

5   ?

6

   .

b Look at the stressed words and try to remember what the unstressed words are. Then listen again to check and write them in.

c Listen again and repeat the sentences. Copy the rhythm.

d (1 50)) Listen and make questions.

)) *It's snowing.* (*How long has it been snowing?*

4 SPEAKING

a Look at the circles, and write something in as many as you can.

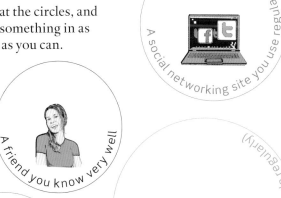
A social networking site you use regularly

A friend you know very well

A sport you play regularly (or a kind of exercise you do regularly)

The car / motorbike / bike you have

The place where you live

A gadget you have which is very important for you

A bar or restaurant you often go to

An organization, club, gym, etc. you are a member of

Something you are learning (to do)

b Compare circles with a partner. Ask your partner at least three questions about the things they've written. One question must be *How long have you…?*

How long have you been using Twitter? (*For about a year.*

Do you write things on it or do you just read other people's tweets?

Why did you buy a Nissan Juke? (*Because it's small, and it's quite 'green'.*

How long have you had it?

5 READING & LISTENING

a In your country, are there charity events to raise money for a good cause? Have you ever taken part in one? What did you do? How much money did you raise?

b You're going to read an article about Helen Skelton, who agreed to kayak down the Amazon for charity. Read the introduction and answer the questions.

1 What did Helen do last year for charity?
2 What is she hoping to do this year?
3 What is dangerous about the trip?
4 What experience does she have?

c Before you read the texts of Helen's first three phone calls, imagine what kind of problems you think she had on her journey. Then read and check. Were you right?

d (1 51))) Read **Phone calls 1–3** again and complete the gaps with the correct word. Then listen and check.

1	a in front	b behind	c back
2	a freezing	b hot	c boiling
3	a exhausted	b angry	c lost
4	a down	b up	c over
5	a long	b wide	c short
6	a ice cream	b coffee	c chocolate
7	a sleep	b paddle	c rest
8	a boring	b interesting	c worrying
9	a being	b feel	c feeling
10	a sick	b well	c hard

e (1 52))) Now listen to the rest of Helen's journey down the Amazon. Did she manage to finish?

f Listen again. Then answer the questions.

Phone call 4

1 Why hasn't she had any music for three days?
2 What does she do to pass the time?
3 Why didn't she celebrate reaching the halfway point?

Phone call 5

4 What have been driving her mad this week?
5 What wildlife has she seen?
6 Why is she starting to feel a bit sad?

The 6.00 news

7 How many kilometres did she do altogether?
8 How long did the journey take?
9 What did Helen miss?
10 What is the first thing she is going to do when she gets home?

g Tell your partner about an adventure sport you've done, or an exciting experience you've had. Was it a positive experience? Why (not)? How did you feel?

TV presenter's Amazon

Helen Skelton hopes to become the first woman to kayak down the Amazon River.

Helen Skelton is a 26-year-old TV presenter of Blue Peter, a BBC programme for young people. She has never been afraid of a challenge. Last year she became the second woman to complete the 78-mile Ultra Marathon in Namibia, running the three consecutive marathons in 23 hours and 50 minutes. But when Blue Peter decided to do something to raise money for the charity Sports Relief (which sponsors projects in the UK and abroad) Skelton said that she wanted an even bigger challenge. So they suggested that she kayak 3,200 kilometres down the Amazon from Nauta in Peru to Almeirim in Brazil.

This is a very risky trip. There are no roads, no towns, only rainforest and the river (which is sometimes more than 40 kilometres wide and infested with crocodiles). If she falls ill, it will take around 11 hours to fly her to a hospital.

Adapted from The Telegraph website

Phone call 1

66 Everything went wrong. I only managed half a day on Wednesday, the first day, and on Thursday we started late, so I'm already ¹_____. I've been suffering from the heat. It's absolutely ²_____, and the humidity is 100% at lunchtime. I went the wrong way and I had to paddle against the current. I was ³_____! They asked me, 'Do you want to give ⁴_____?' but I said, 'No!' Because I've also been having a wonderful time! There are pink dolphins – pink, not grey – that come close to the boat. I think that if I can do 100 kilometres a day, then I can make it. 99

challenge

Helen has only been kayaking once before in her life, so she has been training four hours a day. Last week she arrived at the Amazon in Peru. After two days kayaking she made the first of her phone calls to the BBC.

GUYANA

Almeirim

Amazon

B R A Z I L

Phone call 2

❝I've been on the Amazon for a week now, and I've been paddling for six out of the seven days. The river is incredibly ⁵_____, and it's very hard to paddle in a straight line. The water is so brown that I can't see my paddle once it goes under the surface. It looks like melted ⁶_____. I start at 5.30 in the morning, and I ⁷_____ for at least ten hours, from 5.30 a.m. until dark, with only a short break for lunch. My hands have been giving me problems – I have big blisters. I now have them bandaged in white tape.

I'm usually on the water for at least ten hours; it's ⁸_____ at times, exciting at others. I listen to music on my iPod. I've been listening to *Don't Stop Me Now* by Queen to inspire me! ❞

Phone call 3

❝I haven't been ⁹_____ very well this week. The problem is heat exhaustion. They say it's because I haven't been drinking enough water. I've been travelling 100 kilometres a day, which is my target. But yesterday after 84 kilometres I was feeling ¹⁰_____, and my head was aching and I had to stop and rest. ❞

6 VOCABULARY & PRONUNCIATION
strong adjectives

> 🔍 **Strong adjectives**
> Some adjectives have a strong meaning, e.g.
> *I had to paddle against the current. I was **exhausted**!* (= very tired)
> *I've had a **fantastic** time!* (= very good)
> With strong adjectives you can use *absolutely* or *really*, but NOT ~~very~~.
> *I've been suffering from the heat. It's **absolutely boiling**.* NOT ~~very boiling~~.

a Complete the sentences with a normal adjective.

1 **A** Was Lisa's father _angry_ about the car?
   B Yes, he was **furious**!
2 **A** Is Oliver's flat _____?
   B Yes, it's really **tiny** – just a bedroom and a sitting room.
3 **A** Are you _____ of flying?
   B Yes, I'm **terrified**! I never fly anywhere.
4 **A** Was the food _____?
   B Yes, it was **delicious**.
5 **A** Are you very _____?
   B I'm **starving**! I haven't eaten all day.
6 **A** Is your parents' house _____?
   B It's **enormous**. It has seven bedrooms.
7 **A** Was it _____ in Moscow?
   B It was **freezing**! Minus 20 degrees.
8 **A** Was Jack's kitchen _____?
   B It was **filthy**. It took us three hours to clean it.
9 **A** Are your parents _____ about the wedding?
   B They're **delighted**. In fact, they want to pay for everything!
10 **A** Was the film _____?
   B It was **hilarious**. We laughed the whole way through.
11 **A** Are you _____ you locked the door?
   B I'm **positive**. I remember turning the key.
12 **A** Were you _____ to hear that Ted is getting married?
   B I was absolutely **amazed**! I never thought it would happen.

b (1 53)) Listen and check. How are the strong adjectives pronounced? Practise the dialogues in pairs.

c ▶ **Communication** *Are you hungry?* **A** *p.104* **B** *p.109.*

d Ask and answer with a partner. Ask for more information.

1 Have you ever been swimming in a place where the water was absolutely freezing?
2 Is there anything that makes you furious about car drivers or cyclists in your country?
3 Are there any animals or insects that you're terrified of?
4 What's the most delicious meal you've had recently?
5 Is there a comedian or a comedy series on TV in your country that you think is absolutely hilarious?

7 WRITING

▶ **p.114 Writing** *An informal email.* Write an informal email to thank somebody you have been staying with and to tell them what you have been doing recently.

GRAMMAR

Ⓒircle a, b, or c.

1 My sister _____ fish or seafood.
   a doesn't like   b don't like   c doesn't likes

2 I have a quick breakfast because _____ in a hurry.
   a I usually   b I usually am   c I'm usually

3 I _____ TV when I'm having a meal.
   a never watch   b don't never watch
   c am never watching

4 I usually drink a lot of diet Coke, but at the moment _____ to cut down.
   a I try   b I'm trying   c I'm triing

5 _____ any brothers or sisters?
   a Are you having   b Are you have   c Do you have

6 What _____ when you leave school?
   a you are going to do   b are you going do
   c are you going to do

7 I can't see you this evening because _____ some friends.
   a I'm meeting   b I meet   c I'll meet

8 A Would you like something to drink?
   B Yes, _____ an orange juice, please.
   a I have   b I'm having   c I'll have

9 A I can't open this jar.
   B _____ help you?
   a Shall I   b Will I   c Do I

10 That's a lovely dress. Where _____ it?
   a have you bought   b did you buy
   c did you bought

11 _____ good at saving money.
   a I've never been   b I haven't never been
   c I've never

12 I got $50 for my birthday, but I _____.
   a didn't spend it yet   b haven't spent it yet
   c yet I haven't spent it

13 I've had this computer _____.
   a for about three years   b since about three years
   c for about three years ago

14 A How long _____ in Paris?
   B Since last March.
   a is he living   b has he living   c has he been living

15 _____ the same gym for five years.
   a I'm going to   b I've been going to   c I go to

VOCABULARY

a Ⓒircle the word that is different.

1	prawns	mussels	duck	squid
2	lamb	crab	beef	pork
3	cherry	pear	peach	beetroot
4	raspberry	cucumber	pepper	cabbage
5	fried	baked	chicken	roast

b Write the opposite adjective.

1 honest   _____   4 hard-working   _____
2 mean   _____   5 quiet   _____
3 selfish _____

c Write verbs for the definitions.

1 to spend money on sth that is not necessary   _____
2 to receive money from sb who has died   _____
3 to get money by working   _____
4 to get money from sb that you will pay back   _____
5 to keep money so that you can use it later   _____

d Write the strong adjectives.

1 tired   _____   3 cold   _____   5 angry   _____
2 hungry _____   4 dirty _____

e Complete the phrasal verbs.

1 Shall we eat _____ tonight? I don't feel like cooking.
2 I'm allergic to milk, so I have to cut _____ dairy products from my diet.
3 We live _____ my salary. My wife is unemployed.
4 I'll lend you the money if you promise to pay me _____.
5 I took €200 _____ of my bank account.

PRONUNCIATION

a Ⓒircle the word with a different sound.

1	peach	steak	beef	steamed
2	money	bossy	positive	cost
3	roast	sociable	owe	account
4	filthy	bill	tiny	chicken
5	afford	pork	worth	organized

b Underline the stressed syllable.

1 sal|mon   3 i|mma|ture   5 sen|si|ble
2 in|vest   4 de|li|cious

CAN YOU UNDERSTAND THIS TEXT?

a Read the newspaper article once. How much did winning the lottery change Tony Bryan's life?

Life-changing, or is it...?

You win the lottery. Do you buy a 10-bedroomed mansion, a gold-plated yacht and a Picasso? Or do you just live a bit more comfortably?

In January 2006, Tony Bryan was working in a factory that produces the flavourings they put on fried chicken. He got a message telling him to call his wife, Rachel, urgently. He called his wife, but the line was engaged. Expecting the worst, he jumped into his car and raced home. His seven-year-old daughter opened the door with a smile and said, 'We've won the lottery, Daddy.' He found Rachel in the living room holding a lottery ticket worth £2.6m. Their lives had changed for ever.

Today, he and his family live in a nice house with a lot of land. They have two goats, and ducks and chickens. It seems that they have adapted brilliantly. They are enjoying their money, but they have not stopped working. They run a caravan park in the field next to the house, and they sell their own vegetables. They haven't exactly been relaxing.

'All your life you get up and go to work to earn money to buy a car, or a holiday, or a better house,' says Tony. 'If you take that away, what is the point of getting up? So you quit your job, you start to get up late, you watch morning TV, then you go shopping, then wait for school pick-up time. After a couple of weeks, you begin to wonder what the point of it is. We had six months going on nice holidays, but then we had to sit down and decide what to do in the long-term.'

So they didn't buy an Aston Martin or even a Mercedes. 'I couldn't justify spending £30,000 on a car,' he says. 'It's a ridiculous amount, no matter how much money you have.' They are very careful with their money. 'You don't stop worrying when you win the lottery. You just worry about different things. I felt guilty that we had lots of money. We were just lucky...'

As I leave, the telephone rings. 'It's £8 per night for a caravan...' says their daughter. I set off home, past their vegetable stall at the end of the drive. Tomatoes are 50p a kilo. A cucumber is 50p.

Adapted from The Sunday Times

b Read the article again. Mark the sentences **T** (true), **F** (false), or **DS** (doesn't say).

1 Tony was very worried when he got his wife's message.
2 Tony continued working in a factory for a few months after the lottery win.
3 He and his family now live in the city.
4 They lived very differently for the first six months after the lottery win.
5 Tony thinks that if you don't work, it's hard to know what to do with your life.
6 Their daughter now goes to a private school.

c Choose five new words or phrases from the article. Check their meaning and pronunciation, and try to learn them.

◼ CAN YOU UNDERSTAND THESE PEOPLE?

VIDEO

1 54 ») **In the street** Watch or listen to five people and answer the questions.

| Emma | Andrew | Ben | Zenobia | Simone |

1 Emma says she _____.
   a has liked ice cream since she was a little girl
   b often feels ill after eating chocolate ice cream
   c prefers ice cream to chocolate
2 Andrew likes Asian restaurants because _____.
   a he doesn't like cooking
   b it's cheaper than eating at home
   c he can't cook that type of food at home
3 Ben and his brother went _____ together.
   a running   b to university   c on holiday
4 Zenobia buys a bag _____.
   a if it's cheaper than usual   b every three months
   c if she needs a new one
5 Simone took part in a charity bike ride _____.
   a when she was nine   b for a television programme
   c around a track

CAN YOU SAY THIS IN ENGLISH?

Do the tasks with a partner. Tick (✓) the box if you can do them.

Can you...?

1 ☐ describe your diet and the typical diet in your country, and say how it is changing
2 ☐ agree or disagree with the following statement, and say why: *Our favourite food is usually something we liked when we were children.*
3 ☐ describe members of your family, saying what they look like and what they are like
4 ☐ describe some of your plans and predictions for the future (e.g. your studies, your family life)
5 ☐ ask and answer the following questions:
   • Have you ever won any money? How much did you win? What did you do with it?
   • How long have you been learning English? Where did you first start learning?

◼ VIDEO **Short films** Oxfam
Watch and enjoy a film on iTutor.

G comparatives and superlatives
V transport
P /ʃ/, /dʒ/, and /tʃ/, linking

What's the best way to get around London? Probably the Tube, although buses are cheaper.

3A Race across London

1 VOCABULARY & SPEAKING

transport

a In pairs, can you think of four different forms of public transport in towns and cities in your country?

b ➤ p.155 Vocabulary Bank *Transport*.

2 PRONUNCIATION /ʃ/, /dʒ/, and /tʃ/

a (2 4)) Look at the pictures. What are the words and sounds? Listen and repeat.

ʃ	dʒ	tʃ

b Write three words from the list in each column.

adventure bridge catch coach crash
journey rush station traffic jam

c (2 5)) Listen and check. Practise saying the words.

d Look at the words in the columns. What are the typical spellings for these sounds? Go to the **Sound Bank p.167** and check.

e (2 6)) Listen to the pairs of words. Can you hear the difference? Practise saying them.

/tʃ/ and /dʒ/
1 a cheap   b jeep
2 a chain   b Jane
3 a choke   b joke

/ʃ/ and /tʃ/
4 a ship   b chip
5 a shoes   b choose
6 a wash   b watch

f (2 7)) Listen and circle the word you hear.

g (2 8)) Listen and write five sentences.

3 READING & LISTENING

a You are going to read about a race which the BBC car programme *Top Gear* organized across London. Read the introduction and answer the questions.

1 Where do they have to go from? Where to?
2 What are the four methods of transport?
3 Which one do you think will be the fastest? Why?
4 In what order do you think the other three will arrive? Why?

TopGear Challenge
What's the fastest way to get across London?

On *Top Gear*, a very popular BBC TV series about cars and driving, they decided to organize a race across London, to find the quickest way to cross a busy city. The idea was to start from Kew Bridge, in the south-west of London, and to finish the race at the check-in desk at London City Airport, in the east, a journey of approximately 15 miles. Four possible forms of transport were chosen, a bike, a car, a motorboat, and public transport. The show's presenter, **Jeremy Clarkson**, took the **boat** and his colleague **James May** went by **car** (a large Mercedes). **Richard Hammond** went by **bike**, and **The Stig** took **public transport**. He had an Oyster card. His journey involved getting a bus, then the Tube, and then the Docklands Light Railway, an overground train which connects east and west London.

They set off on a Monday morning in the rush hour…

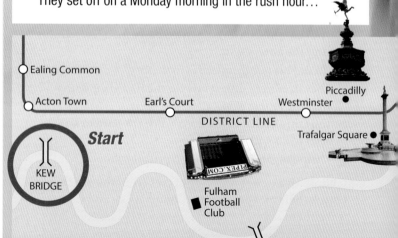

Ealing Common

Acton Town   Earl's Court   Westminster   Piccadilly

DISTRICT LINE

Trafalgar Square

Start

KEW BRIDGE

Fulham Football Club

Wandsworth Bridge

Jeremy in the motorboat

His journey was along the River Thames. For the first few miles there was a speed limit of nine miles an hour, because there are so many ducks and other birds in that part of the river. The river was confusing, and at one point he realized that he was going in the wrong direction. But he **turned round** and got back onto the right route. Soon he was going past Fulham football ground. He phoned Richard and asked him where he was – just past Trafalgar Square. This was good news for Jeremy. He **was ahead of** the bike! He **reached** Wandsworth Bridge. The speed limit finished there, and he could now go as fast as he liked. Jeremy felt like the fastest moving man in all of London. He was flying, coming close to 50 miles an hour! How could he lose now? He could see Tower Bridge ahead. His journey was seven miles longer than the others', but he was now going at 70 miles an hour. Not far to the airport now!

Richard on the bike

Richard could use bus lanes, which was great, but of course he had to be careful not to **crash into** the buses! He hated buses! Horrible things! When the traffic lights **turned red** he thought of cycling through them, but then he remembered that he was on TV, so he had to stop! When he got to Piccadilly he was delighted to see that there was a terrible traffic jam – he could go through the traffic, but James, in his Mercedes, would **get stuck**. He got to Trafalgar Square, and then went into a cycle lane. From now on it was going to be easier…

James in the car

He started off OK. He wasn't going fast but at a steady speed – until he was stopped by the police! They only wanted to check the permit for the cameraman in the back of the car, but it meant that he lost three or four valuable minutes! The traffic was **getting worse**. Now he was going really slowly. 25 miles an hour, 23, 20… 18… It was so frustrating!

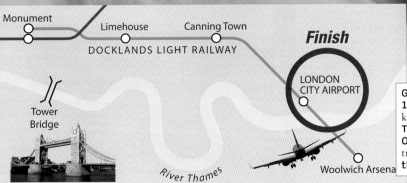

Monument
Limehouse
Canning Town
DOCKLANDS LIGHT RAILWAY
Finish
LONDON CITY AIRPORT
Tower Bridge
River Thames
Woolwich Arsenal

b Now read about the journeys by boat, bike, and car. Do you still think your predictions in **a** 3 and 4 are right?

c Read the three journeys again and answer the questions with **Je** (Jeremy), **R** (Richard), or **Ja** (James).

Who…?

1 ☐ was asked to show a piece of paper
2 ☐ went much faster in the later part of his journey
3 ☐ nearly did something illegal
4 ☐ went more slowly in the later part of his journey
5 ☐ was happy to see that there was a lot of traffic
6 ☐ got slightly lost
7 ☐ had the most exciting journey

d Look at the highlighted verbs and verb phrases. With a partner, work out their meaning from context.

Stig on the Underground

e (2 9))) Now listen to what happened to The Stig. Follow his route on the map.

f Listen again. What information or warning do you hear when you are travelling on the Tube?

g (2 10))) With a partner, write down the order in which you now think the four people arrived. Then listen to what happened. What order did they arrive in? Why do you think that Jeremy Clarkson was annoyed?

h Think of your nearest big city. What kind of public transport is there? If a race was organized there between a bike, a car, and public transport, what order do you think they would arrive in?

i ➤ **Communication** *I'm a tourist – can you help me?* **A** *p.104* **B** *p.109.*

> **Glossary**
> **1 mile** the unit of distance used in the UK and the USA (=1.6 kilometres); 15 miles = approx 25 km
> **The Stig** nickname given to one of the members of the *Top Gear* team
> **Oyster card** a kind of travel card which you use to travel on public transport in London
> **the Tube** nickname for the London Underground

4 GRAMMAR comparatives and superlatives

a Read the sentences. Are the highlighted phrases right or wrong? Tick (✓) or cross (✗) them and correct the wrong sentences.

1 ☐ What's the quicker way to get across London?
2 ☐ Driving is more boring than going by train.
3 ☐ The boat was nearly as fast than the bike.
4 ☐ Oxford is the same distance from London as Brighton.
5 ☐ There aren't as much trains as there were before on this line.
6 ☐ It was the more exciting journey I've ever had.
7 ☐ The worst time of day to travel in London is between 7.30 a.m. and 9.30 a.m.
8 ☐ Women drive more careful than men.

b ➤ p.136 Grammar Bank 3A. Learn more about comparatives and superlatives, and practise them.

5 PRONUNCIATION linking

> 🔍 **Linking**
> We often link words together in English, especially when we speak fast. We link words:
> 1 when a word ends in a consonant sound and the next word begins with a vowel sound, e.g. *more⌣exciting*
> 2 when a word ends in a consonant sound and the next word begins with the same consonant sound, e.g. *a dangerous⌣cyclist*
> 3 when a word ends in /t/ or /d/ and the next word begins with /t/ or /d/, e.g. *the biggest⌣dog*

a (2 14)) Listen and repeat the sentences. Try to link the marked words and copy the rhythm.

1 Riding⌣a motorbike⌣is more⌣exciting than driving.
2 The fastest⌣train⌣only takes⌣an⌣hour⌣and⌣a half.
3 It's more difficult⌣to drive⌣at night than during the day.
4 My father's worse⌣at⌣driving than my mother.
5 The most⌣dangerous road⌣in my town⌣is the ring road.

b Talk to a partner. For each group of three things compare them using the **bold** adjective, i.e. for **1** decide which is the most dangerous, and then compare the other two. Say why.

1 **dangerous:** cycling; riding a motorbike; driving
2 **easy:** learning to drive; learning to ride a bike; learning to ride a horse
3 **relaxing:** flying; travelling by train; driving
4 **difficult:** sleeping on a train; sleeping in a plane; sleeping on a bus
5 **boring:** being stuck in a traffic jam; waiting at an airport; waiting for a bus

I think cycling is the most dangerous because sometimes drivers don't notice cyclists. Riding a motorbike is more dangerous than driving.

6 LISTENING

a Read the text and then talk to a partner.

1 Which of these things do you (or people you know) do when they are driving?
2 Which do you think are the most dangerous? Number them 1–3 (1 = the most dangerous).
3 Which one do you think is the least dangerous?

b (2 15)) Now listen to a safety expert. Number the activities 1–7. Were your top three right?

c Listen again for more information about each activity and why it is dangerous.

Which of these things are the most (and least) **dangerous** when you're driving a car?

A British car magazine tested drivers in a driving simulator. The drivers had to drive in the simulator and do the things in the list below.

⚠ Eating or drinking	☐
⚠ Talking on a mobile (not 'hands free')	☐
⚠ Setting or adjusting a satnav	☐
⚠ Listening to your favourite music	☐
⚠ Listening to music you don't know	☐
⚠ Sending or receiving text messages	☐
⚠ Doing your hair or putting on make-up	☐

7 SPEAKING

a Look at the statements below and decide whether you agree or disagree. Tick (✓) the ones you agree with and put a cross (✗) next to the ones you disagree with. Think about your reasons.

> Slow drivers cause more accidents than fast drivers.

> People who drink and drive should lose their driving licence for life.

> Speed cameras do not stop accidents.

> Drivers who are over 70 are as dangerous as young drivers.

> Cyclists should have to wear helmets.

> The minimum age for riding a motorbike should be 25.

> The speed limit on motorways should be lower.

b In groups, give your opinions on each statement. Try to use expressions from the box. Do you agree?

🔍 **Agreeing and disagreeing**

I agree / don't agree	with this. / with Juan.
I think / don't think	you're right. / that's
I completely / totally	agree. / disagree.

8 WRITING

➤ **p.115 Writing** *An article for a magazine.* Write a magazine article about transport in your town or city.

9 ② 16》 **SONG** *500 Miles* ♫

G articles: *a / an, the,* no article
V collocation: verbs / adjectives + prepositions
P /ə/, sentence stress, /ðə/ or /ði:/?

> Do you think women talk more than men?

> Yes, in general I think they probably do.

3B Stereotypes – or are they?

1 READING & SPEAKING

a In pairs, answer the questions.

1 Are you a talkative or a quiet person?
2 Who is…?
  a the most talkative person in your family
  b the most talkative person you know
3 Do you think that, generally speaking, women are more talkative than men?
4 What topics do a) men talk about more than women? b) women talk about more than men?

b Look at the definition of *stereotype.* Then **A** read the article *Men talk just as much as women* and **B** read the article *A gossip with the girls?* Find answers to questions 1–4.

> **stereotype** /ˈsteriətaɪp/ *noun* a fixed idea about a particular type of person or thing, which is often not true in reality. ▶ **stereotype** *verb In advertisements, women are often stereotyped as housewives.*

1 What was the stereotype that the researchers wanted to investigate?
2 Where was the research done?
3 How was the research done?
4 What did the research show?

c In pairs, tell each other about your article, using questions 1–4 to help you.

d Now read both articles again and look at the highlighted words and phrases, which are commonly used in articles about research. Match them with definitions 1–10.

1 *In fact*   *adverb* really
2 _____ *verb* make less
3 _____ usually do it
4 _____ *adverb* a little bit
5 _____ linking word used to connect or contrast two facts
6 _____ *verb* say that sth is true
7 _____ as said or shown by sb
8 _____ *verb* include several different things in addition to the ones mentioned
9 _____ *adverb* nearly
10 _____ not completely believed, doubted

e Which of the two pieces of research do you think is…?

1 more credible   3 more surprising
2 more important

Men talk just as much as women – can it really be true?

Research by psychologists at the University of Arizona has shown that the stereotype that women talk more than men may not be true. In the study, hundreds of university students were fitted with recorders and the total number of words they used during the day was then counted.

The results, published in the New Scientist, showed that women speak about 16,000 words a day and men speak only slightly fewer. In fact, the four most talkative people in the study were all men.

Professor Matthias Mehl, who was in charge of the research, said that he and his colleagues had expected to find that women were more talkative.

A GOSSIP WITH THE GIRLS? JUST PICK ANY ONE OF FORTY SUBJECTS

Women are experts at gossiping – and they often talk about trivial things, or at least that's what men have always thought. However according to research carried out by Professor Petra Boynton, a psychologist at University College London, when women talk to women their conversations are not trivial at all, and cover many more topics (up to 40) than when men talk to other men.

Women's conversations range from health to their houses, from politics to fashion, from films to family, from education to relationship problems. Almost everything, in fact, except football. Men tend to talk about fewer subjects, the most popular being work, sport, jokes, cars, and women.

However, they had been sceptical of the common belief that women use three times as many words as men. This idea became popular after the publication of a book called *The Female Brain* (2006) whose author, Louann Brizendine, claimed that 'a woman uses about 20,000 words per day, whereas a man uses about 7,000.'

Professor Mehl accepts that many people will find the results difficult to believe. However, he thinks that this research is important because the stereotype, that women talk too much and men keep quiet, is bad not only for women but also for men. 'It says that to be a good male, it's better not to talk – that silence is golden.'

Professor Boynton interviewed over 1,000 women for her study. She also found that women move quickly from one subject to another in conversation, whereas men usually stick to one subject for longer periods of time.

Professor Boynton also says that men and women chat for different reasons. In social situations women use conversation to solve problems and reduce stress, while men chat with each other to have a laugh or to swap opinions.

2 GRAMMAR articles: *a / an, the*, no article

a Complete 1–4 with *a / an, the*, or – (no article).

1 'Have you heard this joke? ____ man with ____ dog walks into ____ bar. ____ man says to ____ barman, "Can I have ____ beer and ____ whisky for my dog…?"'

2 'I've just read ____ article on ____ internet about how eating ____ strawberries makes you look younger…'

3 'I'm sure there's something wrong between us because we never go out to ____ dinner or to ____ cinema any more.

4 'Did you watch ____ match ____ last night? I can't believe that ____ referee didn't see that it was ____ penalty…'

b According to the article *A gossip with the girls?*, who do you think would probably say 1–4, a man or a woman?

c ➤ **p.137 Grammar Bank 3B.** Learn more about articles and practise them.

3 PRONUNCIATION

/ə/, sentence stress, /ðə/ or /ðiː/?

a (2 20)) Listen and repeat the sound and words.

> a about anniversary cinema problem relationship spider usually woman

b (2 21)) Listen and repeat the sentences. Then practise saying them with the /ə/ sound.

1 **What** are we **going** to **have** for **lunch to**d**ay**?
2 I'd **like** to **see** a **good film to**n**ight**.
3 We **need** to **go** in the **other direc**tion.
4 Could you **ask** the **woman over there**?
5 There's a **cinema** and there are **lots** of **shops**.

c (2 22)) Listen and <u>underline</u> five phrases where *the* is pronounced /ðiː/ (not /ðə/). Why does the pronunciation change?

the cinema   the end   the other day   the world   the sun
the internet   the kitchen   the answer   the Earth

4 SPEAKING

Prove that the research in *A gossip with the girls?* is wrong! Work in pairs or small groups.

If you're a **woman**, try to talk for two minutes about:

football   cars   computers

If you're a **man**, try to talk for two minutes about:

fashion   shopping   your family

5 READING & LISTENING

a Do you think it is a stereotype that women are better than men at looking after small children? Do you know any men who stay at home and look after their children? How do they manage?

b Look at an illustration from a new book about looking after young children. Can you name some of the things in the picture?

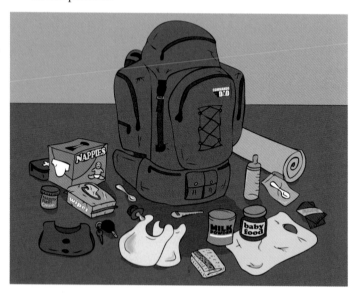

c Read the beginning of an article about the book. Why did Neil Sinclair write it? In what way is it different from other books about bringing up children?

d **2 23))** Listen to two men talking in the park about the book and mark the sentences **T** (true) or **F** (false).

1 Miranda is older than Stephen.
2 Miranda's father slept badly the night before.
3 Stephen's father recommends sleeping tablets.
4 Stephen's father hasn't read *Commando Dad*.
5 He likes the website because he enjoys reading about other men's experiences.
6 Stephen's father really likes the book because it helps him and makes him laugh.
7 In *Commando Dad*, BT means 'Baby Trooper' and 'Base Camp' means the kitchen.
8 The author of *Commando Dad* thinks that women are only better than men when the baby is small.

e Listen again and correct the wrong information.

f Do you think it's a good idea to have a book and a website on childcare especially for men? Why (not)?

For six years Neil Sinclair served as a commando with the British army. He had been in lots of dangerous situations, but nothing prepared him for the day when he brought his first baby home from hospital. 'I put the car seat containing my two-day-old son Samuel down on the floor and said to my wife, 'What do we do now?'

COMMANDO DAD

When he left the army, Sinclair and his wife agreed that he would stay at home and look after the baby, while his wife went back to work.

'I have done a lot of crazy things, but when I put that baby down I thought: I have a tiny baby and he is crying. What does he want? What does he need? I did not know. It was one of the most difficult days of my life.'

It was at that moment that Sinclair had an idea. 'I found myself thinking how much easier life would be if I had a basic training manual for my baby, like the manual you get when you join the army. I realized that somebody needed to write such a manual, and who better to write it than me? I had been a commando, but I was now a stay-at-home dad. I was the man for the job.'

His book, *Commando Dad: Basic Training*, is a set of instructions that explains with military precision and diagrams how new fathers should approach the first three years of their child's life to become a 'first-rate father'.

Adapted from The Times

Glossary
commando *noun* one of a group of soldiers who are trained to make quick attacks in enemy areas
stay-at-home dad *noun* a man who stays at home and looks after the children while his wife goes out to work

6 SPEAKING

a (2 24)) Listen to someone talking about men and women, and complete the gaps.

> 'Generally _____, I think women worry more about their appearance than men. They _____ to spend hours choosing what to wear, doing their hair, and putting on make-up. Women are also _____ better at making themselves look more attractive. But I think that in _____, men are more worried than women about their body image. They feel more insecure about their hair, for instance, especially when they're going bald.'

b In small groups discuss if the statements opposite about men and women are stereotypes or true. Try to use the highlighted expressions for generalizing from **a**.

MEN & WOMEN
stereotypes or true?

- Women worry more about their appearance than men.
- Women spend more time than men on social networking sites.
- Men talk more about things; women talk more about people.
- Men are more interested than women in gadgets like phones and tablets.
- Women are better at multitasking than men.
- Men find it more difficult than women to talk to their friends or family if they have a problem.
- Women spend more time than men talking about celebrities and their lifestyles.
- Men are more interested than women in power.
- Women are less interested in sport than men.
- Men worry more about their health than women.

7 VOCABULARY
collocation: verbs / adjectives + prepositions

a Cover the statements above. Can you remember the missing prepositions?

1 Men worry more ____ their health than women.
2 Women are better ____ multitasking than men.
3 Men are more interested than women ____ power.

b ➤ **p.156 Vocabulary Bank** *Dependent prepositions.*

> 🔍 **When are prepositions stressed?**
> Prepositions are normally only stressed when they are the last word, e.g. in a question. Compare:
>
> We **need** to **talk** about our **holiday**.
> **What** are you **talking about**?
>
> **Freddie** is **afraid** of **flying**.
> **What** are you **afraid of**?

c Complete the questions with a preposition.

1 When you're with friends of the same sex, what do you usually talk ____?
2 Are there any sports or games that you're good ____?
3 Is there anything you're really looking forward ____?
4 Who in your family are you closest ____?
5 What kind of films are you keen ____?
6 Are there any animals or insects that you're afraid ____?
7 What's your town famous ____?
8 Are there any superstitions that you believe ____?

d (2 27)) Listen and check. Then ask and answer the questions with a partner.

1 ◼◀ ROB'S INTERVIEW
VIDEO

a **(2 28)))** Watch or listen to Rob interviewing Kerri. What is she happy / not happy to talk about?

b Watch or listen again. Mark the sentences **T** (true) or **F** (false). Correct the **F** sentences.

1 Kerri's song is about love.
2 Kerri plays in a band.
3 She used to go out with a member of the band.
4 Only one of her parents was a musician.
5 Kerri started playing the guitar when she was six.
6 Her new album is very different from the previous ones.
7 She's been recording and touring recently.
8 She's going to give a big concert in New York.

2 ◼◀ GIVING OPINIONS
VIDEO

a **(2 29)))** Watch or listen to the conversation at lunch. What do they disagree about?

b Watch or listen again. Answer the questions.

1 What does Kerri think about…?
   a the waiters in New York compared to London
   b people in New York compared to London
2 Who agrees with Kerri? Who disagrees? What do they think?
3 Who phones Rob? What about?

c (2 30)) Look at some extracts from the conversation. Can you remember any of the missing words? Watch or listen and check.

1	**Kerri**	_____, I think people in London are a lot more easy-going. London's just not as hectic as New York.
	Don	Sure, we all like peace and quiet. But in my _____, New York is possibly... well, no, is definitely the greatest city in the world. Don't you _____?
	Kerri	To be _____, I definitely prefer London.
	Don	Come on, Rob. You've lived in both. What do you _____?
2	**Don**	OK, I _____, London has its own peculiar charm. But if you _____ me, nothing compares with a city like New York. The whole world is here!
	Kerri	But that's the problem. It's too big. There are too many people. Everybody's so stressed out. And nobody has any time for you.
	Jenny	I don't think that's _____, Kerri. New Yorkers are very friendly.
	Kerri	Oh _____, they can sound friendly with all that 'Have a nice day' stuff.

d (2 31)) Watch or listen and repeat the highlighted phrases. Copy the rhythm and intonation.

e Practise the dialogues in **c** with a partner.

f 👥👥👥 In small groups, practise giving opinions. Discuss the following sentences.

- The best place to live is in a big city.
- Cycling is the most practical way to get round big cities.
- You only get good service in expensive restaurants.
- It's irritating when people in shops or restaurants say *Have a nice day!*

3 🎬 A SURPRISE FOR KERRI
VIDEO

a (2 32)) Watch or listen to the end of the lunch. Why is Kerri surprised?

> 🔍 **British and American English**
> *cell phone* = American English
> *mobile phone* = British English

b Watch or listen again and complete the information.

1 Kerri thinks the waitress is friendly when they leave because Don...
2 Jenny is worried because she thinks Rob...
3 Kerri thinks that the taxi driver is very...

c Look at the **Social English phrases**. Can you remember any of the missing words?

Social English phrases	
Jenny	Did you _____ what you said in the restaurant, Rob?
Jenny	It's _____ that... you seemed homesick in there.
Rob	Oh, _____ on a minute.
Rob	Our taxi's come _____.
Kerri	That was so _____ of him!

d (2 33)) Watch or listen and complete the phrases.

e Watch or listen again and repeat the phrases. How do you say them in your language?

> 👤 **Can you...?**
> ☐ interview someone or be interviewed
> ☐ give your opinion about something
> ☐ agree or disagree with other people's opinions

G can, could, be able to
V -ed / -ing adjectives
P sentence stress

Can you speak French?

No, I've never been able to learn a foreign language.

4A Failure and success

1 GRAMMAR can, could, be able to

a 'If at first you don't succeed, try, try, try again' is a well-known English saying. What does it mean?

b More recently other people have invented different ways of continuing the saying. Which one do you like best?

If at first you don't succeed,
...give up
...blame your parents
...destroy all the evidence that you tried
...do it the way your mother told you to
...skydiving is not for you

c Look at the definition of *be able to*. What other verb is it similar to?

> **be able to (do something)** to have the ability, opportunity, time, etc. to do something: *Will you be able to come to the meeting next week?*

d Read about three people who have tried (but failed) to learn something, and complete the texts with A–G.

A I was able to
B Not being able to
C I just wasn't able to
D I will never be able to
E I would suddenly be able to
F I've always wanted to be able to
G we would never be able to

e Read the article again. Why did they have problems? Have they completely given up trying? Have you ever tried to learn something and given up? Why?

f Look at phrases **A–G** again. What tense or form is *be able to* in each one? What tenses or forms does *can* have?

g ➤ p.138 Grammar Bank 4A. Learn more about *can, could,* and *be able to*, and practise them.

h ➤ **Communication** *Guess the sentence* **A** *p.105* **B** *p.109.*

I've **never** been able to...

...scuba-dive

I really wanted to learn. Maybe it was because of that scene in one of the very first James Bond films, where a beautiful actress comes out of the sea looking fabulous, with oxygen bottles on her back – I could see myself looking just like her. So, two years ago I booked a holiday which included a week's intensive course. On the first day of the course I was incredibly excited. First we had two hours of theory, and then we went into the sea to put it into practice. But as soon as I went under the water I discovered that I suffered from claustrophobia. [1]_____ do it. After about half an hour I gave up. Every evening for the rest of my holiday I had to listen to my scuba-diving classmates talking about all the wonderful things they had seen that day on their diving excursions. [2]_____ join in the conversation was very frustrating.

I still love swimming and snorkelling, but I think that I have to accept that [3]_____ scuba-dive.

Bea, USA

...learn to dance

⁴_____ dance salsa, and when I was working in Ecuador there were free classes, so I joined. But the art of salsa is to keep your arms still and move your hips, and I just couldn't do it. When I hear music my arms start moving, but my hips don't. After about ten hours of classes ⁵_____ do the basic steps, but I was dancing like a robot! I didn't give up, but soon everyone in the class was dancing and I was just slowly moving from side to side and counting out loud 'one, two, three, four'. It was a bit embarrassing. I was sure that one day ⁶_____ do it – but that never happened. I can still remember the first two steps and I still try to dance when I hear a salsa tune – as long as nobody is watching!

Sean, UK

...speak Japanese

I love Manga – Japanese comics – and I tried to learn Japanese, but I found it incredibly difficult and I gave up after two years. I think oriental languages, which have symbols instead of words, are extremely hard to learn for people who are more used to Roman letters. Also my teacher, a Japanese woman, didn't speak Spanish very well, which didn't help! She was a very charming woman, but she was a bit disappointed with us, and you could see that she thought that ⁷_____ learn. However, one day she invited us to dinner and gave us some delicious traditional Japanese food, and since then I often go to Japanese restaurants. So I learnt to love the food, if not to speak the language!

Joaquin, Spain

2 PRONUNCIATION sentence stress

a (2 36))) Listen and repeat the sentences. Copy the rhythm.

> 1 I'd **love** to be **able** to **ski.**
> 2 We **won't** be **able** to **come.**
> 3 I've **never** been **able** to **dance.**
> 4 She **hates not** being **able** to **drive.**

b (2 37))) Listen again. Make new sentences with the verbs or verb phrases you hear.

>))) *I'd love to be able to ski.* **Ride a horse**
> ⤷ *I'd love to be able to ride a horse.*

>))) *We won't be able to come.* **Park**
> ⤷ *We won't be able to park.*

3 SPEAKING

a Look at the topics. Choose two or three and think about what you could say for them.

> Something you've tried to learn, but have never been able to do well.
>
> Something you learnt to do after a lot of effort.
>
> Something you can do, but you'd like to be able to do better.
>
> Something new that you would like to be able to do.
>
> Something you are learning to do and that you hope you'll soon be able to do well.
>
> Something you think all young people should able to do before they leave school.

b Work with a partner. Tell him / her about the things you chose in **a**. Give reasons or explanations for each one.

> ⎰ *I've never been able to ski, and now I don't think I'll ever learn.*
> ⎱ *I always wanted to learn, but I don't live near mountains...*

4 VOCABULARY -ed / -ing adjectives

a Look at the photo. Complete the sentences with *bored* or *boring*.

1 The film was _____.
2 The audience were _____.

> 🔍 **-ed and -ing adjectives**
>
> Many adjectives for feelings have two possible forms, either ending in *-ed* or in *-ing*, e.g. **frustrated** and **frustrating**.
> We use the adjective ending in *-ed* for the person who has the feeling (*I was very frustrated that I couldn't scuba-dive*). We use the adjective ending in *-ing* for a person or situation that produces the feeling (*I couldn't join in the conversation, which was very frustrating*).

b Read the information box. Then complete the adjectives with *-ed* or *-ing*.

1 What do you think is the most **excit**___ sport to watch?
2 What's the most **amaz**___ scenery you've ever seen?
3 What music do you listen to if you feel **depress**___?
4 Have you ever been **disappoint**___ by a birthday present?
5 Which do you find more **tir**___, speaking English or listening to English?
6 What's the most **embarrass**___ thing that's ever happened to you?
7 Are you **frighten**___ of heights?
8 Do you feel very **tir**___ in the morning?
9 Who's the most **bor**___ person you know?
10 Do you ever get **frustrat**___ by technology?

c (2 38)》 Listen and check. Under<u>line</u> the stressed syllable in the adjectives.

d Ask and answer the questions in pairs. Ask for more information.

5 READING & SPEAKING

a Do you know anybody who speaks more than two languages? Which languages do they speak? How did they learn?

b (2 39)》 You are going to read an article about Alex Rawlings, who speaks 11 languages. Before you read, match the languages below with words **1–11**. Then listen and check.

☐ English   ☐ Greek   ☐ German
☐ Spanish   ☐ Russian   ☐ Dutch
☐ 1 Afrikaans   ☐ French   ☐ Hebrew
☐ Catalan   ☐ Italian

c Read the article. Which language(s)…?

1 did he learn as a child
2 is he studying at university
3 does he like best
4 is he planning to learn next
5 did he wish he had been able to speak when he was a child
6 was the first one he taught himself
7 did he find the most difficult

1 Hallo

2 Guten Tag

He's English, but he can speak eleven languages

Alex Rawlings has been named the UK's most multilingual student, in a competition run by a dictionary publisher.

The German and Russian student from London, who is only 20 years old, can speak 11 languages fluently. In a video for the BBC News website he demonstrated his skills by speaking in all of them, changing quickly from one to another. Rawlings said that winning the competition was 'a bit of a shock'. He explained, 'I saw the competition advertised and I heard something about a free iPad. I never imagined that it would generate this amount of media attention.'

As a child, Rawlings' mother, who is half Greek, used to speak to him in English, Greek, and French, and he often visited his family in Greece.
He said that he has always been interested in languages. 'My dad worked in Japan for four years and I was always frustrated that I couldn't speak to the kids because of the language barrier.' After visiting Holland at the age of 14 he decided to learn Dutch with CDs and books. 'When I went back I could talk to people. It was great.'

d Look at the highlighted words and phrases related to language learning, and work out their meaning from the context. Then ask and answer the questions with a partner.

1 Can you or anyone in your family speak another language fluently?

2 Do you know any basic phrases in any other languages?

3 Do you have a personal link to another country or language? Why?

4 Have you ever travelled to another country and felt that there was a real language barrier?

5 What other languages would you like to be able to speak? Why?

He taught himself many of the languages with 'teach yourself' books, but also by watching films, listening to music, and travelling to the countries themselves.

Of all the languages he speaks, Rawlings says that Russian, which he has been learning for a year and a half, is the hardest. He said, 'There seem to be more exceptions than rules!' He added, 'I especially like Greek because I think it's beautiful and, because of my mother, I have a strong personal link to the country and to the language.'

'Everyone should learn languages, especially if they travel abroad. If you make the effort to learn even the most basic phrases wherever you go, it instantly shows the person you're speaking to that you respect their culture. Going around speaking English loudly and getting frustrated at people is tactless and rude.'

The next language Rawlings hopes to learn is Arabic, but 'only once I've finished my degree and got some more time on my hands. For now I need to concentrate on my German and Russian, so I can prepare for my finals.'

Glossary
finals the last exams that students take at university

Adapted from a news website

e Read the grammar information box. Then complete 1–5 with a reflexive pronoun.

> Ⓖ **Reflexive pronouns**
> He taught **himself** many of the languages with 'teach **yourself**' books.
> We use reflexive pronouns (*myself, yourself, himself, herself, itself, ourselves, yourselves, themselves*) when the object of a verb is the same as the subject, e.g. *He taught himself Russian.* = he was his own teacher.
> We also use reflexive pronouns to emphasize the subject of an action, e.g. *We painted the kitchen ourselves.*

1 I always test _____ on new vocabulary – it's a good way to remember it.

2 My uncle built the house _____. It took him three years.

3 This light is automatic. It turns _____ on and off.

4 Did you fix the computer _____? Well done!

5 My sister's so vain! Every time she passes a mirror, she looks at _____ in it!

6 LISTENING & SPEAKING

a ②40)) You're going to listen to six advanced students of English giving a tip which has helped them to learn. Listen once and complete their tip. Then compare your notes with a partner.

TIP 1: Change the language to English on all the _____ you have, for example on your _____, or _____, or _____.

TIP 2: Do things that you _____ _____, but in English.

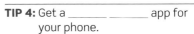

TIP 3: Try to find an English-speaking _____ or _____.

TIP 4: Get a _____ _____ app for your phone.

TIP 5: Book yourself a _____ in an _____-_____ _____.

TIP 6: Listen to as many _____ as possible in English, and then _____ _____ _____ them.

b Listen again. Try to add more details about each tip.

c Talk to a partner.

• Do you already do any of these things?

• Which do you think is the best tip?

• Which tip could you easily put into practice? Try it!

• What other things do you do to improve your English outside class (e.g. visit chat websites, listen to audio books)?

G modals of obligation: *must, have to, should*
V phone language
P silent consonants, linking

Do I have to bring a present?

Yes, I think you probably should.

4B Modern manners?

1 VOCABULARY & SPEAKING
phone language

a **(2 41)))** Listen and match the phone sentences with the sounds.

A ☐ He's **dialling** a number.
B ☐ She's **texting / messaging** a friend.
C ☐ He's just **hung up**.
D ☐ She's choosing a new **ringtone**.
E ☐ He's **calling back**.
F ☐ She **left a message** on his **voicemail**.
G ☐ The line's **engaged / busy**.

b Can you explain what these are?

Skype   a screensaver   silent / vibrate mode
quiet zones   instant messaging

c Use the questionnaire to interview another student. Ask for more information.

YOU AND YOUR PHONE

- What make is your phone? How long have you had it?
- Would you like to get a new one? Why (not)?
- What ringtone do you have?
- What do you use your phone for (apart from talking)?
- Where and when do you normally switch off your mobile?
- Have you ever...?
  - lost your phone
  - sent a message to the wrong person
  - forgotten to turn your phone off (with embarrassing consequences)

2 GRAMMAR
modals of obligation: *must, have to, should*

a Read the extract from Debrett's guide to mobile phone etiquette. Then talk to a partner about questions 1–4.

1 Do you agree with what Debrett's says?
2 Do you ever do any of these things?
3 Are they a problem where you live?
4 Are there any other things people do with their phones that annoy you?

Debrett's, a well-known British publisher, has been producing guides on how people should behave since the 1900s, including *Debrett's Etiquette and Modern Manners* and *The English Gentleman*. Nowadays it still offers advice on what (and what not) to do in social situations.

DEBRETT'S
guide to
mobile phone etiquette

1 *Think what your ringtone says about you*
If you're sometimes embarrassed by your ringtone, it's almost certainly the wrong one and you should change it.

2 *When in doubt, use silent or vibrate mode*
It may surprise your companions when you suddenly answer an invisible, silent phone, but at least they won't have to listen to your ringtone.

3 *Take notice of who is around you*
Make sure your conversation is not disturbing other people. Intimate conversations are never appropriate in front of others.

b Read the text again. Match the **highlighted phrases** with their meaning. Two of the phrases match the same meaning.

A You don't need to do this. It isn't necessary.
B Don't do this. It isn't allowed / permitted.
C It's necesssary or compulsory to do this.
D It's a good idea to do this.

c ➤ **p.139 Grammar Bank 4B.** Learn more about *must, have to,* and *should,* and practise them.

4 *Respect quiet zones*
You must not use your phone in 'quiet zones' on trains or in hotels. That is the reason why they exist.

5 *Never shout*
Your phone is not a megaphone. You don't have to shout. And don't shout because you think reception is poor. It won't make any difference.

6 *People with you deserve more attention than those at the end of a phone*
Wherever possible, turn off your phone in social situations and at mealtimes, or put it on vibrate. If you have to keep your phone on because you are expecting an important call, apologize in advance.

7 *Don't carry on phone conversations when you are in the middle of something else*
This is especially true if you are in banks, shops, etc. It is insulting not to give the people who are serving you your full attention.

8 *Think about where you are calling from*
Don't make (or receive) calls in inappropriate places. Put your phone on vibrate in meetings, cinemas, etc. If you must take a call in the car, use a hands-free set.

Adapted from Debrett's Modern Manners

3 PRONUNCIATION & SPEAKING
silent consonants, linking

a Each of the words in the list has a silent consonant or consonants. With a partner, cross out the silent letters.

should ought mustn't talk wrong listen half dishonest knowledge design whole rhythm doubt foreign calm island

b **2 46**))) Listen and check.

c **2 47**))) Listen and repeat the sentences. Try to copy the rhythm and to link the marked words.

> 1 You must **switch off** your **phone** on a **plane**.
> 2 You should **only call him** in an **emergency**.
> 3 We **have** to **leave** at **eleven**.
> 4 You **mustn't open other people's emails**.
> 5 You **shouldn't talk loudly** on a **mobile phone**.

d Read the definition of *manners*. Then make sentences using *should* / *shouldn't* for something which you think is a question of manners, and with *must* / *mustn't* / *have to* for something which is a law or rule.

manners /ˈmænəz/ *pl noun* a way of behaving that is considered acceptable in your country or culture

- switch off your phone in a theatre
- talk loudly on your phone in public
- send text messages when you are driving
- reply to a message on your phone while you are talking to somebody face-to-face
- play noisy games on a phone in public
- use your phone at a petrol station
- video people on your phone without their permission
- set your phone to silent mode on a train
- send or receive texts in the cinema
- turn off your phone on a plane during take-off and landing

4 READING

a Imagine that you have been invited to stay for a weekend with your partner's family. Think of <u>three</u> things that you think it would be bad manners to do.

b Read the article. Did Heidi do any of those things? What did she do wrong (according to Mrs Bourne)? Now look at the title of the article. What do you think 'from hell' means in this context?

News online

Mother-in-law from hell... or daughter-in-law from hell?

By NEWS ONLINE Reporter

Everyone knows it can be difficult to get on with your in-laws, but for 29-year-old **Heidi Withers**, it may now be impossible. Heidi was invited to spend the weekend with her fiancé Freddie's family at their house in Devon, in south-west England. But soon after they returned to London, Heidi received a very nasty email from Carolyn Bourne, Freddie's stepmother, criticizing her manners.

Here are a few examples of your lack of manners:

- *When you are a guest in another's house, you should not declare what you will and will not eat – unless you are allergic to something.*
- *You should not say that you do not have enough food.*
- *You should not start before everyone else.*
- *You should not take additional helpings without being invited to by your host.*
- *You should not lie in bed until late morning.*
- *You should have sent a handwritten card after the visit. You have never written to thank me when you have stayed.*

Heidi was shocked, and immediately sent the email on to some of her close friends. Surprised and amused, the friends forwarded it to other people, and soon the email had been posted on several websites, with thousands of people writing comments about 'the mother-in-law from hell'.

Adapted from a news website

c Find words or phrases in the article which mean…

1 _____ *noun* a man to whom you are going to be married
2 _____ *adj* unpleasant
3 _____ *verb* saying what is bad or wrong with sb or sth
4 _____ *noun* not having enough of sth
5 _____ *noun* a person who you invite to your house
6 _____ *noun* a person who receives a visitor
7 _____ *verb* sent an email or message you received to another person

 should have
We use *should have* to talk about something that happened in the past that you think was wrong, e.g. *You should have written me a thank-you letter.* = you didn't write to me. I think this was wrong.

d Now read some of the comments that were posted on the internet. Write **H** next to the ones that support Heidi, and **C** next to the ones that support Carolyn.

1 | Mrs Bourne says Heidi should have sent a handwritten thank-you note… however, she sends this letter by email! We are in the 21st century. Nobody sends handwritten letters any more. *13/07/2011 18:52*

2 | Why do we hear nothing about Freddie's role in all this? Why didn't he prepare Heidi? He must know what his stepmother is like. He could also have prepared his family by telling them about any eating problems his girlfriend has. *13/07/2011 16:25*

3 | The email was a private communication. I don't think Heidi should have sent it on to her friends. It makes me think that Mrs Bourne might be right about her bad manners. *13/07/2011 12:40*

4 | The stepmother seems to be extremely jealous of Heidi, perhaps she wants to keep Freddie all to herself. If I were Heidi, I would leave him. *12/07/2011 10:15*

5 | The mother-in-law may have a few good points but she should have spoken to Heidi face-to-face, not sent her an email. *11/07/2011 18:50*

6 | I think that the one with the extremely bad manners is Mrs Bourne. *11/07/2011 14:10*

7 | Mrs Bourne, I agree with every word you say. Young people just don't have any manners nowadays. I hope Freddie sees sense and finds someone better. *11/07/2011 09:48*

e Write your own comment. Then compare with a partner. Do you agree?

f ► **Communication** *The big day p.105.* Read about what Heidi and Freddie did next.

5 LISTENING

a (2 48)) Listen to Miranda Ingram, who is married to Alexander Anichkin, talking about the difference between Russian manners and British manners. What was their problem? How have they managed to solve their differences?

b Listen again and mark the sentences **T** (true) or **F** (false).

1 In Russia you should say please (in Russian) when you ask someone to do something.
2 Before Miranda took Alexander to meet her parents she taught him about English manners.
3 When Alexander smiled at people in the UK, he felt ridiculous.
4 When Miranda went to Russia the first time Alexander's friends were delighted because she smiled all the time.
5 Alexander thinks that the English sometimes use very polite expressions unnecessarily.
6 Alexander thinks the English are too direct.
7 Miranda doesn't think her dinner guests should criticize her cooking.

c What would people from your country do in these situations?

6 SPEAKING

In groups, talk about each thing in the *Good Manners?* questionnaire. Do you think it's good manners, bad manners, or not important / not necessary. Why?

I think it is very rude to criticize the food if you are in somebody's house.

I think it depends. It's OK if you know the person very well or if it's a member of your family...

7 (2 49)) SONG *You Can't Hurry Love* ♫

GOOD MANNERS? BAD MANNERS? NOT IMPORTANT?

WHEN YOU ARE INVITED TO SOMEBODY'S HOUSE...

- [ ] criticize the food (e.g. if it is too cold, salty, etc.)
- [ ] take a present
- [ ] write an email to say thank you
- [ ] arrive more than ten minutes late for lunch or dinner

WHEN GREETING PEOPLE...

- [ ] use more formal language when speaking to an older person
- [ ] kiss a woman on both cheeks when you meet her for the first time
- [ ] use your partner's parents' first names

MEN AND WOMEN – A MAN'S ROLE...

- [ ] pay for the meal on a first date
- [ ] wait for a woman to go through the door first
- [ ] accompany a woman home

WHEN YOU ARE HAVING A MEAL WITH FRIENDS IN A RESTAURANT...

- [ ] leave your mobile on silent on the table in front of you
- [ ] answer or send a text or message
- [ ] make a phone call
- [ ] kiss your partner

ON SOCIAL NETWORKING SITES...

- [ ] post a private message or conversation on an internet site
- [ ] post an embarrassing photo or video clip of a friend without asking their permission
- [ ] post all the details of your break-up with a partner

GRAMMAR

Circle a, b, or c.

1 I walk to work. It's _____ than going by car.
   a healthyer   b as healthy   c healthier

2 Cycling isn't _____ people think.
   a as dangerous as   b as dangerous than
   c so dangerous than

3 This is _____ time of day for traffic jams.
   a the most bad   b the worse   c the worst

4 My wife is a much safer driver than _____.
   a I   b me   c my

5 What _____ beautiful day!
   a a   b –   c an

6 I never drink coffee after _____ dinner.
   a –   b the   c an

7 _____ are usually good language learners.
   a The women   b Women   c Woman

8 We've decided to visit the UK _____.
   a the next summer   b next summer
   c the summer next

9 We won't _____ come to the party.
   a can   b be able   c be able to

10 When he was five he _____ already swim.
    a can   b could   c was able

11 My mother has never _____ cook well.
    a been able to   b could   c be able to

12 Entrance is free. You _____ pay anything.
    a don't have to   b mustn't   c shouldn't

13 I'll _____ work harder if I want to pass.
    a must   b should   c have to

14 I don't think I _____ have a dessert. I've
   already eaten too much!
    a must   b should   c have to

15 You _____ switch on your phone until the
   plane has landed.
    a don't have to   b mustn't   c shouldn't

VOCABULARY

a   Complete with a preposition.

1 We arrived _____ Prague at 5.30.

2 I apologized _____ being late.

3 I'm not very keen _____ horror films.

4 My son is good _____ speaking languages.

5 This song reminds me _____ my holiday.

b   Complete the compound nouns.

1 Slow down! The speed _____ on this road is 100, not 120.

2 I won't start the car until you have all put on your seat _____.

3 It's not a very good town for cyclists – there are very few cycle _____.

4 Try to avoid using the Tube during the _____ hour – between 8.00 and 9.30 in the morning.

5 There's a taxi _____ just outside the station.

c   Complete with the right word.

1 We were late because we got s_____ in a terrible traffic jam.

2 I'm moving into a new flat next week. I've hired a v_____, so that I can take all my things there.

3 The next train to Bristol is now waiting at pl_____ 5.

4 We're going to s_____ off early because we want to get to the hotel before it gets dark.

5 How long does it t_____ to get from here to the airport?

d   Circle the right adjective.

1 The match ended 0–0. It was really *bored | boring*.

2 It was the most *frightened | frightening* experience I've ever had.

3 We're very *excited | exciting* about our holiday!

4 I'm a bit *disappointed | disappointing* with my exam results.

5 This programme is too *depressed | depressing*. Turn it off.

e   Complete the missing words.

1 I'm not in at the moment. Please l_____ a message.

2 The line's **eng**_____. Please hold.

3 I was in the middle of talking to him and he just **h**_____ up!

4 I love the **scr**_____ on your phone. Is it a photo of your kids?

5 I hate it when people have really loud **r**_____ on their mobiles!

PRONUNCIATION

a   Circle the word with a different sound.

1 æ	tram	want	manners	traffic
2	the moon	the sun	the beginning	the end
3	switch	cheap	machine	coach
4	should	crash	permission	gossip
5 dʒ	carriage	message	argue	apologize

b   Underline the stressed syllable.

1 mo|tor|way   3 pe|de|stri|an   5 em|ba|rra|ssing
2 di|sa|ppoin|ted   4 vi|brate

CAN YOU UNDERSTAND THIS TEXT?

a Read the article once. What kind of concert was it? What happened?

Turn it off!

Something historic happened at the New York Philharmonic on the evening of 10 January 2012, about an hour into Mahler's Ninth Symphony. During the beautiful fourth movement, an audience member's cellphone loudly rang. And rang. And rang again. It was the kind of marimba riff we've all heard on the street from a stranger's phone.

From my seat in Row L, I could see the horrified discomfort of the other audience members from their body language. We all wondered whether the conductor Alan Gilbert would react, and how. Suddenly there was silence. The orchestra had stopped playing. Mr Gilbert had halted the performance. He turned to the man, who was seated in the front row, and said:

'Are you going to turn it off? Will you do that?'

There was some 'discussion' between the conductor and the cellphone owner, but we couldn't hear it.

In the Avery Fisher Hall, many members of the audience stood and demanded that the man leave the hall. They were so furious that I could have imagined them dragging him from his seat on to the stage, tying him to a stake, and setting him alight!

When the 'power off' button on the man's phone had finally been located and put to use, Mr Gilbert turned to the audience. 'Usually, when there's a disturbance like this, it's best to ignore it,' he said. 'But this time I could not allow it.'

The audience applauded as if Mahler himself, the orchestra's conductor from 1909 to 1911, had suddenly been resurrected onstage. Mr Gilbert neither smiled nor acknowledged the cheers. Instead he turned to the orchestra, instructing the players to resume, several bars back from the point at which he had stopped the performance. Just before, he raised his baton and turned again to the audience and said, this time with a smile, 'We'll start again.' A few seconds later, the fourth movement resumed.

Mr Gilbert's brave decision that night brought new music to the Philharmonic.

Adapted from The New York Times

---

cellphone (*AmE*) mobile phone

---

b Read the text again and answer the questions.

1 In what part of the symphony did the phone ring? What kind of ringtone was it?
2 Did the owner turn it off immediately?
3 How did the audience react a) to the phone ringing, and b) to what the conductor did?
4 Did the audience really drag the man onto the stage?
5 Did Mr Gilbert restart the music from the same place where he had stopped?
6 Does the journalist think Mr Gilbert made the right decision?

c Choose five new words or phrases from the text. Check their meaning and pronunciation and try to learn them.

◼️ CAN YOU UNDERSTAND THESE PEOPLE?
VIDEO

2 50))) In the street Watch or listen to five people and answer the questions.

Christopher   Maria   Harry   Sean   Liz

1 Christopher likes using the subway because _____.
   a he only needs to take one train
   b he gets to work in less than half an hour
   c it runs all day and night
2 Maria thinks that women are better than men at looking after young children because _____.
   a they have had a lot of practice
   b they know when children are hungry
   c they know what to do when children are ill
3 Harry says that men in her family _____.
   a don't enjoy telling stories
   b talk about the same things as women
   c try to talk about things that interest them
4 Sean _____.
   a started learning yoga three years ago
   b can touch his toes
   c is thinking of giving up yoga
5 It annoys Liz when people _____.
   a make phone calls all the time
   b play games on their phones
   c use their phones when they are with other people

CAN YOU SAY THIS IN ENGLISH?

Do the tasks with a partner. Tick (✓) the box if you can do them.

Can you...?

1 ☐ compare different methods of public transport in your town / country
2 ☐ agree or disagree with this statement, and say why: *All towns and cities should have a lot more cycle lanes.*
3 ☐ talk about typical stereotypes about men and women, and say if you think they are true
4 ☐ describe something you would like to be able to do, but have never been able to
5 ☐ talk about things which are / aren't good manners in your country if you are staying with someone as a guest, and what you think is the right thing to do

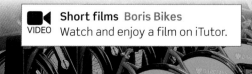

◼️ **Short films** Boris Bikes
VIDEO Watch and enjoy a film on iTutor.

G past tenses: simple, continuous, perfect
V sport
P /ɔː/ and /ɜː/

Why did he lose the match?

Because he wasn't feeling very well in the last set.

5A Sporting superstitions

1 VOCABULARY sport

a Do the quiz in small groups.

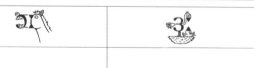

SPORTS QUIZ

What sport do you associate with...?

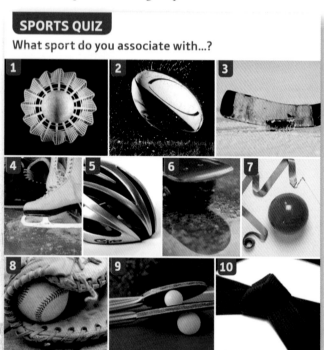

b ➤ p.157 Vocabulary Bank *Sport*.

2 PRONUNCIATION /ɔː/ and /ɜː/

a Write the words in the correct column. Be careful with *or* (there are two possible pronunciations).

ball caught court draw fought hurt score serve shirt sport warm up world worse work out

b (3 6)) Listen and check.

c ➤ p.166 Sound Bank. Look at the typical spellings of these sounds.

d (3 7)) Listen and write six sentences.

3 SPEAKING

In pairs, interview your partner about sport using the questionnaire. Ask for more information.

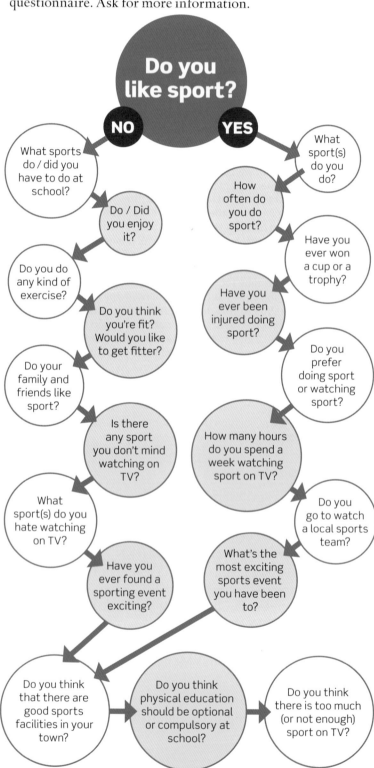

Do you like sport?

NO

YES

What sports do / did you have to do at school?

Do / Did you enjoy it?

Do you do any kind of exercise?

Do you think you're fit? Would you like to get fitter?

Do your family and friends like sport?

Is there any sport you don't mind watching on TV?

What sport(s) do you hate watching on TV?

Have you ever found a sporting event exciting?

What sport(s) do you do?

How often do you do sport?

Have you ever won a cup or a trophy?

Have you ever been injured doing sport?

Do you prefer doing sport or watching sport?

How many hours do you spend a week watching sport on TV?

Do you go to watch a local sports team?

What's the most exciting sports event you have been to?

Do you think that there are good sports facilities in your town?

Do you think physical education should be optional or compulsory at school?

Do you think there is too much (or not enough) sport on TV?

4 READING

a Do you know of any sports players who are superstitious? What do they do?

b Read an article about sport superstitions and complete it with **A–F**.

  A It is not only the players who are superstitious
  B A good example is Serena Williams
  C Superstitions and rituals are very common among fans
  D After my wife had left the room, Murray lost the fourth set
  E The superstitions and rituals are not confined to the court
  F ~~Tennis players are strange people~~

c Read the article again. Who does the article say are superstitious: sports players, sports fans, TV spectators, or all of them?

d <u>Underline</u> five words or phrases you want to remember from the article.

e Look at the photos of four more famous sports people who are superstitious. Do you know what any of their superstitions are or were?

Tiger Woods

Laurent Blanc

Kolo Touré

Alexander Wurz

f ▶ **Communication** *Other sporting superstitions* **A** *p.106* **B** *p.110*. Read and tell each other about the people in the photos.

g Do *you* have any superstitions, e.g. when you are playing or watching sport, or before an exam?

If I bounce the ball five times...

MATTHEW SYED writes about sporting superstitions

1 *Tennis players are strange people*. Have you noticed how they always ask for three balls instead of two; how they bounce the ball the same number of times before serving, as if any change from their routine might result in disaster?

2 _____, the ex-world number 1 female tennis player. When she was once asked why she had played so badly at the French Open she answered, 'I didn't tie my shoe laces right and I didn't bounce the ball five times and I didn't bring my shower sandals to the court with me. I didn't have my extra dress. I just knew it was fate; it wasn't going to happen.'

3 _____. Goran Ivanišević, Wimbledon champion in 2001, was convinced that if he won a match he had to repeat everything he did the previous day, such as eating the same food at the same restaurant, talking to the same people and watching the same TV programmes. One year this meant that he had to watch *Teletubbies* every morning during his Wimbledon campaign. 'Sometimes it got very boring,' he said.

4 _____. As we were watching British tennis player Andy Murray play the fourth set at Wimbledon, my wife suddenly got up and went to the kitchen. 'He keeps losing games when I'm in the room,' she said. 'If I go out now, he'll win.'

5 _____. Last year, a survey of British football supporters found that 21 per cent had a lucky charm (anything from a scarf to a lucky coin), while another questionnaire revealed that 70 per cent of Spanish football fans performed pre-match rituals (like wearing 'lucky' clothes, eating the same food or drink, or watching matches with the same people).

6 _____. She returned, and he won the fifth. I laughed at her, and then remembered my football team, Spurs, who were losing 1–0 in the Carling Cup. 'If I leave the room now, Spurs will score,' I told my kids, after 27 minutes of extra time. I left the room and they scored. Twice.

> **Glossary**
> **Teletubbies** a British television series for very young children
> **Spurs** Tottenham Hotspur, a London football team

Adapted from The Times

5 LISTENING

a In your country, are referees a) well-paid b) respected c) unpopular? Why do you think somebody would want to become a referee?

b (3 8))) You're going to hear to an interview with an ex-Champions League football referee from Spain. Listen to **Part 1** and choose a, b, or c.

Juan Antonio Fernandez Marin refereed 200 league and 50 international matches

1 Why did he become a referee?
  a His father was a referee.
  b He liked sport, but wasn't good at it.
  c He was always attracted by the idea.
2 What was the most exciting match he ever refereed?
  a His first professional match.
  b He can't choose just one.
  c Real Madrid against Barcelona.
3 The worst experience he ever had as a referee was when _____ attacked him.
  a a player b a woman c a child
4 Why does he think there is more cheating in football today?
  a Because football is big business.
  b Because the referees are worse.
  c Because footballers are better at cheating.
5 How does he say footballers often cheat?
  a They fall over when no one has touched them.
  b They accept money to lose matches.
  c They touch the ball with their hands.

c (3 9))) Now listen to **Part 2**. Complete the sentences with one to three words.

1 The most difficult thing for him about being a referee is making _____ during a match.
2 One of the reasons why it's difficult is because football today is so _____.
3 Making correct decisions often depends on the referee's interpretation of _____.
4 He thinks that players who cheat are still _____.
5 A study that was done on Leo Messi shows that he can run exceptionally fast _____.
6 He thinks Messi isn't the _____ footballer.

d Do you agree with the referee that there is more cheating in football than before? Is it true in other sports as well? Would *you* like to be a sports referee (or umpire)? Why (not)?

6 GRAMMAR past tenses: simple, continuous, perfect

a In your country, is cheating considered a serious problem in sport? In what sports do you think cheating is most common? What kind of things do people do when they cheat?

b Read *Taking a short cut* about a marathon runner who cheated. How did she cheat?

c Look at the highlighted verbs in the text. Which of them are used for…?

1 a completed action in the past
2 an action that happened *before* the past time we are talking about
3 an action in progress (or not) at a particular moment in the past

d ➤ p.140 Grammar Bank 5A. Learn more about past tenses and practise them.

e Read *The hand of God?* and complete it with the verbs in the right tenses.

Famous (cheating) moments in sport

Although it isn't true that everybody in sport cheats, it is certainly true that there are cheats in every sport...

Taking a short cut

On 21 April 1980, 23-year-old Rosie Ruiz was the first woman to cross the finish line at the Boston Marathon. She finished the race in the third-fastest time for a female runner (two hours, 31 minutes, 56 seconds). But when the organizers congratulated Rosie after the race, they were surprised because she wasn't sweating very much. Some spectators who were watching the race told them what had really happened. During the last half mile Rosie suddenly jumped out of the crowd and sprinted to the finish line. The marathon organizers took Ruiz's title away and awarded it to the real winner, Jacqueline Gareau. It was later discovered that three months earlier Rosie had also cheated in the New York Marathon where she had taken the subway!

The hand of God?

It was 22 June 1986. Argentina ¹*were playing* (play) England in the quarter-finals of the World Cup and both teams ²_____ (play) well. The score ³_____ (be) 0–0. In the 51st minute the Argentinian captain, Diego Maradona, ⁴_____ (score) a goal. The English players ⁵_____ (protest), but the referee ⁶_____ (give) the goal. However, TV cameras showed that Maradona ⁷_____ (score) the goal with his hand! Maradona ⁸_____ (say) the next day, 'It was partly the hand of Maradona, and partly the hand of God.'

Later in the game Maradona ⁹_____ (score) another goal and Argentina ¹⁰_____ (win) the match 2–1. They went on to win the World Cup.

7 SPEAKING

a You are going to tell your partner two anecdotes. Choose two of the topics below and plan what you are going to say. Ask your teacher for any words you need.

TELL YOUR PARTNER ABOUT...

- **a time you cheated (in a sport / game or in an exam)**
  When and where did this happen? What were you doing? Why did you cheat? What happened in the end?

- **a really exciting sports event you saw**
  Where and when was it? Who was playing?
  What happened? Why was it so exciting?

- **a time you had an accident or got a sports injury**
  When and where did this happen? What were you doing? How did the accident happen? What part of your body did you hurt? What happened next? How long did it take you to recover?

- **a time you saw or met a celebrity**
  When was this? Where were you? Who were you with? What was the celebrity doing? What was he / she wearing? Did you speak to him / her? What happened in the end?

- **a time you got lost**
  Where were you going? How were you travelling? Why did you get lost? What happened in the end?

b Work with a partner. Tell each other your two stories. Give as much detail as you can.

 Starting an anecdote
I'm going to tell you about a time when...
This happened a few years ago...
When I was younger...

8 WRITING

➤ **p.116 Writing** *Telling a story*. Write a story about something that happened to you.

9 ③14)) **SONG** *We Are the Champions* ♫

G *usually* and *used to*
V relationships
P linking, the letter s

How do you usually get to work? — I used to take the bus, but now I cycle.

5B Love at Exit 19

1 READING

a How do you think people usually meet friends and partners nowadays? Number the phrases 1–5 (1 = the most popular). Then compare with a partner. Do you agree?

A ☐ at work
B ☐ at school or university
C ☐ on the internet (e.g. on forums, on social networking sites, etc.)
D ☐ in a bar, club, etc.
E ☐ through friends

b (3 15)) Read and listen to an article about Sonya Baker and Michael Fazio. Why did their relationship nearly never happen?

♥ Love at Exit 19

He was a tollbooth operator, she was a soprano who sang in Carnegie Hall. Their eyes met at Exit 19 of the New York State Thruway, when he charged her 37¢. The romance that followed was even less likely than the plot of an opera!

Sonya Baker was a frequent commuter from her home in the suburbs to New York City. One day, when she was driving to an audition, she came off the Thruway and stopped at the tollbooth where Michael Fazio was working. She chatted to him as she paid to go through, and thought he was cute. For the next three months, they used to exchange a few words as she handed him the money, and he raised the barrier to let her pass. 'It was mostly "What are you doing today? Where are you going?"' she said. They learned more about each other, for example that Sonya loved Puccini and Verdi, while Michael's love was the New York Yankees. But their conversations suddenly came to an end when Michael changed his working hours. 'He used to work during the day,' said Sonya, 'but he changed to night shifts.' Although Michael still looked out for Sonya's white Toyota Corolla, he did not see her again for six months.

When Michael's working hours changed back to the day shift, he decided to put a traffic cone in front of his lane. He thought, 'It will be like putting a candle in a window.' Sonya saw it, and their romance started up again. 'I almost crashed my car on various occasions,' she said, 'trying to cross several lanes to get to his exit.' Finally, she found the courage to give Michael a piece of paper with her phone number as she passed through the toll. Michael called her and for their first date they went to see the film *Cool Runnings*, and then later they went to an opera, *La Bohème*, and to a Yankees game.

They are now married and living in Kentucky, where Sonya is a voice and music professor at Murray State College and Michael runs an activity centre at a nursing home. It turned out that she had given him her number just in time. A short while later she moved to New Jersey and stopped using the New York State Thruway. 'I might never have seen him again,' she said.

Glossary
a tollbooth a small building by the side of a road where you pay money to use the road
Carnegie Hall a famous concert hall in New York City
New York State Thruway a motorway
New York Yankees a baseball team based in the Bronx in New York
a traffic cone a plastic object, often red and white, used to show where vehicles can or can't go

Adapted from The Times

c Read the article again and number the events in the order they happened.

A ☐ Michael changed his working hours.
B ☐ Michael tried to find Sonya.
C ☐ They got married.
D ☐ Sonya moved to New Jersey.
E ☐ Sonya gave Michael her phone number.
F ☐ Michael changed his working hours again.
G ☐ 1 Sonya chatted to Michael.
H ☐ They stopped seeing each other.
I ☐ They had their first date.
J ☐ Sonya and Michael moved to Kentucky.

d Read the article again and look at the **highlighted** words and phrases. Try to work out what they mean. Then match them with 1–10 below.

1 _____ a period of time worked by a group of workers
2 _____ a person who travels into a city to work every day
3 _____ attractive, good-looking (*AmE*)
4 _____ what had happened was
5 _____ manages
6 _____ probable
7 _____ sth which is used to give light, made of wax
8 _____ have short conversations
9 _____ they looked at each other romantically
10 _____ was brave enough

2 GRAMMAR *usually* and *used to*

a Think of a couple you know well, e.g. your parents or friends. How did they meet? Do you know any couples who met in unusual circumstances?

b (3 16)) Listen to four people talking about where they met their partner. Match each one with a place from **1a**.

Speaker 1 ☐   Speaker 2 ☐   Speaker 3 ☐   Speaker 4 ☐

c Listen to each story again and take notes on how the people met. Compare your notes with your partner and listen again if necessary. Which meeting do you think was the most romantic?

d Look at two extracts from the listening. Answer the questions with a partner.

> We used to go to bars and clubs together on Saturday night.
> It used to be quite difficult to meet people.

1 When do we use *used to*? How do you make negatives and questions?
2 How would you change these sentences (using *usually*) if you wanted to talk about present habits or situations?

e ➤ **p.141 Grammar Bank 5B.** Learn more about *usually* and *used to*, and practise them.

3 PRONUNCIATION & SPEAKING linking

> 🔍 **used to**
> Remember that *used to* and *use to* are normally linked and pronounced /juːstə/.

a (3 18)) Listen and repeat the sentences. Copy the linking and the sentence rhythm.

1 I **used to live** in London.
2 She **didn't use to wear glasses**.
3 **Where** did you **use to work before**?
4 They **used to see each other** a **lot**.
5 **Didn't** you **use to have** a **beard**?

b In pairs, tell each other about *three* of the following. Give as much information as you can. How do you feel about these people and things now?

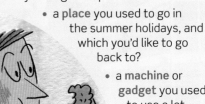

Is there...

• a kind of **food** or **drink** you didn't use to like at all, but which you now like?

• a **TV series** you used to be addicted to? Why did you like it?

• a **singer** or a **kind of music** you used to listen to a lot (but don't any more)?

• a **sport** or **game** you used to play a lot, but which you've given up?

• a **place** you used to go in the summer holidays, and which you'd like to go back to?

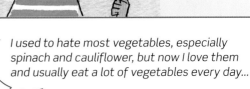

• a **machine** or **gadget** you used to use a lot, but which is now out of date?

> *I used to hate most vegetables, especially spinach and cauliflower, but now I love them and usually eat a lot of vegetables every day...*

4 VOCABULARY relationships

a Explain the difference between these pairs of phrases.

1 to meet somebody and to know somebody
2 a colleague and a friend
3 to argue with somebody and to discuss something with somebody

b ➤ **p.158 Vocabulary Bank** *Relationships*.

c Think of one of your close friends. In pairs, ask and answer the questions.

- How long have you known him / her?
- Where did you meet?
- Why do you get on well?
- What do you have in common?
- Do you ever argue? What about?
- How often do you see each other?
- How do you keep in touch?
- Have you ever lost touch? Why? When?
- Do you think you'll stay friends?

5 PRONUNCIATION
the letter *s*

a **3 21))** Listen to the words in the list. How is the *s* (or *se*) pronounced? Write them in the correct columns.

busy   close (*adj*)   close (*verb*)   conversation   decision
discuss   eyes   friends   lose   music   pleasure
practise   raise   school   somebody   sport   sugar
summer   sure   unusual   used to   usually   various

b **3 22))** Listen and check.

c Answer with a partner.

1 How is *s* usually pronounced at the beginning of a word? What are the two exceptions?
2 What two ways can *s* (or *es*) be pronounced at the end of a word?
3 How is *s* pronounced in *-sion*?

6 LISTENING

a Talk to a partner. Do you think the following are **T** (true) or **F** (false)?

1 22-year-olds have an average of 1,000 friends.
2 Men have more online friends than women.
3 People who spend a lot of time on *Facebook* become more dissatisfied with their own lives.

b  (3 23))) Listen to the introduction to a radio programme. According to research, are 1–3 in **a** true or false?

c (3 24))) Listen to four people who phone the programme, George, Beth, Caitlin, and Ned. Who is the most positive about *Facebook*? Who is the most negative?

d Listen again. Answer with **G**eorge, **B**eth, **C**aitlin, or **N**ed.

Which caller…?
1 ☐ does not want to share personal information with strangers
2 ☐ has fewer *Facebook* friends than he / she used to have
3 ☐ has over a thousand friends
4 ☐ uses it to keep in touch with friends who don't live near
5 ☐ thinks people use *Facebook* to give themselves more importance
6 ☐ used to use *Facebook* more than he / she does now
7 ☐ uses *Facebook* instead of phoning
8 ☐ does not use social networking sites

e Do you use *Facebook* or any other social networking sites? Do you agree with anything the speakers said?

7 SPEAKING

a Read sentences **A–F** below. Tick (✓) the ones you agree with and cross (✗) the ones you don't agree with. Think about your reasons.

A ☐ You can only have two or three close friends.
B ☐ Nowadays people are in touch with more people but have fewer close friends.
C ☐ Men keep their friends longer than women.
D ☐ You should never criticize your friend's partner.
E ☐ You should never lend money to a friend (or borrow money).
F ☐ It's impossible to stay good friends with an ex-partner.

b In groups, compare opinions. Try to give real examples from your own experience or of people you know. Use the phrases below to help you.

> 🔍 **Giving examples**
> **For example**, I have a friend who I've known since I was five years old…
> **For instance**, I once lent some money to a cousin…

1 ▶ JENNY HAS COFFEE WITH A FRIEND
VIDEO

a ③25))) Watch or listen to Jenny and Monica. What's Monica's news?

b Watch or listen again and answer the questions.

1 Who's Scott?
2 When did they get engaged?
3 Who has Monica told the news to?
4 What did she use to do a lot at night? What does she do now?
5 Who's going to organize the wedding?
6 What does Jenny tell Monica about her relationship with Rob?
7 What does Monica think about Rob being British?

2 ▶ PERMISSION AND REQUESTS
VIDEO

a ③26))) Watch or listen. What two favours does Rob ask Jenny?

b Watch or listen again. Mark the sentences **T** (true) or **F** (false). Correct the **F** sentences.

1 Rob orders a cappuccino.
2 Rob says Monica looks different from her photos.
3 Monica gets a good impression of Rob.
4 Monica leaves because she has to go to work.
5 Jenny says that most of their friends are in serious relationships.
6 Paul is going to stay for a fortnight.
7 Paul used to be very quiet when they were younger.
8 Jenny is keen to meet Paul.

c (3 27))) Look at some extracts from the conversation. Can you remember any of the missing words? Watch or listen and check.

Asking permission

1 **Rob** Do you _____ if I join you?
  Monica Of _____ not. Come on, sit down.

2 **Rob** Is it _____ if we change our plans a bit this week?
  Jenny Er...sure.

Requests: asking someone to do something

1 **Rob** _____ you pass the sugar?
  Jenny _____.

2 **Rob** Could you do me a big _____? I have to work late this evening, so... would you mind _____ him at the airport?
  Jenny _____ at all. I'd like to meet him.

3 **Rob** And do you think you _____ take him to my flat? I'll give you the keys.
  Jenny No _____, Rob.

d Look at the highlighted phrases and answer the questions.

1 How do you respond to *Do you mind if…?* and *Would you mind…?* when you mean *OK, no problem*?

2 Which two forms of request should you use if you want to be very polite or are asking a very big favour?

e (3 28))) Watch or listen and repeat the highlighted phrases. Copy the rhythm and intonation.

f Practise the dialogues in **c** with a partner.

g 👥 ➤ **Communication** *Could you do me a favour? p.105.*

3 ▇◄ PAUL ARRIVES
VIDEO

a (3 29))) Watch or listen. How do Rob and Jenny feel about Paul's arrival?

b Watch or listen again and (circle) the right answer.

1 Paul's appearance *has changed a lot | hasn't changed much.*
2 His flight was *on time | late.*
3 On the journey from the airport Paul *talked a lot about himself | asked Jenny a lot of personal questions.*
4 Rob suggests *eating in | eating out.*
5 Paul feels *exhausted | full of energy.*
6 Jenny *feels like | doesn't feel like* going out.

c Look at the **Social English phrases**. Can you remember any of the missing words?

Social English phrases	
Paul	Hey _____!
Paul	It's great to see you, _____.
Rob	How _____ you're so late?
Paul	No _____, man!
Jenny	Rob, I think I'll go home if you don't_____.
Rob	Just like the old _____!
Paul	Rob, we've got a lot to talk _____!

d (3 30))) Watch or listen and complete the phrases.

e Watch or listen again and repeat the phrases. How do you say them in your language?

👤	**Can you...?**
	☐ use different expressions to ask permission to do something and respond
	☐ use different expressions to ask another person to do something and respond
	☐ greet someone you haven't seen for a long time

G passive (all tenses)
V cinema
P sentence stress

6A Shot on location

Where was the film shot?

I think it was shot in New York.

1 READING

a Look at the photos with the article. Do they remind you of any films or TV series that you have seen?

b Now read the article and complete it with a past participle from the list.

based   designed   inhabited   inspired   ~~owned~~
photographed   transformed   used   welcomed

You are standing in *the place where...*

A Highclere Castle *near Newbury in Berkshire, UK*

The castle has been ¹ *owned* by the Carnarvon family since 1679, and the Earl and Countess Carnarvon currently live there. In 2010, film director Julian Fellowes, a close friend of the family, was planning a new TV series about an aristocratic family and their servants during the early 20th century. While he was staying at Highclere Castle, he realized that it would be the perfect place to set his historical drama, and the castle was ² _____ into *Downton Abbey*, the home of the fictional Crawley family. The series was a huge success and it has been sold all over the world. Both the interior and exterior scenes were shot in and around the castle itself.

In the second TV series the castle is used as a hospital during the First World War. These scenes are ³ _____ on a real-life event. In 1914, Lady Almina Carnarvon allowed soldiers who had been wounded to be looked after in the castle.

Go there

Highclere Castle and gardens are open to the public during the Easter and summer holidays, and on many Sundays and public holidays from 10.30 a.m. to 6.00 p.m. Visit the Egyptian Gallery which contains many objects brought back from his travels by Lady Almina's husband, the fifth Earl of Carnarvon, who famously discovered the tomb of the young Pharaoh Tutankhamun. www.highclerecastle.co.uk

B Cortlandt Alley *New York, USA*

In Hollywood's version of New York City, the giant metropolis is full of secret alleys where crimes take place, and criminals are chased by the police. In fact there are hardly any alleys in New York today at all. One of the few remaining ones, Cortlandt Alley, has been ⁴ _____ for almost all the alley scenes in films and TV series that are set in New York. Films with scenes that were shot there include *Crocodile Dundee* and *Men in Black 3*, and TV series like *Blue Bloods*, *Boardwalk Empire*, *NYPD Blue*, and *Law & Order*.

Go there

Thousands of tourists want to be ⁵ _____ in Cortlandt Alley. It is on the edge of Chinatown, in Manhattan, between Franklin Street and Canal Street. In fact it is a perfectly safe place to visit. In real life, it is not ⁶ _____ by gangsters, but is the home for perfectly respectable businesses such as the New York Table Tennis Federation Training Center.

C Christ Church College

Oxford, UK

This wonderful 16th-century college, with a spectacular tower, which was ⁷_____ by the famous architect Sir Christopher Wren, has an important connection with children's literature. It was at Christ Church that Charles Dodgson, professor of mathematics, first met the children of the Dean (the head of the College). He used to tell them stories, and was ⁸_____ by one of the girls, Alice, to write *Alice in Wonderland*, in 1865, under the pen-name of Lewis Carroll. Many years later, Christ Church was used as the setting for several film adaptations of some other famous children's books, the Harry Potter novels. The first time Harry and his friends enter Hogwarts, they walk up the Christ Church staircase where Professor McGonagall is waiting for them at the top. The dining room in Hogwarts is the Christ Church Dining Hall. It could not be used for filming, because it was being used by students at the time, so it was recreated in a studio.

Go there

Visitors are ⁹_____ throughout the year. However, as the college is a working academic institution, some areas may occasionally be closed to the public. Opening times: Monday to Saturday: 9 a.m.–5 p.m., Sunday: 2 p.m.–5 p.m. www.chch.ox.ac.uk

> **Glossary**
> **Earl and Countess** titles given to British aristocrats (people of a high social position)
> **Hogwarts** the fictional boarding school where Harry Potter goes

Adapted from a travel website

---

c Read the article again. Answer the questions with **A** (Highclere Castle), **B** (Cortlandt Alley), or **C** (Christ Church College).

Which place…?

1 is not really as it seems in films
2 has a permanent exhibition there
3 was used for the same thing both in real life and on TV
4 is where a famous author met a person who inspired him
5 is one of the few places of its kind that still exists
6 is only open during holiday periods
7 was built in the 1500s
8 is sometimes not open because people are working there

d Have you seen any of the films or TV series mentioned? Which of the three places would you most like to visit? Why?

2 GRAMMAR passive (all tenses)

a Read the *Highclere Castle* text again. <u>Underline</u> an example of the present passive, the past passive, the present perfect passive, the past perfect passive, and a passive infinitive. How do you form the passive? What part of the passive changes when you want to change the tense?

b ➤ p.142 Grammar Bank 6A. Learn more about the passive and practise it.

3 PRONUNCIATION sentence stress

a ③ 32)) Listen and write the stressed words in the large pink rectangles.

1   *film*   *based*   *famous*   *book* .

2

3 .

4 .

5 ?

6 ?

b Look at the stressed words and try to remember what the other (unstressed) words are. Then listen again to check and write them in.

4 VOCABULARY cinema

a Look at some extracts from the texts in **1**. What do you think the highlighted phrases mean?

1 Cortlandt Alley has been used for almost all the alley scenes in films and TV series that are set in New York.

2 These scenes are based on a real-life event.

3 Both the interior and exterior scenes were shot in and around the castle itself.

b ▶ p.159 Vocabulary Bank *Cinema*.

c Explain the difference between these pairs of words and phrases.

1 a plot and a script
2 a horror film and a thriller
3 a musical and a soundtrack
4 the main cast and the extras

5 SPEAKING

a Read the cinema interview and think about your answers and reasons.

THE **Cinema** INTERVIEW

1 **CAN YOU THINK OF A FILM WHICH...?**

– was incredibly funny
– had a very sad ending
– sent you to sleep
– made you feel good
– you've seen several times
– made you buy the soundtrack

2 **DO YOU PREFER...?**

– seeing films at home, or in the cinema
– seeing a) American films
        b) other foreign films
        c) films from your country
– seeing foreign films dubbed or with subtitles

3 **TELL ME ABOUT A REALLY GOOD FILM YOU'VE SEEN THIS YEAR**

– What kind of film is it?
– Is it based on a book or on a real event?
– Where and when is it set?
– Who's in it? Who is it directed by?
– Does it have a good plot?
– Does it have a good soundtrack?
– Why did you like it?

b In pairs, interview each other. Ask for and give as much information as you can. Do you have similar tastes?

6 SPEAKING & LISTENING

a Look at the images from some famous films. What kinds of films are they? Have you seen any of them? What are they about? What do you think they have in common?

War Horse

Indiana Jones and the Temple of Doom

E.T. the Extra-Terrestrial

Minority Report

Catch Me If You Can

b Now look at some photos of Steven Spielberg and Dagmara Walkowicz, who worked as an interpreter on one of his films. In pairs, answer the questions.

1 Where do you think they are?
2 Which Spielberg film do you think was being made?
3 What do you think Dagmara is doing in the photo on the right?
4 Do you think Dagmara found Spielberg easy to work with?

c **3 36**))) Listen to the first part of an interview with Dagmara and check your answers to **b** 1 and 2.

d Listen again and mark the sentences **T** (true) or **F** (false).

1 When the film company came to Krakow, Dagmara was working as a teacher.
2 She got a part-time job doing translations for them.
3 There was party at the hotel to celebrate Spielberg's birthday.
4 When she arrived she was asked to interpret Spielberg's speech, because the interpreter was late.
5 Spielberg was very pleased with the way she had done her job.

e **3 37**))) Now listen to the second part of the interview and check your answers to **b** 3 and 4.

f Listen again and make notes under the headings below.

What she had to do during the film
go to the film set every day, translate Spielberg's instructions

The worst thing about the job

One especially difficult scene

What it was like to work with Spielberg

Being an extra

What happened after the film was finished

g Would you have liked to have done Dagmara's job? Do you think she made the right decision in the end?

7 WRITING

➤ p.117 Writing *A film review*. Write a review of a film.

G modals of deduction: *might, can't, must*
V the body
P diphthongs

6B Judging by appearances

> She can't be his mother. She must be his sister.

> No, she's his mother. She looks very young for her age.

Annabel, 27

Martin, 39

Sean, 19

Sarah, 22

1 READING & SPEAKING

a Answer the questions in pairs.

1 Do you have a profile photo of yourself which you use on social networking sites, or on your ID?

2 Why did you choose it?

3 What do you think the photo says about you?

b Look at the four profile photos. Why do you think the people have chosen these photos?

c Read the article and complete it with the headings below. Then look at the four photos again. Which of the 12 categories do you think they belong to?

A **Photo of you as a child**

B **Holiday photo**

C **Logo of your business or company**

D **Photo with a celebrity**

E **Photo with a partner**

F **Photo with your baby or child**

d Read the article again. Look at the highlighted phrases. With a partner, try to work out their meaning.

e Think about the profile photos or ID card photos of your family and friends. Which categories do they fit in? Do you agree with the text? Has the article made you want to change your profile picture? Why (not)?

What does your profile picture say about you?

Whether it's a photo of you on a night out or of you with your newborn baby, the image you choose to represent you on social networking sites says a lot about you.

Profile pictures on *Facebook* and similar sites are the visual projection to friends and family of who you are and what you are like. On *Twitter*, where people follow both friends and strangers, profile pictures are smaller and perhaps more significant. They are often the first and only visual introduction people have to each other. So what does *your* profile photo say about you?

According to communications consultant Terry Prone, there are 12 categories that cover most types of profile pictures.

1 **The professionally taken photo**
You use social media mainly for business or career purposes.

2
You want to show what you have achieved in your family life, and are generally more interested in a response from women than from men.

3
You see your other half as the most important thing in your life, and you see yourself as one half of a couple.

4 **Having fun with friends**
Generally young and carefree, you want to project an image of being fun and popular.

5
You are a bit of an escapist and keen to show a different side of yourself from what you do on a day-to-day basis.

6
This kind of image says that you don't really want to grow up and face the future. You are nostalgic for your childhood.

7 **Caricature**
Using a caricature is a way of saying that your image isn't rigid and that you don't take yourself too seriously.

8 **Photo related to your name, but not actually you (a shop sign, or product label for example)**
You want to be identifiable, but you feel your name is more important than what you look like.

9 **Photo related to your political beliefs or a team that you support**
You think that your beliefs and interests are more important than your personality.

10
You think that showing yourself with a well-known person will make you seem more important.

11 **Self-portrait taken with webcam / camera phone**
Functional. It says, 'Look, I don't dress up; take me as I am.'

12
You only use social media in a professional capacity, and you identify more with your work role than with your private life.

Adapted from The Irish Times

2 **VOCABULARY** the body

a ③ **38**)) Look at the four pictures and listen. Which one is the thief? Describe the four pictures with a partner.

b ➤ p.160 **Vocabulary Bank** *The body.*

3 **PRONUNCIATION** diphthongs

a ③ **41**)) Read the information about diphthongs. Then listen and repeat the six words and sounds.

1	2	3	4	5	6
aɪ	eɪ	əʊ	aʊ	eə	ɪə

🔍 **Diphthongs**
Diphthongs are a combination of two short vowel sounds, e.g. the /ɪ/ sound and the /ə/ sound said together make the longer /ɪə/ sound.

b Write these words in the correct columns.

bite beard eyes face hair mouth nose
shoulders smile stare taste throw toes

c ③ **42**)) Listen and check. Then practise saying the phrases below.

fair hair   narrow shoulders   a wide mouth
brown eyes   a Roman nose   a round face

d Do the quiz with a partner. Answer with *my | your | their* + a part of the body.

WHICH PART(S) OF THE BODY...?

1	do you wear	a ring	on
		gloves	
		socks	
		a cap	

2 do ballet dancers stand on
3 do footballers often injure
4 do women put make-up on
5 do people brush
6 do people carry a rucksack on

4 ③ **43**)) **SONG** *I Got Life* ♫

5 **GRAMMAR** modals of deduction

a Look at the photos of three people. Then in two minutes, match three sentences with each person.

- ☐ He / she might be a criminal.
- ☐ He / she might not know how to use the internet.
- ☐ He / she could be a model.
- ☐ He / she could be German or Scandinavian.
- ☐ He / she may not have a job.
- ☐ He / she may be a millionaire.
- ☐ His / her hair must be dyed.
- ☐ He / she must be retired.
- ☐ He / she can't be a business person.

b Compare with a partner.   *I think he could be a model.*

c ➤ **Communication** *Judging by appearances p.106.* Find out about the three people. Did you guess correctly?

d Look at the sentences in **a** and answer the questions.

1 Which modal verbs mean *it's possible*?
   *might*_____ _____ _____
2 Which modal verb means *it's very probable*? _____
3 Which modal verb means *it's impossible*? _____

e ➤ **p.143 Grammar Bank 6B.** Learn more about modals of deduction and practise them.

6 **LISTENING & READING**

a In pairs, look at the man in the photo. Make sentences about him using *might / may / could (not) be, must be*, or *can't be* and words from the list.

> Italian   English
> very rich   homeless
> intellectual   hungry

b (3 47)) Listen to a woman talking about the man in **a** and answer the questions.

1 Where were the speaker and her friend Adriana?
2 What were they doing when they saw the man?
3 What did he look like?
4 What did Adriana want to do?
5 What did the speaker do?

c (3 48)) Why do you think the speaker stopped Adriana? Listen and find out. Who was the man?

d Look at the two photos of Susan Boyle in the article. Do you know who she is? Can you guess why she has changed her appearance?

e Read the article once and choose the best summary.

1 We now realize that it is wrong to judge people by their appearance.
2 Judging people by appearance can be useful, and is often right.
3 If you try to judge people by their appearance, you will usually be wrong about them.

f Read the article again and mark the sentences **T** (true) or **F** (false). Say why the **F** ones are false.

1 Most people predicted that Susan Boyle would be successful as a singer.
2 After her appearance on TV, people started saying that we shouldn't judge people by their appearance.
3 Scientists think that judging by appearance is an important skill.
4 It is more important to be able to make quick judgements about people than it used to be.
5 When we judge people by their appearance, we are usually wrong.
6 Susan Boyle has probably realized that people will never stop judging her by her appearance.

Yes, appearance matters.

When Susan Boyle first walked onto the stage of the *Britain's Got Talent* TV show people immediately thought that she looked like a 47-year-old single woman, who lived alone with her cat (which in fact she was). Nobody thought for a minute that she had a chance of doing well on the show, or could ever become a star. But when she opened her mouth and started singing *I Dreamed a Dream*, from the musical *Les Misérables*, everybody was amazed. After the video of her performance went viral, journalists started talking about how wrong it is to stereotype people into categories, and how we should learn, once and for all, 'not to judge a book by its cover'.

But social scientists say that there are reasons why we judge people based on how they look. On a very basic level, judging people by their appearance means putting them quickly into categories. In the past, being able to do this was vitally important, and humans developed the ability to judge other people in seconds. Susan Fiske, a professor of psychology and neuroscience at Princeton University, said that traditionally, most stereotypes are linked to judging whether a person looks dangerous or not. 'In prehistoric times, it was important to stay away from people who looked aggressive and dominant,' she said.

One reason why our brains persist in using stereotypes, experts say, is that often they give us generally accurate information, even if all the details aren't right. Ms Boyle's appearance, for example, accurately told us a lot about her, including her socio-economic level and lack of worldly experience.

People's enthusiasm for Susan Boyle, and for other underdogs who end up winning, is unlikely to stop us from stereotyping people. This maybe one of the reasons why, although Ms Boyle expressed the hope that 'maybe this could teach them a lesson, or set an example,' she did begin to change her appearance, wearing make-up, dying her grey hair, and appearing in more stylish clothing.

Adapted from The New York Times

---

g Find a word or phrase in the article for the definitions.

Paragraph 1

1 _____ _____ was sent all over the internet

2 _____ a _____ by _____ _____
judge a person by his / her appearance

Paragraph 2

3 _____ _____ absolutely essential

Paragraph 3

4 _____-_____ _____ what social class she is and how much money she has

Paragraph 4

5 _____ people who are not expected to succeed

h Talk to a partner.

1 Do you think people in your country tend to judge other people by their appearance? In what way?

2 How important do you think appearance is for the following people?
- politicians
- TV presenters
- business people
- singers
- doctors

Do you think it is right that their appearance matters?

3 On what occasions might *you* judge someone by their appearance?

5&6 Revise and Check

GRAMMAR

Circle a, b, or c.

1 Elliot served, but the ball _____ into the net.
   a went   b was going   c had gone
2 The athlete fell at the end of the race when she _____ towards the finishing line.
   a run   b was running   c had run
3 I didn't realize that you two _____ before.
   a didn't meet   b weren't meeting   c hadn't met
4 A I can't find my glasses anywhere.
   B _____ them when you left home this morning?
   a Did you wear   b Were you wearing   c Had you worn
5 _____ walk to work, or do you drive?
   a Do you use to   b Do you usually   c Use you to
6 When I was a child I _____ like vegetables.
   a don't used to   b didn't used to   c didn't use to
7 _____ do any sport when you were at university?
   a Did you use to   b Use you to   c Did you used to
8 Lots of famous films _____ in Cortlandt Alley.
   a have shot   b have been shot   c has been shot
9 He's an actor who hates _____ about his private life.
   a asking   b being asking   c being asked
10 Why _____ in New Zealand?
   a is the film being made   b is the film making
   c is making the film
11 Many people believe that Columbus _____ America.
   a didn't really discover   b wasn't really discovered
   c weren't really discovered
12 A I've just rung the doorbell, but there's no answer.
   B They _____ in the garden. Have a look.
   a can't be   b might be   c can be
13 He's a bit older than me, so he _____ in his 30s now.
   a must be   b may be   c can't be
14 A Did you know Ann and Simon have broken up?
   B That _____ true! I saw them together just now.
   a mustn't be   b might be   c can't be
15 A Does your sister know Liam?
   B She _____ him. I'm not sure.
   a can't know   b may know   c can know

VOCABULARY

a Write the parts of the body that you use to do these actions.

1 kiss _____   3 smell _____   5 bite _____
2 stare _____   4 clap _____

b Circle the right verb or phrase.

1 Arsenal *won* / *beat* Chelsea 2–0.
2 Can you book a tennis *course* / *court* on Friday?
3 Sports players are usually very careful not to *get injured* / *get fit* before important events.
4 Real Madrid *scored* / *kicked* a goal just before half-time.
5 I *do* / *go* swimming every morning during the week.

c Complete the words.

1 Luke is a very **cl**_____ friend. I've known him all my life.
2 My wife and I have a lot in **c**_____.
3 Gina and I lost **t**_____ after we both changed jobs.
4 We met in our first class at university, and we **g**_____ to know each other very quickly.
5 Linda is getting married next month. Her **f**_____ is Italian. He's very nice.

d Write words beginning with *s* for the definitions.

1 _____ the music of a film
2 _____ the translation of the dialogue of a film
3 _____ _____ images often created by computer
4 _____ the most important actor in a film
5 _____ one part of a film which happens in one place

e Complete the sentences with one word.

1 I love working _____ at the gym. I go every evening.
2 The player was sent _____ for insulting the referee.
3 My sister and her boyfriend have split _____.
4 Jane and Nora used to be great friends, but they fell _____ because of a boy they both liked.
5 Is there anything good _____ TV tonight?

PRONUNCIATION

a Circle the word with a different sound.

1 score   draw   court   couple
2 taste   lose   propose   nose
3 face   eyes   audience   course
4 hair   stare   ears   parents
5 drama   arm   war   cast

b Underline the stressed syllable.

1 re|fe|ree   3 spec|ta|tors   5 co|lleague
2 re|view   4 di|rec|tor

62

CAN YOU UNDERSTAND THIS TEXT?

a Read the text. Do you know of any similar theatrical superstitions in your country? What are they?

b Read the text again and choose a, b, or c.

1 Before a performance, actors often…
   a wish each other good luck
   b wish each other bad luck
   c touch each others' legs.

2 Whistling in a theatre is considered unlucky because…
   a it used to cause problems for the scene changers
   b it was associated with being out of work
   c it confused the actors

3 It is bad luck to…
   a rehearse any part of a play without an audience
   b rehearse a play in front of family members
   c get to the end of a play when nobody is watching

c Choose five new words or phrases from the text. Check their meaning and pronunciation and try to learn them.

THEATRICAL SUPERSTITIONS

Along with sports players, theatre professionals are considered some of the most superstitious people around. These are some of their more common beliefs and practices.

NOT WISHING "GOOD LUCK"

Generally, it is considered bad luck to wish someone 'good luck' in a theatre. Before a performance, it is traditional for the cast to get together and prevent bad luck by wishing each other <u>bad</u> luck. English actors used to say to each other 'I hope you break a leg', and even today actors and musicians often say 'break a leg' to each other instead of 'good luck' before they go on stage.

WHISTLING

It is considered bad luck for an actor to whistle on or off stage. Original stage crews were often hired from ships which were in port, and whose sailors were temporarily unemployed. These sailors, as they did on ships, often used special whistles to communicate scene changes to each other. If an actor whistled, this could confuse the sailors into changing the set or scenery at the wrong time.

NOT WITHOUT AN AUDIENCE

It is considered bad luck to complete a performance of a play when there is no audience. For this reason actors never say the last line of a play during rehearsals, or some production companies allow a limited number of people (usually friends, family, and reviewers) to attend the dress rehearsals.

CAN YOU UNDERSTAND THESE PEOPLE?

VIDEO

3 49)) **In the street** Watch or listen to five people and answer the questions.

Maria   Adrian   Ryder   Helen   Liz

1 Maria _____.
   a prefers doing sport to watching sport
   b started watching Formula 1 because of her father
   c likes watching athletics because it's exciting

2 An old friend of Adrian's who was using online dating _____.
   a thought the person looked less attractive in real life
   b thought the person looked younger on the internet
   c married the person they met on the internet

3 Ryder hasn't cheated by _____.
   a using his phone
   b bringing a book to an exam
   c looking at another student's exam

4 Helen likes *Dirty Dancing* because _____.
   a she loves the soundtrack
   b some of the actors in it are attractive
   c it makes her laugh

5 Liz chose her profile photo because she looks _____ in it.
   a attractive   b silly   c unusual

CAN YOU SAY THIS IN ENGLISH?

Do the tasks with a partner. Tick (✓) the box if you can do them.

Can you…?

1 ☐ tell an anecdote about something that happened to you using the past simple, past continuous, and past perfect

2 ☐ talk about three past and three present habits of yours

3 ☐ describe a film, saying where is was set, what it is based on, who it was directed by, and what you thought of it

4 ☐ make deductions about a famous person using *might be*, *must be* and *can't be*

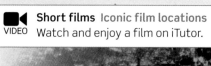
Short films Iconic film locations
VIDEO Watch and enjoy a film on iTutor.

G first conditional and future time clauses + *when, until,* etc.
V education
P the letter *u*

What will you do if you don't pass your exams?

I'll probably retake them.

7A Extraordinary school for boys

1 VOCABULARY education

a You have two minutes. Answer as many of questions 1–8 as you can in **one** minute. How many did you get right?

b (4 2)) Now match the questions with these school subjects. Then listen and check.

- ☐ biology
- ☐ chemistry
- ☐ geography
- ☐ history
- ☐ information technology
- ☐ literature
- ☐ maths
- ☐ physics

c ➤ p.161 Vocabulary Bank *Education.*

1 How many wives did King Henry VIII have?

2 What is the capital of Brazil?

3 Who wrote David Copperfield?

4 How many megabytes are there in a gigabyte?

5 Who developed the theory of relativity?

6 What is 5 × 18 ÷ 4?

7 How many legs does an insect have?

8 What is water made of?

2 PRONUNCIATION & SPEAKING
the letter *u*

> 🔍 **The letter *u***
> The letter *u* is usually pronounced /ju/, e.g. *uniform* or /ʌ/, e.g. *lunch* and sometimes /uː/, e.g. *true*, or /ʊ/, e.g. *put*.

a Put the words in the correct column.

education full lunch music nun pupil put result
rude rules student study subject true university

👢	🔼	🐂	/juː/

b (4 6)) Listen and check. Practise saying the words. Why do we say *a university* but *an umbrella*?

c (4 7)) Listen and write four sentences.

d Interview your partner using the questionnaire. Ask for more information.

YOUR EDUCATION

- What kind of secondary school / you go to?
- / you like it?
- How many pupils / there in each class? Do you think it / the right number?
- How much homework / you usually get?
- / you think it / too much?
- / you have to wear a uniform? / you like it? Why (not)?
- / your teachers too strict or not strict enough? Why? What kind of punishments / they use?
- / pupils behave well?
- Which subjects / you good and bad at?
- Which / your best and worst subject?

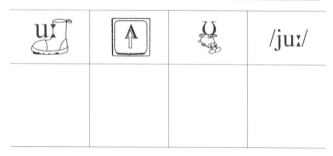

What kind of secondary school did (do) you go to?

3 LISTENING

Gareth Malone first made his name on TV as a choirmaster in BBC Two's *The Choir*, a series in which he brought together all kinds of different people who had never sung before and turned them into accomplished singers.

Last April, Gareth took on what was perhaps an even bigger challenge. He became a primary school teacher for a term. His mission was to teach a group of 11-year-old boys from a mixed primary school in Essex in the south of England. Many of the boys weren't doing very well at school and, like many other boys in Britain, they were a long way behind the girls in reading and writing. The result is *Gareth Malone's Extraordinary School for Boys* – a three-part series for BBC Two…

a Look at the photos above. What can you see? Now read about Gareth Malone's *Extraordinary School for Boys*. In your country, are boys usually behind girls in reading and writing?

b (4 8)) Listen to **Part 1** of a radio programme about the experiment and answer the questions.

1 How long did Gareth have to teach the boys?
2 What was his aim?
3 What three things did he believe were important?

c (4 9)) Listen to **Part 2**. Complete the chart.

Gareth made some general changes, for example:	1
	2
To improve their language skills he organized:	1 A _____ competition
	2 A _____ 'World Cup'
	3 A _____, which the boys (and girls) had to both write and perform

d Listen again. How successful were the three activities?

e (4 10)) Now listen to **Part 3** to find out what the result of the experiment was. Did the boys' reading improve?

f What do you think of Gareth's ideas? Do you think they are appropriate for girls? Are any of them used in your country?

4 SPEAKING

a In groups of three, each choose one (different) topic from the list below. Decide if you agree or disagree and write down at least three reasons.

- Boys and girls both learn better in single-sex schools.
- Schools should let children wear whatever they want at school.
- Cooking and housework should be taught at school.
- Schools don't teach children the important things they need to know to be an adult.
- Physical education should be optional.
- School summer holidays should be shorter.
- Children spend too much time at school on maths and IT, and not enough on things like music, art, and drama.
- Private schools are usually better than state schools.

> **Debating a topic: organizing your ideas**
> - The topic I've chosen is…
> - I | completely agree | that…
> | partly agree |
> | completely disagree |
> - First of all, (I think that…)
> - My second point is that…
> - Another important point is that…
> - Finally,…

b Explain to the rest of your group what you think about your topic. The others in the group should listen. At the end, they can vote for whether they agree or disagree with you and say why.

5 GRAMMAR first conditional and future time clauses + *when, until*, etc.

a In pairs, answer the questions.

1 When was the last time you did an exam? Did you pass or fail?
2 What's the next exam you are going to do? How do you feel about it?
3 How do you usually feel before you do an exam?
4 What do you usually do the night before an exam?
5 Have you ever failed an important exam you thought you had passed (or vice versa)?

b **11, 12**)) Listen to Olivia and Tomasz, who are waiting for their exam results, and answer the questions.

1 Do they think they have passed?
2 When and how will they get the results of the exam?
3 How will they celebrate if they get good results?
4 What do they want to do if they get good results?
5 What will they do if they fail, or if they don't get the results that they need?

> ### ○ Exams
> Exam results can be given as **marks** (usually out of 10 or 100) or as **grades** (A, B, C, etc.). **A level** marks are given in grades. **IELTS** = International English Language Testing System. It is an accepted qualification in universities and institutions all over the world.

c **4 13**)) Listen and complete the sentences.

1 They won't give me a place **unless** _____.
2 **When** _____ I'll take the letter upstairs and open it.
3 I don't want to plan any celebrations **until** _____.
4 **If** I don't get into Cambridge, _____.
5 I'll take the exam again **as soon as** _____.

d **4 14**)) Listen to Olivia and Tomasz. What grades / marks did they get? What are they going to do?

e ➤ **p.144 Grammar Bank 7A.** Learn more about first conditionals and future time clauses, and practise them.

f Ask and answer with a partner. Make full sentences.

What will you do…?
• as soon as you get home
• if you don't pass your English exam
• when this course finishes
• if it rains at the weekend

g ➤ **Communication**
Three in a row p.106.

6 READING & SPEAKING

a Read the article once. What is a 'tiger mother'?

Your 12-year-old daughter is delighted. She got an A-minus in maths, second prize in a history competition, and top marks in her piano exam. Do you **a)** say *Well done!*, give her a hug, and tell her she doesn't need to practise the piano today, and can go to a friend's house, or **b)** [1]*ask why she didn't get an A in maths*, why she didn't get first prize in the history exam, and tell her she'll be punished if she doesn't do her piano practice? If you chose **a)**, you are definitely not Amy Chua.

A lot of people wonder why so many Chinese children are maths geniuses and musical prodigies. Amy Chua explains why in her book *Battle Hymn of the Tiger Mother*. It is a book which caused great controversy among parents when it was first published. [2]_____, Chua married a man who she met at Harvard University, and when their two daughters were born she was determined that they would be as successful as she was.

Her system had strict rules. Her two daughters were expected to be number one in every subject (except gym and drama) and [3]_____. Playing with friends and TV was forbidden. Music was compulsory.

The system seemed at first to be working. From a very early age her daughters Sophia and Lulu were outstanding pupils and musical prodigies.

Do you want to practise for five hours or six?

Amy Chua brought up her daughters the Chinese way...

At 13 Sophia played a piano solo at the Carnegie Hall in New York, and at 12, Lulu a violinist, was the leader of a prestigious orchestra for young people. Chua chose maths and music for her daughters, but it seems that they could have excelled in anything. 4_____.

Eventually Chua realized that she was pushing her daughters too hard. Lulu had always rebelled the most, and when she was 13 she refused to co-operate at all. After a series of violent arguments, Chua decided to give her daughters a little more freedom, and Lulu immediately gave up violin lessons and took up tennis. 5_____.

Many people have been shocked by the book. 6_____. She once sent her daughter Lulu, aged three, into the garden without her coat when it was -6° because she had behaved badly at her first piano lesson.

However, the girls do not seem to resent their mother. Sophia said that she herself chose to accept the system, and after the book was published she wrote an article defending her mother. Lulu says that although she no longer wants to be a violinist, she still loves playing the violin. 7_____. Sophia is now studying law at Harvard, and Lulu is doing well at high school and winning tennis trophies.

Interestingly Chua, who was brought up in a family of four girls, has no idea whether she could apply her Chinese parenting system to boys. 8_____.

Adapted from The Times

b Read the article again and put the phrases **A–H** in the correct places.

A 'They are a mystery to me,' she says
B Later Sophia was even allowed to go to a rap concert
C ~~ask why she didn't get an A in maths~~
D Chua spent much of her daughters' childhood shouting at them and criticizing every mistake they made
E Born in the Unites States to Chinese immigrant parents
F In fact, she is glad her mother made her learn
G to be at least two years ahead of their classmates in maths
H 'There's no musical talent in my family,' she says, 'it's just hard work'

c In pairs, look at the highlighted words and phrases and work out their meaning from the context.

d Read three responses that were posted after the article was published. Do you agree with any of them?

Wow, what a different way of looking at how to learn! Amy Chua certainly shows that strict discipline works. But personally I think that being positive and encouraging children is better than being so strict.

I disagree with the idea that children on their own never want to work. My son was motivated by himself to succeed in music. If having strict and pushy parents is what it takes to be a child prodigy, then I feel sorry for the child. Yes, they might be very successful but at what cost? What is the rest of their life going to be like?

I agree that no matter what we do in life, hard work is required to be successful. That's a great lesson to learn. BUT, it should be accompanied by love and respect for the child.

e Talk to a partner.

1 What do **you** think of Amy Chua's system?
2 Were (are) your parents strict about your education?
3 Did they (do they)...?
  • help you with your homework
  • make you study a certain number of hours every day
  • punish you if you didn't (don't) pass exams
  • let you go out with friends during the week
  • let you choose your extra activities
  • make you do extra activities that you didn't (don't) really want to do

🔍 **make and let**
After *make* and *let* we use the infinitive without *to*.
My parents made me work very hard.
They didn't let me go out during the week.

G second conditional
V houses
P sentence stress

7B Ideal home

> If I could afford it, I'd move out tomorrow.

> I wouldn't. I like living with my parents.

1 GRAMMAR second conditional

a Work with a partner. Describe the two photos, then answer the questions.

1 Which of the two houses would you prefer to live in? Why?
2 Who do you live with? Do you get on well? Do you argue about anything? What?

b Read the article. How many of the people would like to leave home?

Still living at home?

More and more young people in their 20s all over the world are living with their parents, because it is too expensive for them to rent or buy a place of their own. Are you living at home? Are you happy with it? Post a comment at #stilllivingathome

c Read the article again. Who…?

1 is not happy living at home because of family conflict
2 thinks his / her parents think of him / her as still being a teenager
3 thinks that the advantage of living at home is not having to do any work
4 would like to be able to decorate his / her home in his / her own taste

d Look at the article again, and answer the questions.

1 In the highlighted phrases, what tense is the verb after *if*?
2 What tense is the other verb?
3 Do the phrases refer to a) a situation they are imagining or b) a situation that will probably happen soon?

e ➤ p.145 Grammar Bank 7B. Learn more about the second conditional and practise it.

Comments

Vivienne @Montreal, Canada
If I had the money, I would move out immediately. All I want is somewhere that's my own, where I can do what I want, where I can have my own furniture and pictures, where no one can tell me what to do. If it was my place, I'd be happy to do the cleaning and things like that, I would look after it. But at the moment it's just a dream, because I can't find a job.

Marco @Naples, Italy
I'm perfectly happy living at home. If I lived on my own, I'd have to pay rent, do the housework, and the cooking. Here my mother does my washing, she cleans my room, and of course she cooks, and her food is wonderful. I have a nice room, I have my computer where I can watch TV… Why would I want to leave? Even if I could afford it, I wouldn't move out. Not until I get married…

Andrea @Melbourne, Australia
It isn't that my parents aren't good to me, they are. If they weren't, I wouldn't live with them. But I just don't feel independent. I'm 29, but I sometimes worry that if I come back very late after a night out, I'll find them still awake waiting up for me. It's never happened, but it still makes me want to move out.

Carlos @Valencia, Spain
I'd love to move out. I get on well with my parents, but I think I'd get on with them even better if I didn't live at home. My mother drives me mad – it isn't her fault, but she does. And I'd really like to have a dog, but my mother is allergic to them.

2 PRONUNCIATION & SPEAKING
sentence stress

a **④ 18))** Listen and repeat the sentences. Copy the rhythm.

> 1 If I **lived** on my **own**, I'd **have** to **pay rent**.
> 2 **Would** you **leave home** if you **got** a **job**?
> 3 **Even** if I **could afford** it, I **wouldn't move out**.
> 4 If it were **my flat**, I'd be **happy** to **do** the **cleaning**.
> 5 I'd **get** on **better** with my **parents** if I **didn't live** at **home**.

b ➤ **Communication** *Guess the sentence* A *p.107* B *p.111.*

c Choose three of the sentence beginnings below and complete them in a way which is true for you.

…could live anywhere in my town or city, I'd live…
…won a 'dream holiday' in a competition, I'd go…
…could choose any car I liked, I'd have a…
…could choose my ideal job, I'd be…
…had more time, I'd learn…
…had to go abroad to work, I'd go to…

d Work with a partner. **A** say your first sentence. Try to get the right rhythm. **B** ask for more information. Then say your first sentence.

If I could live anywhere in my city, I'd live in the old town. *Why in the old town?*

3 VOCABULARY houses

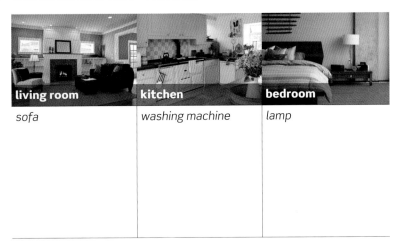

living room	kitchen	bedroom
sofa	*washing machine*	*lamp*

a With a partner, write five words in each column.

b ➤ **p.162 Vocabulary Bank** *Houses.*

c Answer the questions with a partner.

What's the difference between…?
1 the outskirts and the suburbs
2 a village and a town
3 a roof and a ceiling
4 a balcony and a terrace
5 a chimney and a fireplace
6 the ground floor and the first floor
7 wood and wooden

4 READING

a Do you know where Tchaikovsky was from and what he did?

b Look at the photos of Tchaikovsky's house. Which do you think shows…?

   a the place where he composed
   b the place where he wrote letters
   c his favourite place

c **4 22))** Read and listen to the audio guide once to check.

d Read the guide again. What is the connection between these things and Tchaikovsky's house?

  1 Maidanovo
  2 The *Pathétique* symphony
  3 Alexei
  4 Lilies of the valley
  5 Doroshenko
  6 The International Tchaikovsky Competition

e Look at the **highlighted** words and first try to work out their meaning from context. Then match them with definitions 1–8.

  1 _____ in good order
  2 _____ stay or continue
  3 _____ having a view of
  4 _____ fixed to a wall with a cord
  5 _____ make sth become
  6 _____ without a pattern or decoration
  7 _____ sth that is owned (by someone)
  8 _____ a piece of furniture with shelves to keep books in

f Have you ever visited the house where a famous person was born or lived? Where was it? What do you especially remember about it?

Tchaikovsky's house

In 1885 Tchaikovsky wrote to a friend,

'These days I dream of settling in a village not far from Moscow where I can feel at home.'

First he rented a small house in the village of Maidanovo. But Maidanovo was too full of tourists in the summer, and Tchaikovsky had too many visitors, when what he wanted was peace and quiet. Eventually he found the perfect house, in the small town of Klin. It was 85 kilometres northwest of Moscow and he lived there until his death on 6 November 1893. It is the place where he wrote his last major work, his *6th Symphony*, or the *Pathétique* as it is sometimes called.

It's a grey wooden house with a green roof. Tchaikovsky's servant Alexei lived on the ground floor, and the kitchen and dining room were on the first floor. Tchaikovsky himself lived on the second floor. The sitting room and study, where his piano is located, is the largest room in the house and there is a fireplace and a bookcase with his music books. His writing desk, where he wrote letters every morning after breakfast, is at the end of the room. But the place where he composed music was in his bedroom, on a plain, unpainted table overlooking the garden.

In his final years, Tchaikovsky's great love was his garden. It was not a tidy English-style garden, but more like a forest. He adored flowers, particularly lilies of the valley, and after his death, his brother Modest, who had decided to turn the house into a museum, planted thousands of lilies of the valley around the garden.

In 1917, after the Bolshevik revolution, an anarchist named Doroshenko lived there with his family. People say that he fired shots at the portrait of Pope Innocent hanging in one of the bedrooms. He was finally arrested in April, and the house became the property of the state.

Since 1958, the winners of the annual International Tchaikovsky Competition have all been invited to come to Klin to play his piano, and there is a tradition that each musician plants a tree in his garden in the hope that, like his music, it will remain beautiful forever.

5 LISTENING & SPEAKING

a **4 23»)** Listen to four American architecture students describing their 'dream house'. Which speaker's house is…?

- [ ] the most hi-tech
- [ ] the most luxurious
- [ ] the most eco-friendly
- [ ] the most romantic

b Listen again and make notes about the location and special features of each house.

Speaker 1
Speaker 2
Speaker 3
Speaker 4

c **4 24»)** Now listen to four sentences the students said. Why do the speakers use *would*?

d Think for a few minutes about what your dream house or flat would be like and make brief notes. Use ➤ **p.162 Vocabulary Bank** *Houses* to help you.

Where would it be?
What kind of house or flat would it be?
What special features would it have?

e In groups, describe your dream houses. Try to describe your house in as much detail as possible. Whose do you like best?

6 WRITING

➤ **p.118 Writing** *Describing a house or flat.* Write a description of your house or flat for a house rental website.

7 **4 25»)** SONG *If I Could Build My Whole World Around You* ♫

1 ◼◀ ROB AND PAUL CATCH UP
VIDEO

a (4 26)》 Watch or listen to Rob and Paul. What does Paul think of Jenny?

b Watch or listen again. Mark the sentences **T** (true) or **F** (false). Correct the **F** sentences.

1 Rob used to play pool when he was younger.
2 Rob has a lot of free time.
3 Rob had fair hair the last time Paul saw him.
4 Paul thinks Rob has changed a lot.
5 Jenny's parents gave Rob the shirt he's wearing.
6 Rob doesn't want to keep Jenny waiting.

2 ◼◀ MAKING SUGGESTIONS
VIDEO

a (4 27)》 Watch or listen to Paul, Rob, and Jenny talking about what to do after dinner. What do Paul and Rob decide to do? What excuse does Jenny give? What does she do in the end?

b Watch or listen again. Answer with **P**aul, **R**ob, or **J**enny.

Who suggests…?
1 ☐ going dancing
2 ☐ doing some exercise
3 ☐ going to a club
4 ☐ going to an art gallery
5 ☐ staying at home
6 ☐ going to a gig
7 ☐ meeting Kerri

c (4 28)) Look at some extracts from the conversation. Can you remember any of the missing words? Watch or listen and check.

1 **Paul** What shall we _____ now?
   Rob What do you want to do?
   Paul Well... I haven't been on a dance floor for weeks now. I've got to move my body. _____ go dancing!

2 **Jenny** I'm going running in the morning. Why _____ you join me?
   Paul No thanks. I'm not very _____ on running. But I've read about this place called Deep Space, where they play great music. We _____ go there.

3 **Jenny** _____ about going to the late show at MOMA?
   Paul MOMA? What's that?

4 **Jenny** _____ about staying in and watching a movie on TV?
   Paul I'm in New York. I can watch TV anywhere.

5 **Paul** I didn't think so. So _____ we go there?
   Rob _____ not?

6 **Rob** We _____ meet her outside and go together.
   Paul That's a great _____!

🔍 **Verb forms**
Remember to use the infinitive without *to* after:
Shall we... We could... Why don't you / we... Let's...
Remember to use the gerund after:
What about...? How about...?

---

d Look at the highlighted expressions for making and responding to suggestions. Which of the ways of making suggestions do you think is the most emphatic?

e (4 29)) Watch or listen and repeat the highlighted phrases. Copy the rhythm and intonation.

f Practise the dialogues in **c** with a partner.

g 👥👥 In small groups, practise making suggestions and responding.

You are going to have an end-of-term class party. You need to decide:
• When to have it
• Where to have it
• What time to have it
• What food and drink to have

a (4 30)) Watch or listen to Rob and Jenny talking on the phone. What's the problem?

b Watch or listen again. Complete the sentences with 1–3 words.
1 Rob says that he's feeling _____.
2 Kerri invited Rob and Paul to _____.
3 Rob says that he can't make _____.
4 Jenny is upset because it's an _____.
5 Rob promises that _____ again.
6 Rob also says that Paul _____ that afternoon.
7 Jenny tells Don that Rob is such _____.

c Look at the **Social English phrases**. Can you remember any of the missing words?

Social English phrases	
Jenny	Where are you _____?
Rob	That's _____ I'm calling. I'm not going to make it.
Rob	It won't _____ again.
Rob	He's _____ to Boston this afternoon.
Jenny	I mean, _____ not that I don't like Paul, but...
Don	I wanted to have a _____ with him before the meeting.
Jenny	He's _____ a professional.

d (4 31)) Watch or listen and complete the phrases.

e Watch or listen again and repeat the phrases. How do you say them in your language?

👤 **Can you...?**
☐ use different ways of making suggestions
☐ respond to suggestions
☐ apologize and make an excuse

G reported speech: sentences and questions
V shopping, making nouns from verbs
P the letters *ai*

She said that she was going to complain.

Did they give her a refund?

8A Sell and tell

1 GRAMMAR reported speech: sentences and questions

a Look at the home page of a new website. What do you think you can sell or buy there?

NEVER LIKED IT ANYWAY

Welcome, **Visitor!** [Register | Login]

| HOME | BUY IT | SELL IT | TELL IT |

search breakin' deals   GO

Welcome!

Never Liked It Anyway™ is a place where once loved gifts from once loved lovers get a second chance…

We've all been there.
We've all got stories to tell and things to sell. This is a place full of marvellous deals.

Let the fun begin!

BARGAIN OF THE WEEK

Sweet & Simple Engagement Ring
sold by brjen

"Well when I first met him he was charming and sweet and funny – most of you know how that goes right? After a couple of years, things started happening… I found things that indicated he was cheating…"

Real World Price: $2,500.00
Break-up Price: $900.00

STUFF READY TO MOVE ON

NEVER LIKED IT ANYWAY

b (4 32)) Listen to part of a radio programme about this new website. Did you guess right?

c Listen again and answer the questions.

1 Why did Annabel Acton set it up?
2 What kind of things do people sell on it?
3 What else do they do apart from selling things?

d Now look at three things from the website and answer the questions with a partner.

1 Would you like to buy any of them?
2 Which break-up do you think was the worst?
3 Do you have anything you would like to sell on the website?

e Look at four sentences from the website. What do you think were the actual words that the people used when they said these things?

1 My fiancé told me that he was in love with another woman.
2 She said that she'd come and pick it up.
3 I asked if it was new.
4 I asked her who had given it to her.

1 'I'm in love with another woman.'

f ➤ p.146 Grammar Bank 8A. Learn more about reported sentences and questions, and practise them.

g (4 35)) Imagine you were stopped in a shopping mall last Saturday by a woman doing a survey. Listen and write down the questions she asked. Then write your answers.

h Work in pairs. Take it in turns to tell your partner about the survey, what the woman asked you, and what you said.

Last Saturday I was in shopping mall and a woman who was doing a survey stopped me. She asked me if I usually…

Wedding dress

sold by Marianne

Real World Price: $1,200.00
Break-up price: $500.00

The Product:
Never worn, still has price tags. Selling matching veil and other extras.

The Story:
Two weeks before our wedding was supposed to take place, my fiancé phoned and told me that he was in love with another woman. I'm over it now, but selling the dress will help me to move on.

BUY IT

Apple Macbook pro

sold by Carl

Real World Price: $850
Break-up price: $250

The Product:
Everything works fine. A few scratches.

The Story:
My ex-girlfriend left it here when she walked out. She said that she'd come and pick it up, but she never did. Her new guy must have a lot of money!

BUY IT

Tiffany heart necklace

sold by Ellie

Real World Price: $1,400.00
Break-up price: $650.00

The Story:
I got this truly lovely necklace as a Christmas present from my boyfriend Andy. A year later I went to a party at his office and I saw a girl wearing the exact same necklace. I asked if it was new, and she yes, it was a present, so I asked her who had given it to her, and she said Andy. I dumped him the next day.

BUY IT

2 VOCABULARY & SPEAKING
shopping

a In pairs, say if you think these are the same or different. Then check with your teacher.

1 buy something online and buy something on the internet
2 a chemist's and a pharmacy
3 an outlet store and a department store
4 a shopping centre and a shopping mall
5 a library and a bookshop
6 *put on a shirt* and *try on a shirt*
7 *It fits you* and *It suits you.*
8 a sale and the sales

b With your partner, explain the meaning of the words in the list.

a bargain	a discount	a price tag
a receipt	a refund	take sth back

c Work with a different partner. Interview him / her with the questionnaire below. Ask for and give as many details as you can.

Shopping – in town or online?

1 What's your favourite shop or website to buy...?
○ a clothes
○ b shoes
○ c books and music
○ d presents
○ e food

2 Do you ever shop...? What do you buy?
○ a in street markets
○ b in supermarkets
○ c in shopping centres or malls
○ d online

3 What do you...?
○ a enjoy buying
○ b hate buying

4 Do you prefer shopping for clothes...?
○ a by yourself or with somebody
○ b at the beginning of the season or in the sales

5 What do you think are the advantages and disadvantages of buying clothes online?

Email address   **Submit**

3 READING

a In your country, if people have a problem with something they've bought, or with the service in a shop or restaurant, do they usually complain? If not, why not?

b Read the article *The King of Complainers*. Which of these adjectives (or any others) would you use to describe Clive? Why?

admirable clever crazy eccentric mean obsessive

c What does Clive think is the best way to complain? What did he get as a result of complaining about…?

1 the smell of biscuits
2 a friend's faulty car
3 his wife's fall during a holiday
4 some old strawberries

d Now read *Clive's top tips*. Complete the tips with a heading from the list.

DON'T BE TOO SPECIFIC
DON'T LOSE YOUR TEMPER
KNOW WHO YOU ARE WRITING TO
THREATEN ACTION
WRITE A LETTER
USE FLATTERY

e Now look at the highlighted verbs and verb phrases. With a partner, try to work out their meaning from the context.

f Which two tips do you think are the most important?

The **King** of Complainers

Clive Zietman loves complaining – but not shouting in hotel lobbies, or angrily telling a shop assistant to call the manager, or making a waitress cry. He loves complaining properly and in writing. Over the last twenty years he has written over 5,000 letters of complaint. His successes include refunded holidays, countless free meals, and complimentary theatre tickets.

So how has he achieved this? 'Screaming and shouting is a complete waste of time and is usually directed at a person who is not in a position to do anything,' he says. 'I like to write a polite letter to the company. People won't want to help you if you are aggressive, they respond much better to good manners.'

It all started many years ago, on a boring train journey home to West London. The train passed by the McVitie's biscuit factory, and the smell of the biscuits made Clive feel hungry. He wrote a letter to the managing director to complain, in a humorous way, about the fumes coming through the carriage window. The result? Some free packets of biscuits. But since then there have been more serious victories as well. On one occasion he managed to get a Volkswagen Golf GTI within 24 hours for a friend who had been complaining for almost a year (without any success) about his faulty vehicle. On another occasion he got a travel agent to refund the cost of a holiday worth £2,000, after Clive's wife Bettina broke her leg when she slipped in a puddle of water in their holiday apartment in Spain.

These days, there is almost nothing he won't complain about. After Clive was served mouldy strawberries on a British Airways flight, he used a courier service to send the fruit to the airline's chief executive. To compensate, BA invited his daughters, Nina and Zoë, to Heathrow to personally inspect the airline's catering facilities. 'I just can't bear bad service,' says Clive. 'We have a right to good service, and should expect it and demand it. In fact, what irritates me more than anything is that, unlike Americans, we British are hopeless at complaining.'

So how do Bettina, his wife, and daughters Nina, 22, Zoë, 18, and 12-year-old son Joe cope with living with Britain's biggest complainer? Surely he must be a nightmare to live with? Has he ever asked Bettina to explain why a meal she made is badly cooked? 'Oh no, of course not,' says Clive. It seems there are some things even he knows you should never complain about!

Adapted from the Daily Mail website

How to complain successfully: Clive's top tips

1

Never shout and swear – it achieves nothing. Don't spoil your meal or your holiday by getting into an argument with a waiter or customer services call centre operator. Make a mental note of the circumstances and write a letter later.

2

Don't send emails, or standard, printed-out complaints forms. Companies may not read these but they probably will read a letter. And unless you are particularly fond of Vivaldi, don't waste your time ringing a customer complaints line! Your letter should be short and to the point and should fit on one side of A4 paper. And type it. Reading other people's handwriting is hard work.

3

Write to the company's marketing director or finance director, as they're probably the least busy. Find their name on the internet, or by phoning. Writing *Dear Sir / Madam* is lazy. Taking the time to find a person's name and title shows initiative.

4

If your complaint is serious enough, make it clear you will not hesitate to change to another bank / mobile phone company. Smart companies know that changing an angry customer into a satisfied one will make the customer more loyal.

5

Don't say exactly what you expect to receive as compensation. Leave it to the company.

6

Use phrases like 'I can only imagine this is an unusual departure from your usual high standards,' and 'I would love to shop with you again if you can demonstrate to me that you are still as good as I know you used to be'.

Glossary
lose your temper become angry
threaten *verb* warn that you may punish sb if they do not do what you want
flattery *noun* saying good things about sb that you may not mean

---

4 PRONUNCIATION the letters *ai*

a Say the words aloud, then write them in the correct column.

airline bargain certain complain email fair obtain hairdresser mountain paid painting repair

eɪ	eə	(magnifier)

b (4 36)) Listen and check, and then answer the questions.

1 What is the pronunciation of *ai* when it is a) stressed b) unstressed?
2 How is *air* usually pronounced?
3 Is *said* pronounced /seɪd/ or /sed/?

c (4 37)) Listen and write four sentences. Practise saying them.

5 VOCABULARY making nouns from verbs

a Look at some nouns from the article. What verbs do they come from?

complaint argument compensation

b ➤ p.163 Vocabulary Bank *Word building*. Do Part 1.

6 LISTENING & SPEAKING

a (4 40)) Listen to part of a radio consumer programme where people are talking about bad service. What did the people complain about…?

1 in the taxi   2 in the hotel   3 in the restaurant

b Listen again and answer the questions.

1 Who did each person complain to?
2 What did the people they complained to do as a result?

c Talk to a partner.

1 Who's best at complaining in your family? Give examples.
2 Can you remember a time when you (or someone in your family) complained…?
   • to a taxi driver   • to a hotel receptionist
   • to a waiter   • to someone else
   Why did you complain? What did you say? What happened?

d ➤ **Communication** *I want to speak to the manager* **A** *p.107* **B** *p.111*. Role-play a customer complaining to a shop assistant and a restaurant manager.

7 WRITING

➤ p.119 Writing *A letter of complaint*. Write a letter to complain about something you bought online.

G gerunds and infinitives
V work
P word stress

Do you like your job?

Yes. I'm an accountant – I enjoy working with numbers.

8B What's the right job for you?

1 VOCABULARY work

a Look at the picture story. Match sentences A–I with pictures 1–9.

A ☐ She decided to **set up** an online business selling birthday cakes.

B ☐ Her business is **doing very well**. Clare is a success!

C ☐ She was **unemployed**, and had to **look for a job**.

D ☐ They had an argument, and Clare **was sacked**.

E ☐ *1* Clare **worked for** a marketing company.

F ☐ She **applied for** a lot of jobs, and **sent in CVs**.

G ☐ She had a **good salary**, but she didn't like **her boss**.

H ☐ She had some interviews, but didn't **get the jobs**.

I ☐ She had to work very hard and **do overtime**.

b (4 41)) Listen and check. Then cover the sentences and look at the pictures. Tell the story from memory.

c ➤ p.164 Vocabulary Bank *Work*.

2 PRONUNCIATION & SPEAKING
word stress

a Underline the stressed syllable in each word. Use the phonetics to help you.

1 a|pply /əˈplaɪ/
2 sa|la|ry /ˈsæləri/
3 re|dun|dant /rɪˈdʌndənt/
4 ex|pe|ri|ence /ɪkˈspɪəriəns/
5 o|ver|time /ˈəʊvətaɪm/
6 per|ma|nent /ˈpɜːmənənt/
7 qua|li|fi|ca|tions /kwɒlɪfɪˈkeɪʃnz/
8 re|sign /rɪˈzaɪn/
9 re|tire /rɪˈtaɪə/
10 tem|po|ra|ry /ˈtemprəri/

b (4 45)) Listen and check. Practise saying the words.

c Do you know anybody who…

– is applying for a job? What kind of job?
– is doing a temporary job? What?
– has a part-time job? What hours does he / she work?
– is self-employed? What does he / she do?
– has been promoted recently? What to?
– was sacked from his / her job, or was made redundant? Why?
– has just retired? How old is he / she?

d Think of someone you know who has a job. Prepare your answers to the questions below.

- What / do?
- Where / work (in an office, at home, etc.)?
- What qualifications / have?
- What hours / work?
- / have to do overtime?
- / get a good salary?
- / like the job? Why (not)?
- Would *you* like to do his / her job? Why (not)?

e Work in pairs. **A** interview **B** about their person's job. Ask more questions if you can. Then swap.

I'm going to tell you about my cousin. Her name's Corinne.

What does she do?

She's a journalist. She works for a local newspaper…

3 GRAMMAR gerunds and infinitives

a Complete *The right job for you* questionnaire by putting the verbs in the correct form, the gerund (e.g. *working*) or *to* + infinitive (e.g. *to work*).

b Read the questionnaire and tick (✓) only the sentences that you strongly agree with. Discuss your answers with another student.

c Now see in which group(s) you have most ticks, and go to ➤ **Communication** *The right job for you p.107.* Do you agree with the results?

d Look at the sentences in the questionnaire. Complete the rules with **the gerund** or *to* + **infinitive**.

1 After some verbs,
e.g. *enjoy, don't mind* use… _____
2 After some verbs,
e.g. *would like* use… _____
3 After adjectives use… _____
4 After prepositions use… _____
5 As the subject of a phrase or
sentence use… _____

e ➤ **p.147 Grammar Bank 8B.** Learn more about gerunds and infinitives, and practise them.

f Choose *five* of the circles below and write something in them.

- something you **enjoy doing** on Sunday mornings
- somebody you find very **easy to talk** to
- something you are **planning to do** in the summer
- a job you **hate doing** in the house
- a country **you'd like to visit** in the future
- a sport, activity, or hobby you **love doing**, but never have time for
- something you're **afraid of doing**
- somebody you **wouldn't like to go** on holiday with
- a job **you'd love to do**

g Work in groups. Tell the others about what you put in your circles, and answer their questions.

> *I'm going to tell you about someone I find really easy to talk to. It's my uncle…*

The right job for you –
MATCH YOUR PERSONALITY TO THE JOB

1 I'd like *to work* as part of a team.	work
2 I enjoy _____ people with their problems.	help
3 I don't mind _____ a very large salary.	not earn
4 I'm good at _____ to people.	listen

5 I'm good at _____ quick decisions.	make
6 _____ risks doesn't worry me.	take
7 I'm happy _____ by myself.	work
8 I'm not afraid of _____ large amounts of money.	manage

9 I'm good at _____ myself.	express
10 I always try _____ my instincts.	follow
11 It's important for me _____ creative.	be
12 I enjoy _____.	improvise

13 _____ complex calculations is not difficult for me.	do
14 I enjoy _____ logical problems.	solve
15 I find it easy _____ theoretical principles.	understand
16 I am able _____ space and distance.	calculate

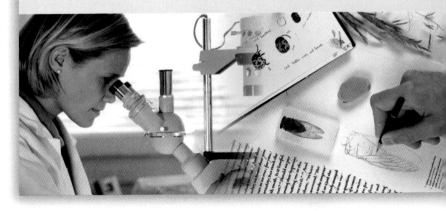

4 READING

a Read the first paragraph of an article about the TV programme *Dragons' Den*. Answers the questions.

1 Who are the 'Dragons'?
2 What is their 'Den'?
3 How does the programme work?
4 Is there a similar TV programme in your country? How does it work?

b Look at the photos and read about three products that were presented on the show, a sauce (**A**), coffee tables (**B**), and suitcases for children (**C**). Which product...?

1 has been very successful although the Dragons didn't invest in it
2 was presented by a musician
3 became successful very quickly
4 has two different functions
5 combines history with practicality
6 is sold outside the UK

IN THE DRAGONS' DEN

Peter Jones and Duncan Bannatyne have been Dragons on the show since it started. Deborah Meaden joined in 2006.

Dragons' Den is a UK TV series, with similar versions in many different countries. In the UK programme, contestants have three minutes to present their business ideas to five very successful business people. These people are nicknamed the 'Dragons', and the intimidating room where they meet the contestants is the 'Den' (the dragons' home). The Dragons, who are often multi-millionaires, are prepared to invest money in any business that they believe might be a success. In return, they take a share in the profits. The contestants are usually young entrepreneurs, product designers, or people with a new idea for a service. After the contestants have made their presentations, the Dragons ask them questions about the product and its possible market, and then say if they are prepared to invest or not. If they are not convinced by the presentation, they say the dreaded words 'I'm out'.

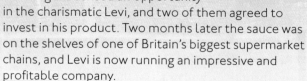

So far, the Dragons have agreed to invest in 110 businesses. They were very pleased with their investment in Levi Roots, the Rastafarian singer who had the idea for Reggae Reggae Sauce. He came into the Den with a guitar, a couple of bottles of sauce he had made in his kitchen – and nothing else. But the Dragons sensed an opportunity in the charismatic Levi, and two of them agreed to invest in his product. Two months later the sauce was on the shelves of one of Britain's biggest supermarket chains, and Levi is now running an impressive and profitable company.

A

Paul Simpson wanted the Dragons to invest in his handmade coffee tables. They have a wooden base, which look like 14th-century castles, and a glass top. Nobody was enthusiastic, and the Dragons rejected his idea. But Paul hasn't given up. Now he is making a new table, this time a replica of Windsor Castle, which he thinks might be popular with tourists. And that is what makes a real entrepreneur – they never give up. If the Dragons invest in them, there is a good chance they will be successful. But if they leave the Den empty-handed, the determination to make it on their own is as great as ever.

B

And of course the Dragons don't always get it right. Inventor Rob Law's product, a suitcase for children which they can also ride on, was rejected as 'worthless'. One Dragon thought it was not strong enough, and another Dragon, who runs a holiday company, said she didn't think there was a market for the product. A third Dragon simply said 'I meet people like you all the time. You think you have something, but you don't'. However, today Trunki cases are best-sellers, and are sold in 22 different countries.

C

c Which (if any) of the three products would you be interested / definitely not interested in buying? Why?

d Look at the **highlighted** words and phrases which are all related to business. Try to work out their meaning from the context.

> **🔍 Words with different meanings**
> Sometimes the same word can have two completely different meanings, e.g. *I **work** in a shop.* (= it's my job) and *My laptop **doesn't work**.* (= it's broken).

e With a partner, say what the difference in meaning is between the pairs of sentences.

1 He's **running** a business. *and*
  He's **running** a marathon.
2 Marion **was fired** last week. *and*
  When the man **fired** the gun, everyone screamed.
3 There's a **market** for this product. *and*
  There's a **market** where you can buy vegetables.
4 He's set up a **company**. *and*
  He's very good **company**.

5 LISTENING

a (**4** 49)) Look at the photos of two more products which were presented on *Dragons' Den*. Now listen and find out exactly what makes them special.

b Listen again. Do you think the Dragons invested in…? Why?

a both of them
b neither of them
c one of them (which?)

c (**4** 50)) Now listen to what happened. Were you right? What influenced the Dragons' choice?

d Do you think either of these products would be successful in your country? Why (not)?

6 SPEAKING

a Work with a partner. Imagine you are going to appear on the programme. You can choose one of the products below, or you can invent your own.

| a watch   a sandwich   an app   a chair |
| a dessert   a pen   a lamp   a drink   a gadget |

Think about the following aspects of your product.

- What is the product?
- What is its name?
- Who is it for?
- How much will it cost?
- Why is it different from other similar products?
- Do you have an advertising slogan for it?

b Present your product to the class together. Spend a few minutes preparing your presentation. Take turns to give the information, and use language from the box to help you.

> **🔍 Presenting a product**
> Good morning. We're going to tell you about our new product.
> It's a… and it's called…
> We think it will be very popular with…
> It is completely different from / better than anything else on the market because…

c You also have money to invest in one of the products your classmates present, so listen to their presentations and decide which one to vote for.

7 WRITING

➤ **p.120 Writing** *A covering email with your CV.* Write an accompanying email to send with your CV to apply for a job.

8 (**4** 51)) **SONG** *Piano Man* ♫

GRAMMAR

Circle a, b, or c.

1 We'll miss the train if we _____.
   a don't hurry   b won't hurry   c didn't hurry

2 If you help me with the washing-up, _____ in five minutes.
   a we'll finish   b we finish   c we finished

3 I won't get into university unless _____ good grades in my A levels.
   a I'll get   b I got   c I get

4 If we bought a house, we _____ a dog.
   a can have   b could have   c will have

5 I'd be sad if my brother and his wife _____.
   a break up   b 'll break up   c broke up

6 If I had a job, I _____ live with my parents.
   a won't   b wouldn't   c didn't

7 If I won a lot of money, _____ a big house.
   a I'd buy   b I'll buy   c I buy

8 He said he _____ to his lawyer tomorrow.
   a will speak   b spoke   c would speak

9 I asked Sally if _____ coming to the party.
   a she is   b she was   c was she

10 The little girl _____ that she was lost.
   a told   b said us   c told us

11 The policeman asked me where _____.
   a did I live   b I was live   c I lived

12 Tom's really good at _____ problems.
   a solve   b solving   c to solve

13 _____ clothes online saves a lot of time.
   a Buying   b To buy   c Buy

14 I wouldn't _____ that car if I were you.
   a get   b getting   c to get

15 It's really important _____ the receipt.
   a keep   b to keep   c keeping

VOCABULARY

a Complete with one word.

1 The UK school year has three _____.
2 Children under five can go to _____ school.
3 UK high schools are called _____ schools.
4 Children who _____ very badly at school may be expelled.
5 A school where you study, eat, and sleep is called a _____ school.

b Circle the right word.

1 We live in a residential area *in* / *on* the outskirts of Oxford.
2 The *roof* / *ceiling* in our flat is very low, so don't hit your head!
3 Close the garden *gate* / *door* or the dog might get out.
4 Our flat is *in* / *on* the fifth floor of a large block of flats.
5 On the shelf above the *chimney* / *fireplace* there are some photos.

c Complete the sentences with a noun made from the **bold** word.

1 I don't like shopping in supermarkets because there is too much _____. **choose**
2 My flatmates and I have an _____ about who does what in the house. **agree**
3 I'm sure the new company will be a _____. **succeed**
4 I made a _____ about the service in the hotel. **complain**
5 We went on a _____ to support the unemployed. **demonstrate**
6 The government is planning to raise the _____ age to 70. **retire**
7 If you want to get a job, you need good _____. **qualify**
8 My sister has been working as a _____ for the EU. **translate**
9 Some _____ say that drinking coffee may be good for us. **science**
10 I want an _____ for what happened yesterday. **explain**

d Complete the missing words.

1 I did a lot of **ov**_____ last week – two hours extra every day.
2 He works night **sh**_____ at the local factory.
3 It's only a **t**_____ job, from March to September.
4 I'd like to **s**_____ up a small business, making children's clothes.
5 Lewis loves being **s**_____-_____, because it means he is his own boss and can choose the hours that he works.

PRONUNCIATION

a Circle the word with a different sound.

1	↑	country	study	pupil	punished
2	ʊ	choose	roof	wooden	school
3	aɪ	village	primary	resign	private
4	eɪ	paid	complain	sale	said
5		certain	attach	entrance	educate

b Underline the stressed syllable.

1 se|con|dary   3 de|li|ve|ry   5 a|chieve|ment
2 un|em|ployed   4 a|pply

CAN YOU UNDERSTAND THIS TEXT?

a Read the blog once. Complete the main message of the article in your own words.

It is better to do a job that _____ than a job which you _____, but which _____.

The importance of doing what you love

When I was growing up, all I wanted to be was an artist. When I got to high school and could choose what classes to take, I took every art class that was available. Painting, drawing, photography, you name it – I took the class.

Then I took a chemistry class. I LOVED it. It was fun! And I was good at it. I started thinking: wouldn't I make more money if I went into the sciences instead of being a starving artist?

So I threw away the art school applications and went to study chemistry. College was fun, and when I graduated with my chemistry degree, I went to graduate school in Washington DC to do a PhD program in chemistry! It was OK to start with, but after the first year, I was completely depressed. I hated the program. It was dry and boring. But I didn't know what to do about it.

So I quit. I spent the next month feeling bad about my failure, unsure what to do next. Finally, I went to a work agency to get a job. Something – anything – that would pay money.

I got a temporary job filling envelopes at an NGO. One day they needed some graphic design and I volunteered. This was the major turning point in my career. Over the next few months, they gave me more and more design work. What began as a temporary post turned into a permanent job. I was finally doing something I loved and I was making money doing it.

It's been difficult at times, but I really love my job. Believe me, it is FAR more important that you are happy and get to do what you are passionate about every day and get paid less for it, than to dread getting up in the morning because you dislike what you do.

Adapted from workawesome.com

b Read the blog again and mark the sentences **T** (true), **F** (false), or **DS** (doesn't say).

1 She used to get very good marks for art at high school.
2 She thought she would earn more money working as a chemist than being an artist.
3 She enjoyed Graduate school but not college.
4 She lived at home after she quit Graduate school.
5 She was quite well-paid for filling envelopes at the NGO.
6 She feels passionate about design.

c Choose five new words or phrases from the text. Check their meaning and pronunciation and try to learn them.

CAN YOU UNDERSTAND THESE PEOPLE?

4 52)) **In the street** Watch or listen to five people and answer the questions.

Lizzie   Ian   Simon   Joe   Simone

1 Lizzie says she learnt better at _____ school.
   a a mixed   b a single-sex   c primary
2 Ian likes shopping online because _____.
   a it's convenient
   b it's cheaper
   c he doesn't like trying on clothes
3 Simon was _____ with what he sold on eBay.
   a satisfied   b delighted   c disappointed
4 Joe would like to _____.
   a paint the walls of his flat
   b have more paintings in his flat
   c invite more people to his house
5 Simone would like to have a job _____.
   a in banking   b that's well paid   c that's enjoyable

CAN YOU SAY THIS IN ENGLISH?

Do the tasks with a partner. Tick (✓) the box if you can do them.

Can you...?

1 ☐ describe the schools you went to (or have been to) and say what you liked or didn't like about them
2 ☐ say what you will do a) if you don't pass your English exam at the end of the course and b) when you can speak English fluently
3 ☐ describe your ideal holiday house
4 ☐ say what you would do if a) you won a lot of money and b) you had more free time
5 ☐ report three questions that someone has asked you today and what you answered

Short films Trinity College, Dublin
VIDEO Watch and enjoy a film on iTutor.

G third conditional
V making adjectives and adverbs
P sentence stress

9A Lucky encounters

> You were really lucky!

Yes. If he hadn't helped me, I would have missed the train.

1 READING & SPEAKING

a Answer the questions with a partner. Say what you would do and why.

What would you do if...?

1 somebody in the street asked you for money on your way home tonight
2 you were driving home at night and you saw somebody who had run out of petrol
3 you saw an old man being attacked in the street by a couple of teenagers
4 you were in a queue at a station or airport and someone asked to go in front of you because he / she was in a hurry

b Read the beginning of a true story by the writer Bernard Hare, about something that happened to him when he was a student. Then in pairs, decide what you think happened next.

c (5 2)) Now listen to what happened. Were you right?

d Listen again and answer the questions.

1 What did Bernard have to do as soon as he got off the train?
2 How did Bernard react?
3 What did the ticket inspector then ask him to do?

The ticket inspector

I was living in a student flat in North London, when the police knocked on my door one night. I thought it was because I hadn't paid the rent for a few months, so I didn't open the door. But then I wondered if it was something to do with my mother, who I knew wasn't very well. There was no phone in the flat and this was before the days of mobile phones, so I ran down to the nearest phone box and phoned my dad in Leeds, in the north of England. He told me that my mum was very ill in hospital and that I should go home as soon as I could.

When I got to the station I found that I'd missed the last train to Leeds. There was a train to Peterborough, from where some local trains went to Leeds, but I would miss the connection by about 20 minutes. I decided to get the Peterborough train – I was so desperate to get home that I thought maybe I could hitchhike from Peterborough.

'Tickets, please.' I looked up and saw the ticket inspector. He could see from my eyes that I'd been crying. 'Are you OK?' he asked. 'Of course I'm OK,' I said. 'You look awful,' he continued. 'Is there anything I can do?' 'You could go away,' I said rudely.

But he didn't. He sat down and said 'If there's a problem, I'm here to help'. The only thing I could think of was to tell him my story. When I finished I said, 'So now you know. I'm a bit upset and I don't feel like talking any more, OK?' 'OK,' he said, finally getting up. 'I'm sorry to hear that, son. I hope you make it home.'

I continued to look out of the window at the dark countryside. Ten minutes later, the ticket inspector came back.

e After this story was on the BBC, several people wrote in with their stories about being helped by strangers. **A** read *The students*, **B** read *The angel*.

The students

I was living in South Korea at the time, teaching English. I had to leave the country and return again because of problems with my visa, so I booked a ferry to Fukuoka in Japan. I intended to change some Korean money into Japanese yen when I got there, but when I arrived I discovered it was a holiday in Japan and all the banks were closed. I didn't have a credit card, so I walked from the ferry terminal towards the town wondering what I was going to do without any Japanese money. I was feeling lonely and depressed when suddenly I heard a young couple speaking French. I asked them if they spoke any English, and they told me (in good English) that they were Belgian students. When I explained my problem, they immediately offered to take me around the city and look for somewhere where I could change money. They paid for my bus ticket, and they took me to several places and in the end we found a hotel where I was able to change my cash. They then invited me to join them and their friends for the evening. I had a fantastic night and have never forgotten how they changed all their plans just to help a stranger. – *Karina*

The angel

It was a cold Sunday evening in Manchester. I was a university student, and my girlfriend and I had been invited to dinner with our tutor at his house 30 km away. We decided to go on my motorbike, but we hadn't realized how cold it was, so we hadn't dressed properly, and after ten minutes on the bike we were absolutely freezing. When we were about half way there, the bike started to make a funny noise and then stopped. We had run out of petrol. We stood at the side of the road, shivering with cold, and not sure what to do.

Suddenly a passing car stopped. The driver got out, opened the boot of his car, and took out a can of petrol. He walked up to my bike, opened the petrol tank, and poured the petrol in. He then closed the tank and got back into his car, without saying a single word, and drove away. We couldn't believe our luck. We sometimes wonder if the man who rescued us was an angel... – *Andy*

f In pairs, tell each other your story. Tell your partner:

Where it happened
What the problem was
What the stranger(s) did to help

g Which of the three stories do you think was a) the most surprising b) the most moving? Why?

h Have you ever helped a stranger, or been helped by a stranger? What happened?

2 GRAMMAR third conditional

a Match the sentence halves from the story.

1 ☐ If the inspector hadn't stopped the train to Leeds, …
2 ☐ If the couple hadn't helped Karina, …
3 ☐ If the man in the car hadn't stopped, …

A she would have been alone without any money.
B they would have had to walk for miles in the cold.
C he would have missed his connection.

b Now look at the sentences below. Which one describes what really happened? Which one describes how the situation might have been different?

1 If the inspector hadn't stopped the train, he would have missed his connection.
2 The inspector stopped the train, so he didn't miss his connection.

c ➤ p.148 Grammar Bank 9A. Learn more about the third conditional and practise it.

3 PRONUNCIATION
sentence stress

a ⑤4》 Listen and repeat the sentences. Copy the rhythm.

1 If I'd **known** you were **ill**, I would have **come** to **see** you.
2 If the **weather** had been **better**, we would have **stayed longer**.
3 If I **hadn't stopped** to **get petrol**, I **wouldn't** have been **late**.
4 We would have **missed** our **flight** if it **hadn't** been **delayed**.

b ⑤5》 Listen and write five third conditional sentences.

c ➤ **Communication** *Guess the conditional* **A** *p.108* **B** *p.111.*

4 SPEAKING

a Read the questions and think about your answers.

1 Look at some quotes about luck. Do you think they are true?

'The more I practise, the luckier I get.'

Gary Player, golf player

'You've got to think lucky. If you fall into a lake, check your back pocket – you might have caught a fish.'

Darrell Royal, American football coach

'You never know what worse luck your bad luck has saved you from.'

Cormac McCarthy, writer

'If you have two friends in your lifetime, you are lucky. If you have one **good** friend, you are more than lucky.'

Susan Hinton, writer

2 Do you consider yourself in general to be a lucky person? Why (not)?
3 Can you remember a time when you were either very lucky or very unlucky? What happened?
4 Do you know anyone who you think is particularly lucky or unlucky? Why?

b In groups of three or four, discuss your answers. Give as much detail as possible.

5 READING & LISTENING

a Think of some very successful people, e.g. business people, musicians, sports stars. Which of these three things do you think was probably most important in making them successful: a) talent b) hard work c) luck?

b Read the article *A question of luck?* about a book by Malcolm Gladwell, and answer the questions.

1 What three factors does he think being successful really depends on?
2 Why is it an advantage for sports players to be born in the first months of the year in some countries?
3 What is the 10,000 hours theory?

c **5 6))** Now listen to two other examples Gladwell mentions, The Beatles and Bill Gates. What two main reasons does he give for their extraordinary success?

d Listen again and answer the questions.

THE BEATLES

1 Where did they play and between which years?
2 Where did the club owner usually get bands from?
3 How much did they have to play?
4 How many times had they performed live by 1964?

BILL GATES

5 When did his school start a computer club?
6 Why was this unusual?
7 What did he and his friends do at weekends?
8 How many hours did he spend at the computer club every week?

e What do you think? Answer these questions with a partner.

1 Do you agree that luck and practice are just as important as talent? Is luck more important than practice or the other way around?
2 Think of something you are quite good at or very good at. Were you lucky to be able to have the opportunity to start doing it? How many hours do you think you have spent practising it? Do you think you have spent more hours doing it than other people you know?

A question of luck?

What is the question we always ask about successful people? We want to know what they're like – what kind of personalities they have, or how intelligent they are, or what kind of lifestyles they have, or what special talents they might have been born with. And we assume that it is those personal qualities that explain how that individual gets to the top of his or her profession.

But according to Malcolm Gladwell, in his book *Outliers*, we are asking the wrong questions. He thinks that while talent is obviously a factor, there are two other more important ones that make a person successful. The first of these factors is luck.

He begins with the example of sports players. In recent research done on various groups of elite ice hockey players from Canada and the Czech Republic, one fascinating fact came to light. In both countries, it was discovered that 40% of the players in the top teams were born between January and March, 30% between April and June, 20% between July and September, and only 10% between October and December. The explanation was simple. The school year in these countries runs from January to December. A boy who is ten on January 2nd will be in the same class as one whose 10th birthday is on December 30th. The chances are the first boy will be bigger, stronger, and more coordinated. He is much more likely than the other boy to be chosen to play in junior teams. He will then get better coaching than the others, and will play many more games, so will also get more practice. In the beginning his advantage isn't so much that he is more talented, simply that he is older. He was lucky enough to be born in the first months of the year. But by the age of 13 or 14, with the extra coaching and practice, he really <u>will</u> be better than the others, and far more likely to be successful.

The extra practice is vital, because the second factor that Gladwell believes is of great importance in determining whether somebody is going to be successful or not is what he calls the '10,000 hours theory'. This theory, based on studies in many different fields, says that in order to get to the very top you need to put in 10,000 hours of practice, whether it is playing an instrument or a sport, or programming a computer.

Adapted from a British newspaper

6 VOCABULARY
making adjectives and adverbs

> One of these is **luck**, for example being **lucky** enough to be in the right place at the right time.

a Look at the **bold** words in the sentence above. Which is a noun and which is an adjective? Using the word *luck*, can you make…?

1 a negative adjective
2 a positive adverb
3 a negative adverb

b ➤ p.163 Vocabulary Bank *Word building.* Do Part 2.

7 WRITING

a Read the rules for the sentence game.

The **sentence** game

1 You must write correct sentences with the exact number of words given (contractions count as one word).

2 The sentences must make sense.

3 You must include a form of the word given (e.g. if the word is *luck*, you can use *lucky*, *luckily*, etc.).

b Work in teams of three or four. Play the sentence game. You have five minutes to write the following sentences.

1 **fortune** (11 WORDS)
2 **comfort** (9 WORDS)
3 **luck** (7 WORDS)
4 **care** (6 WORDS)
5 **patience** (12 WORDS)

c Your teacher will tell you if your sentences are correct. The team with the most correct sentences is the winner.

8 (5 9)) **SONG** *Karma* ♫

G quantifiers
V electronic devices, phrasal verbs
P *ough* and *augh*, linking

9B Too much information!

> You look a bit stressed!

> Yes, I have too much work and not enough time to do it.

1 GRAMMAR quantifiers

a Look at the illustration. How many electronic devices can you see? Which ones do you have? What do you use them for?

b Circle the correct phrase in 1–6.

1 I used to have *a lot of | lot of* different gadgets, but now I use my phone for almost everything.
2 I'd like to buy a better computer, but I don't have *enough money | money enough* at the moment.
3 I spend *too much | too many* time every day online.
4 I only have *a little | a few* friends on Facebook, and *no | none* of them are close friends.
5 I never watch TV or films on my phone because the screen isn't *enough big | big enough*.
6 I like Apple products because of their design, but I think they are *too | too much* expensive.

c ➤ **p.149 Grammar Bank 9B.** Learn more about quantifiers and practise them.

d Talk to a partner. Are the sentences in **b** true for you? Say why (not).

2 PRONUNCIATION *ough* and *augh*

> 🔍 **ough and augh**
> Be careful with the letters **ough** and **augh**. They can have different pronunciations.
> Try to remember how to pronounce the most common words which have this combination of letters, e.g. *although*.

a Write the words in the list in the correct column.

although bought brought caught cough daughter
enough laugh thought through tough

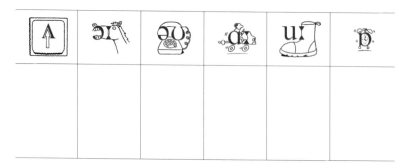

b ⑤14))) Listen and check. Which is the most common sound? Which four words finish with the sound /f/?

c ⑤15))) Listen to sentences 1–5 and practise saying them.

1 I thought I'd brought enough money with me.
2 My daughter's caught a bad cold.
3 I bought it although it was very expensive.
4 We've been through some tough times.
5 I didn't laugh! It was a cough.

Information overload

If you type the words 'information overload' into Google, you will immediately get an information overload – more than 7 million hits in 0.05 seconds. Some of this information is interesting – for example, you learn that the phrase 'information overload' was first used in 1970, actually before the internet was invented. But much of the information is not relevant or useful: obscure companies and even more obscure bloggers.

Information overload is one of the biggest irritations in modern life. There are news and sports websites to watch, emails that need to be answered, people who want to chat to you online, and back in the real world, friends, family, and colleagues who also have things to tell you. At work, information overload is also causing problems. A recent survey has shown that many company managers believe that it has made their jobs less satisfying, and has even affected their personal relationships outside work. Some of them also think that it is bad for their health.

Clearly there is a problem. It is not only the increase in the quantity of information, it is also the fact that it is everywhere, not just in the home and in the workplace. Many people today do not go anywhere without their smartphones. There is no escape from the internet.

3 READING & SPEAKING

a Look at the title of the article. What do you think it means? Read the first paragraph to check.

b Now read the whole article. Choose a, b, or c.

1 Many of the managers surveyed think that as a result of information overload __.
   a they have to work harder
   b they enjoy their jobs less
   c they are ill more often

2 Scientists think that information overload makes people __.
   a more anxious but more productive
   b more productive but less creative
   c more stressed and less creative

3 One solution to information overload would be for people to spend less time __.
   a searching for information
   b using the internet
   c talking on the phone

c Read the article again and work out the meaning of the **highlighted** words and phrases related to the internet and technology.

d Do you suffer from information overload in your own life? Talk to your partner about how information overload affects different parts of your life.

> your work   your studies
> your social life   your family life

Scientists have highlighted three big worries. Firstly, information overload can make people feel anxious: there is too much to do and not enough time to do it. People end up **multitasking**, which can make them even more stressed. Secondly, information overload can make people less creative. Research shows that people are more likely to be creative if they are allowed to focus on one thing for some time, without interruptions. Thirdly, information overload can make people less productive. People who multitask take much longer and make many more mistakes than people who do the same tasks one after another.

What can be done about information overload? One solution is technological: there is now a computer program or app you can install called 'Freedom', which disconnects you from the web at preset times. The second solution involves willpower. **Switch off** your mobile phone and the internet from time to time. The manager of an IT company puts 'thinking time' into his schedule, when all his **electronic devices** are switched off so that he isn't disturbed. This might sound like common sense. But nowadays, although we have more information than ever before, we do not always have enough common sense.

Adapted from a news website

4 VOCABULARY & PRONUNCIATION electronic devices, phrasal verbs, linking

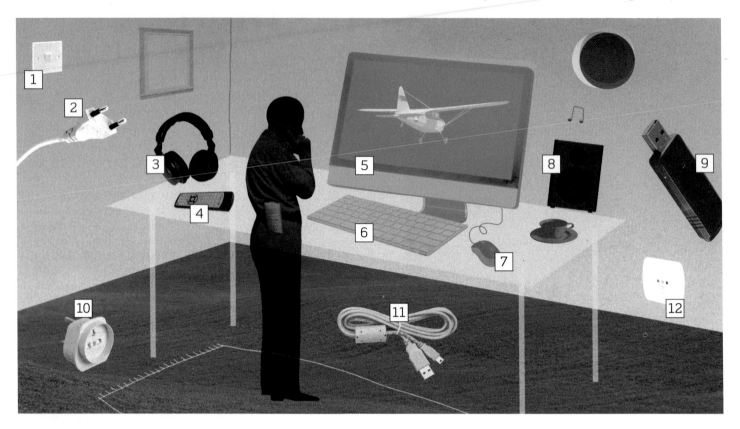

a Match the words and pictures.

☐ a mouse	☐ a memory stick	☐ a socket
☐ a speaker	☐ a plug	☐ *1* a switch
☐ a USB cable	☐ a remote control	☐ an adaptor
☐ a keyboard	☐ a screen	☐ headphones

b (5 16)) Listen and check. Then test each other.

A **What's 6?** (*B* (words covered) **It's a keyboard.**

c Match the sentences.

1 ☐ I changed the heating from 20° to 18°.   A I **switched it off**.
2 ☐ I disconnected my iPod from the computer.   B I **switched it on**.
3 ☐ I made the volume on the TV louder.   C I **turned it down**.
4 ☐ I pressed the 'off' button on the TV.   D I **turned it up**.
5 ☐ I programmed the alarm on my phone.   E I **plugged it in**.
6 ☐ I put my phone charger into a socket.   F I **unplugged it**.
7 ☐ I pressed the 'on' button on my laptop.   G I **set it for 7.30**.

d (5 17)) Listen and check.

e (5 18)) Listen and repeat A–G. Try to link the words. Now cover A–G and look at sentences 1–7. Say A–G from memory.

> **Separable phrasal verbs**
> Remember that many phrasal verbs are separable, i.e. the object can go between the verb and particle (**Switch** *the TV* **on**.) or after the particle (**Switch on** *the TV*.).
> However, if the object is a pronoun, it <u>must</u> go between the verb and particle, e.g. *Switch it on*. NOT ~~Switch on it~~.

f Answer the questions with a partner. Give reasons for your answers.

1 How many devices do you have with screens? Which one do you use the most?

2 Do you prefer to use a keyboard with or without a mouse?

3 Do you normally listen to music with headphones or with speakers?

4 How many remote controls do you have? Do you think you have too many?

5 How many pins do plugs in your country have? Do you need a travel adaptor if you go abroad?

6 In your house do you usually agree about what the temperature should be, or is someone always turning the heating or air conditioning up and down?

5 LISTENING & SPEAKING

a Look at the book cover and the book review information. What do you think the book is about? How do you think the three teenagers feel?

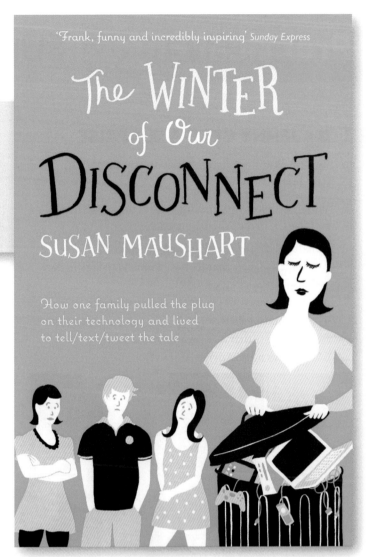

'Frank, funny and incredibly inspiring' *Sunday Express*

The WINTER of Our DISCONNECT

SUSAN MAUSHART

How one family pulled the plug on their technology and lived to tell/text/tweet the tale

> *The wise and hilarious story of a family who discovered that having fewer tools to communicate with actually led them to communicate more.*
>
> When Susan Maushart first announced her intention to pull the plug on her family's entire collection of electronic gadgets for six months her three kids didn't react at all. Says Maushart, 'Looking back, I can understand why. They didn't hear me.'

> * The title is a play on words. Shakespeare's play *Richard III* opens with the famous phrase 'Now is the winter of our discontent...'

b (5 19)) Listen to **Part 1** of a radio breakfast show where the guests are discussing the book. Answer questions 1–6.

1 Why did Susan Maushart decide to do the experiment?
2 Was it just her children who were spending too much time using technology?
3 Who are 'digital immigrants' and 'digital natives'?
4 What gadgets did Susan Maushart's family have to switch off? Where?
5 What were they allowed to use?
6 How did she get the children to agree to the experiment?

c (5 20)) Listen to **Part 2**. In general, was the experiment positive or negative? Why?

d Listen again and complete the sentences in your own words.

1 At the beginning the children complained that…
2 Later they started to…
3 Her son started to…
4 Their mother found it difficult to…
5 Another negative thing was that…
6 They now have new house rules, for example…

e (5 21)) Now listen to **Part 3**. What does each guest say he / she would miss most if they had to do the experiment?

1 Sally	
2 Andrew	
3 Jenny	
4 Nick	

f Discuss the questions with a partner.

1 Have you ever had to live without the internet for a few days or more, e.g. when you were on holiday somewhere? Did you miss it a lot? Why (not)?
2 Do you think Susan Maushart's experiment was a good idea? Why (not)?
3 If you had to do the experiment, what do you think you would miss the most? Why?

> 🔍 **Useful language**
> The thing I'd miss most is…
> I can't live without it because…
> I need / use it (for)…
> I'm addicted to it…
> I depend on it (for)…

6 WRITING

> ➤ **p.120 Writing** *A magazine article – advantages and disadvantages.* Write an article about the advantages and disadvantages of smartphones.

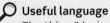

1 ◼◀ JENNY GETS A SURPRISE
VIDEO

a ⑤22)) Watch or listen. How do you think Jenny and Rob feel at the end?

b Watch or listen again. Mark the sentences **T** (true) or **F** (false). Correct the **F** sentences.

1 Jenny didn't expect Paul to be there.
2 Paul tells Jenny that Rob is planning to stay in New York.
3 Rob arrives with croissants for breakfast.
4 Rob accuses Paul of lying.
5 Rob insists that he's serious about Jenny.
6 Rob says he will drive Paul to Boston.

2 ◼◀ INDIRECT QUESTIONS
VIDEO

a ⑤23)) Watch or listen to Rob and Jenny talking in the office. Do they resolve their problems?

b Watch or listen again and answer the questions.

1 What reason does Rob give for Paul being in his flat?
2 How does Rob know that Paul is really leaving?
3 Why doesn't Jenny believe that Rob wants to stay in New York?
4 According to Jenny, how did Rob behave when he was with Paul?
5 What does Jenny think about their relationship?

c ⑤24)) Look at some extracts from the conversation. Can you remember any of the missing words? Watch or listen and check.

1	**Jenny**	Could you _____ me why Paul is still in your apartment?
	Rob	Well, he couldn't get a ticket to Boston...
2	**Jenny**	Do you _____ if he's got one now?
	Rob	I bought it! He's leaving this evening.
3	**Jenny**	Look Rob, I'd _____ to know what you really want.
	Rob	What do you mean?
4	**Jenny**	I _____ if you really want to be here. I wonder if...
	Rob	Jenny, what is it?
5	**Don**	I need a word. _____ you tell me what you decided at the last meeting?
	Jenny	Right away, Don. Rob was just leaving.

d ⑤25)) Watch or listen and repeat the highlighted phrases. Copy the rhythm and intonation.

e Practise the dialogues in **c** with a partner.

f Read the information about indirect questions. Then make questions 1–5 more indirect by using the beginnings given.

> 🔍 **Indirect questions**
>
> We often put *Can / Could you tell me...?, Do you know...?, I'd like to know..., I wonder...* before a question to make it less direct. When we do this, the direct question changes to an affirmative sentence, i.e. the word order is subject + verb, and we don't use *do / did* in the present and the past.
>
> Compare:
>
> **Why is Paul** in your apartment?
> Could you tell me why Paul is still in your apartment?
>
> **Has he got** one now?
> Do you know if (or whether) he's got one now?
>
> What **do you really want**?
> I'd like to know what you really want.
>
> **Do you really want** to be here?
> I wonder if (or whether) you really want to be here.
>
> **What did you decide** at the last meeting?
> Can you tell me what you decided at the last meeting?

1 *Where's the station?*

Excuse me, can you tell me _____
_____?

2 *What did he say?*

I'd like to know _____
_____.

3 *Does she like me?*

I wonder _____
_____.

4 *Is your brother coming tonight?*

Do you know _____
_____?

5 *What time does the shop close?*

Could you tell me _____
_____?

g 👥 ➤ **Communication** *Asking politely for information* **A** *p.106* **B** *p.110.*

3 📹 ROB GETS SERIOUS

a (5 26))) Watch or listen to Rob and Jenny. How do you think Jenny will answer Rob's final question?

b Watch or listen again and complete the sentences with 2–4 words.

1 Rob is trying to convince Jenny that he _____.
2 Jenny says that she's sure that Rob wants to _____.
3 Rob says that he loves his _____.
4 Jenny and Rob are going to visit _____.
5 Rob promises not to forget _____.
6 Rob asks Jenny to _____.

c Look at the **Social English phrases**. Can you remember any of the missing words?

Social English phrases	
Jenny	It's _____ you want to go back.
Rob	Of _____ I miss London, but I love my life here.
Rob	And I won't forget the chocolates this time _____.
Jenny	Well, that's a start, I _____.
Rob	_____ if I proposed to you?
Jenny	Rob, _____ it. It's embarrassing.

d (5 27))) Watch or listen and complete the phrases.

e Watch or listen again and repeat the phrases. How do you say them in your language?

> 👤 **Can you...?**
>
> ☐ make indirect questions, e.g. beginning with *Can you tell me...?*
> ☐ discuss a problem

G relative clauses: defining and non-defining
V compound nouns
P word stress

10A Modern icons

Is that the first Apple computer?

No, it's the one they made in 1990.

1 READING

a In pairs, do the quiz. Choose a, b, or c.

b 🔊 5 28))) Compare with another pair, and listen and check.

What do you know about Steve Jobs?

1 He was born in...
   a New York
   b San Francisco
   c Texas

2 At college...
   a he was a star pupil
   b he dropped out
   c he was expelled

3 His first job was with a company which made...
   a video games   b TVs   c computers

4 The Apple Macintosh was the first successful computer to use...
   a a mouse
   b a keyboard
   c a USB port

5 In 1986 he co-founded...
   a Pixar
   b HandMade Films
   c DreamWorks

6 Steve Jobs died of cancer in...
   a 2010   b 2011   c 2012

7 He was _____ years old.
   a 46   b 56   c 66

c Look at the photos and guess what the connection is between each of the things, people, or places and Steve Jobs.

d Now read paragraphs 1–5 and check.

1 The Macintosh Classic was the
personal computer which was made by Apple in 1990. It had a 23 cm monochrome screen and a 4 megabyte (MB) memory. It was cheaper than earlier Apple computers and very easy to use. It was their first commercially successful computer.

2 Stephen Wozniak is the American
computer engineer and programmer whose computer designs became the original Apple I and Apple II computers. He and Steve Jobs became friends when they were both working at Hewlett Packard. They started making computers in Jobs's parents' garage and together they founded Apple Computers (now Apple Inc.) in 1976.

3 Mona Simpson is Steve Jobs's sister.
Jobs was adopted when he was born, but in the 1980s he found his biological mother, who told him that he had a sister. Mona and Steve met for the first time in 1985 (when she was 25 and he was 30) and they became very close. They kept their relationship secret for a year until Mona introduced Steve as her brother at the party which she gave to celebrate the publication of her first novel, *Anywhere But Here*.

4 Mountain View is the area in
California where Steve Jobs grew up. He was born in San Francisco and was adopted by Paul and Clara Jobs. When he was six years old the family moved to Mountain View, which was becoming a centre for electronics. People began to call the area 'Silicon Valley' because silicon is used to manufacture electronic parts.

5 This is the logo which was designed
by Jonathan Mak, a Chinese design student from Hong Kong, as a tribute to Steve Jobs when he died. The design, which used Jobs's silhouette incorporated into the 'bite' of a white Apple logo, became a worldwide internet sensation. The teenager said that Jobs had inspired him to become a designer.

2 GRAMMAR relative clauses

a Cover the text. Complete the sentences with *who*, *whose*, *which*, or *where*.

1 The Macintosh Classic was the personal computer _____ was made by Apple in 1990.

2 Stephen Wozniak is the American computer engineer _____ founded Apple Computers with Steve Jobs and _____ computer designs became the original Apple I and Apple II computers.

3 Mona introduced Steve as her brother at the party _____ she gave to celebrate the publication of her first novel.

4 Mountain View is the area in California _____ Steve Jobs grew up.

5 Jonathan Mak's design, _____ used Jobs's silhouette incorporated into the 'bite' of a white Apple logo, became a worldwide internet sensation.

b Answer the questions in pairs.

1 In which phrase is the relative pronoun (*who, that*, etc.) not necessary?

2 In which sentence could you leave out the relative clause, but the sentence would still make sense?

c ➤ **p.150 Grammar Bank 10A.** Learn more about defining and non-defining relative clauses, and practise them.

d Cover the text and look at the photos. Can you remember the connections with Steve Jobs? Try to use a relative clause.

3 WRITING

a ➤ **p.121 Writing** *A biography.* Write a biography of an interesting or successful person you know about.

b ➤ **Communication** *Relatives quiz* **A** *p.108* **B** *p.112.* Write quiz questions to ask a partner.

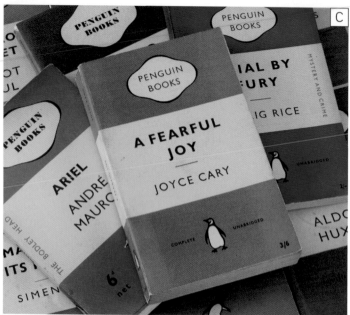

GREAT BRITISH DESIGN ICONS

Some of the things which were voted the best in a recent survey of British design icons.

4 LISTENING

a Look at the photos which show four famous examples of British design. What are they? What do you know about them?

b (5 31)) Now listen to an exhibition audio guide about them. Complete sentences 1–4.

1 Harry Beck was the man who…
2 Julia Barfield and David Marks are the couple who…
3 Allen Lane was the man who…
4 Peter Blake is the man who…

c Listen again and answer the questions.

Which icon…?

1 is the most recent
2 is the oldest
3 has been used in many different products
4 used different colours to show different products
5 didn't make its designer much money
6 was the result of something that happened to its designer when he was travelling
7 was not expected to be popular
8 makes places look nearer than they really are

d Which of the four do you find the most attractive design? What would you consider to be examples of iconic design in your country?

5 SPEAKING

a Write the names of people, things, or places in as many of the circles as you can.

b In groups, talk about your people, things, and places. Explain why you admire them.

a famous dead person (who) you admire

a famous living person (that) you admire

an iconic landmark (that) you really like

a country whose design you admire

an everyday object (that) you own that you think has a beautiful design

an object (which) you would like to own that you think has a beautiful design

a DVD cover, film poster, or book cover (that) you think has great design

6 VOCABULARY & PRONUNCIATION

compound nouns, word stress

> **Compound nouns**
> We often put two nouns together, where the first noun describes the second one, e.g. an *album cover* (= the cover of an album), the *Tube map* (= the map of the Tube). Compound nouns can be two words, e.g. *tourist attraction* or one word, e.g. *website*.

a Match a noun from column **A** with a noun from column **B** to make compound nouns.

A	B
football	picture
speed	case
sun	hall
town	pitch
book	mate
class	glasses
profile	camera

b (5 32)) Listen and check. Which three are written as one word? Which noun is usually stressed more in compound nouns? Practise saying the compound nouns in **a** with the right stress.

c In pairs, try to answer all the questions in **three minutes** with compound nouns from Files 1–10.

COMPOUND NOUNS RACE

1 Where can you take money out without going into a bank?
2 What do you need to have before you can get on a plane?
3 What might you have to pay if you park in a bus lane?
4 What should you put on when you get into a car?
5 What do you call a long line of cars that can't move?
6 What do you need to book if you want to play tennis with someone?
7 Where do people go if they want to watch a basketball or handball match?
8 What do you call the noise a phone makes?
9 What kind of books or films are about the future, and often outer space?
10 What do you call a school which is paid for by the government?
11 If you are in a lift and you press G, where do you want to go to?
12 What device do you use when you want to transfer files from one computer to another?

7 (5 33)) **SONG** *Greatest Love of All* ♫

G question tags
V crime
P intonation in question tags

10B Two murder mysteries

You were a detective with Scotland Yard, weren't you?

Yes, I was.

1 VOCABULARY crime

a Have you heard of Jack the Ripper? What do you know about him?

b Match the words and definitions.

detectives evidence murder murderer
prove solve suspects victims witnesses

1 _____ *noun* police officers who investigate crimes

2 _____ *noun* people who see something which has happened, and then tell others (e.g. the police) about it

3 _____ *noun* people who are hurt or killed by somebody in a crime

4 _____ *noun* a person who plans and kills another person

5 _____ *noun* the crime of killing a person illegally and deliberately

6 _____ *noun* the facts, signs, etc. which tell you who committed a crime

7 _____ *noun* people who are thought to be guilty of a crime

8 _____ (a mystery) *verb* to find the correct answer to why something happened

9 _____ (sth) *verb* to use facts and evidence to show something is true

c (5 34)) Listen and check. Practise saying the words.

d Read *Who was Jack the Ripper?* and complete the gaps with words from **b**.

e Read the article again and find the answer to these questions.

1 Where and when did the murders take place?

2 How many murders were there?

3 How long did the murders go on for?

4 Who are the main suspects?

5 What does Patricia Cornwell usually do?

6 How did she try to solve the mystery?

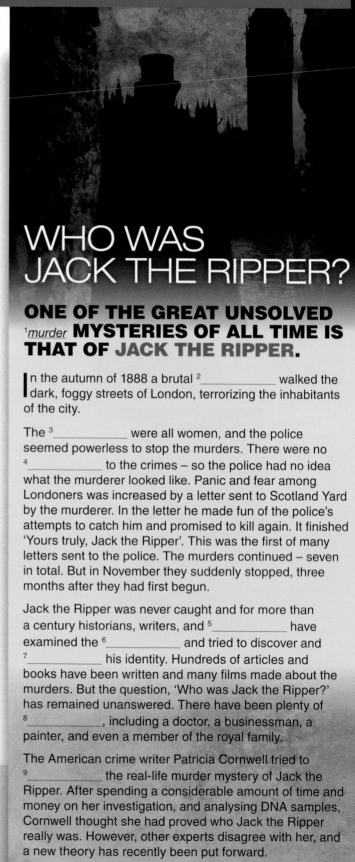

WHO WAS JACK THE RIPPER?

ONE OF THE GREAT UNSOLVED ¹*murder* MYSTERIES OF ALL TIME IS THAT OF JACK THE RIPPER.

In the autumn of 1888 a brutal ²_____ walked the dark, foggy streets of London, terrorizing the inhabitants of the city.

The ³_____ were all women, and the police seemed powerless to stop the murders. There were no ⁴_____ to the crimes – so the police had no idea what the murderer looked like. Panic and fear among Londoners was increased by a letter sent to Scotland Yard by the murderer. In the letter he made fun of the police's attempts to catch him and promised to kill again. It finished 'Yours truly, Jack the Ripper'. This was the first of many letters sent to the police. The murders continued – seven in total. But in November they suddenly stopped, three months after they had first begun.

Jack the Ripper was never caught and for more than a century historians, writers, and ⁵_____ have examined the ⁶_____ and tried to discover and ⁷_____ his identity. Hundreds of articles and books have been written and many films made about the murders. But the question, 'Who was Jack the Ripper?' has remained unanswered. There have been plenty of ⁸_____, including a doctor, a businessman, a painter, and even a member of the royal family.

The American crime writer Patricia Cornwell tried to ⁹_____ the real-life murder mystery of Jack the Ripper. After spending a considerable amount of time and money on her investigation, and analysing DNA samples, Cornwell thought she had proved who Jack the Ripper really was. However, other experts disagree with her, and a new theory has recently been put forward.

do it out straight. My knife's so nice and sharp I want to get to work right away if I get a chance. Good luck!
yours truly
Jack the Ripper

2 LISTENING

a (5 35)》 Now listen to the first part of an interview with a retired police inspector, who is an expert on Jack the Ripper. Complete the information about the suspects.

Prince Albert,
Queen Victoria's _____

_____ Maybrick,
a cotton merchant

Walter Sickert,
an _____

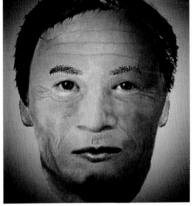

Carl Feigenbaum,
a _____

b (5 36)》 Listen to the second part of the interview and mark the sentences **T** (true) or **F** (false).

1 Cornwell's evidence is mainly scientific.
2 She took DNA samples from a letter written by Sickert.
3 Art lovers were angry with Cornwell.
4 There is evidence that Sickert was abroad at the time of some of the murders.
5 There is a letter that some people think Maybrick wrote confessing to the crimes.
6 Inspector Morton thinks that Prince Albert was a serial killer.
7 Carl Feigenbaum was executed in London for another murder.
8 Trevor Marriott found that Feigenbaum had travelled to London at the time of the murders.
9 The Inspector doesn't want to say who he thinks the murderer is.
10 He doesn't think the mystery will ever be solved.

c Listen again. Say why the **F** sentences are false.

d Do you know of any famous unsolved crimes in your country?

3 GRAMMAR question tags

a Look at four questions from the interview and complete them with the missing words.

1 'You were a detective with Scotland Yard, _____ _____?'
2 'It's incredible, _____ _____?'
3 'But you don't think she's right, _____ _____?'
4 'There's been another recent theory, _____ _____?'

b (5 37)》 Listen and check. What's the difference between these questions and direct questions, e.g. between **1** and *Were you a detective with Scotland Yard?*

c ▶ **p.151 Grammar Bank 10B.** Learn more about questions tags and practise them.

4 PRONUNCIATION & SPEAKING
intonation in question tags

a (5 39)》 Listen and complete the dialogue between a policeman and a suspect.

P Your surname's Jones, _____?
S Yes, it is.
P And you're 27, _____?
S Yes, that's right.
P You weren't at home last night at 8.00, _____?
S No, I wasn't. I was at the theatre.
P But you don't have any witnesses, _____?
S Yes, I do. My wife was with me.
P Your wife wasn't with you, _____?
S How do you know?
P Because she was with me. At the police station. We arrested her yesterday.

b (5 40)》 Listen and repeat the question tags. Copy the rhythm and intonation.

c ▶ **Communication** *Just checking* **A** *p.108* **B** *p.112*. Role-play a police interview.

d Which detective TV series or films are popular in your country at the moment? Do you enjoy watching these kinds of programmes?

5 READING & LISTENING

a Do you enjoy reading crime novels? If so, which ones? If not, why not? Have you read a crime story recently? What was it about?

b (5 41)) Read and listen to **Part 1** of a short story. Use the glossary to help you. Then answer the questions with a partner.

1 Where did the murder take place?
2 What did the prisoner look like?
3 How many witnesses saw him?
4 Why did Mrs Salmon go to the window?
5 When did Mr MacDougall see Adams?
6 Did Mr Wheeler see Adams's face?

The Case for the Defence is a short story written by novelist Graham Greene. The story takes place in England around the time it was written, in the late 1930s, when the death penalty for murder still existed. It was abolished in 1965.

The Case for the Defence
BY GRAHAM GREENE
PART 1

It was the strangest murder trial I have ever attended. They named it the Peckham murder in the headlines, although Northwood Street, where Mrs Parker was found murdered, was not actually in Peckham.

The prisoner was a well-built man with bloodshot eyes. An ugly man, one you wouldn't forget in a hurry – and that was an important point. The prosecution intended to call four witnesses who hadn't forgotten him and who had seen him hurrying away from the little red house in Northwood Street.

At two o'clock in the morning Mrs Salmon, who lived at 15 Northwood Street, had been unable to sleep. She heard a door shut and so she went to the window and saw Adams (the accused) on the steps of the victim's house. He had just come out and he was wearing gloves. Before he moved away, he had looked up – at her window.

Henry MacDougall, who had been driving home late, nearly ran over Adams at the corner of Northwood Street because he was walking in the middle of the road, looking dazed. And old Mr Wheeler, who lived next door to Mrs Parker, at number 12, and was woken up by a noise and got up and looked out of the window, just as Mrs Salmon had done, saw Adams's back and, as he turned, those bloodshot eyes. In Laurel Avenue he had been seen by yet another witness.

Glossary 1
trial /'traɪəl/ the process where a judge listens to evidence and decides if sb is guilty or innocent
Peckham /'pekəm/ an area in South London
the prosecution /prɒsɪ'kjuːʃn/ the lawyer(s) who try to show that sb is guilty of a crime

PART 2

'I understand,' the lawyer for the prosecution said, 'that the defence intends to plead "mistaken identity". Adams's wife will tell you that he was with her at two in the morning on February 14. However, after you have heard the witnesses for the prosecution and examined carefully the features of the prisoner, I don't think you will be prepared to admit the possibility of a mistake.'

Mrs Salmon was called again. She was the ideal witness, with her slight Scottish accent and her expression of honesty and kindness. There was no malice in her, and no sense of importance. She told them what she had seen and how she had rung the police station.

'And do you see the man here in court?'

She looked straight at the big man in the dock, who stared hard at her with his bloodshot eyes, without emotion.

'Yes,' she said, 'there he is.'

'You are quite certain?'

She said simply, 'I couldn't be mistaken, sir.'

'Thank you, Mrs Salmon.'

The lawyer for the defence began to cross-examine Mrs Salmon.

'Now, Mrs Salmon, you must remember that a man's life may depend on your evidence.'

'I do remember it, sir.'

'Is your eyesight good?'

'I have never had to wear spectacles, sir.'

'You're fifty-five years old, aren't you?'

'Fifty-six, sir.'

'And the man you saw was on the other side of the road, is that right?'

'Yes, sir, he was.'

'And it was two o'clock in the morning. You must have remarkable eyes, Mrs Salmon?'

'No, sir. There was moonlight, and when the man looked up, he had the lamplight on his face.'

'And you have no doubt whatever that the man you saw is the prisoner?'

'None whatever, sir. It isn't a face you can easily forget.'

> **Glossary 2**
> **the defence** /dɪˈfens/ the lawyer(s) who try to show that sb is not guilty of a crime
> **plead (guilty)** /pliːd/ to say in court that you are guilty (or not guilty) of a crime
> **court** /kɔːt/ the place where crimes are judged
> **dock** /dɒk/ the place in a court where a person who is accused sits or stands
> **cross-examine** /krɒs ɪɡˈzæmɪn/ to question a witness carefully about answers they have already given

c (5 42)) Now read and listen to **Part 2**. Then answer the questions with a partner.

1 Adams's defence was 'mistaken identity'. What does this mean?

2 Where did Adams say that he was?

3 What did the prosecution lawyer ask Mrs Salmon?

4 What three reasons did she give to explain how she had seen Adams's face so clearly?

d (5 43)) Read the glossary for **Part 3** of the story, and check how the words are pronounced. Then listen to **Part 3** and answer the questions with a partner.

> **Glossary 3**
> **swear** /sweə/ to make a public promise that something is true
> **case** /keɪs/ something that is being officially investigated by the police, e.g. a murder case
> **alibi** /ˈæləbaɪ/ evidence that proves sb was in a different place at the time that a crime was committed
> **be acquitted** /bi əˈkwɪtɪd/ to be declared not guilty of a crime

1 Who was the man at the back of the court?

2 How was he dressed?

3 What did the defence lawyer say to Mrs Salmon?

4 What was the man's alibi?

5 Why was the man acquitted?

6 Why was there a big crowd outside the court?

7 Why did the brothers refuse to leave by the back entrance?

8 What happened to one of the brothers?

9 Why does the writer ask the question at the end, *If you were Mrs Salmon, could you sleep at night?*

e Do you like the way the story ends? Why (not)?

GRAMMAR

Circle a, b, or c.

1 If you _____ here on time, we wouldn't have missed the start of the film.
   a were   b had been   c would have been

2 What _____ if that man hadn't helped you?
   a you would do   b you would have done
   c would you have done

3 If she _____ me that she was arriving this morning, I would have gone to the airport to pick her up.
   a told   b would tell   c had told

4 I would have finished the exam if I _____ about another ten minutes.
   a would have had   b had had
   c would have

5 I'm afraid there's _____ time left.
   a no   b none   c any

6 There are _____ good programmes on tonight. I don't know what to watch.
   a lots of   b a lot   c plenty

7 Is there _____ in the car for me too?
   a room enough   b enough room
   c too much room

8 Most people have _____ close friends.
   a very little   b very few   c not much

9 Is he the man _____ you met at the party?
   a –   b whose   c which

10 Is that the woman _____ husband is a famous writer?
   a who   b that   c whose

11 The *Mona Lisa*, _____ was painted in about 1510, is the Louvre in Paris.
   a which   b what   c that

12 I'm very fond of Susan, _____ I used to share a flat with at university.
   a who   b –   c that

13 They're very rich, _____?
   a are they   b aren't they   c isn't it

14 Your brother's been to New Zealand, _____?
   a wasn't he   b isn't he   c hasn't he

15 You won't be late, _____?
   a will you   b won't you   c are you

VOCABULARY

a Complete the sentences with a word formed from the **bold** word.

1 I got to the airport late, but _____ the flight was delayed. **luck**
2 He's _____ with his work. It's always full of mistakes. **care**
3 This sofa is really _____. It's much too hard. **comfort**
4 I found a great jacket online, but _____ it was sold out. **fortunate**
5 Don't be so _____! The bus will be here soon. **patience**

b Complete with a verb.

1 It was too hot in the room, so I _____ the heating down a bit.
2 I need to _____ my alarm for 5.30 as I have an early flight.
3 It's always a good idea to _____ your computer during a storm.
4 Could you _____ up the volume? I can't hear very well.
5 If you're not watching the TV, please _____ it off.

c Complete with the right words.

1 you use it to change the TV channel   r_____ c_____
2 you use this on a computer to write   k_____
3 you use this to transfer files or photos   m_____ st_____
4 you use these to listen to music, e.g. on a plane   h_____ s
5 you use this to move the cursor on a computer   m_____

d Complete the compound nouns.

1 football p_____   3 ground fl_____   5 speed c_____
2 pr_____ picture   4 petrol s_____

e Complete the missing words.

1 The d_____ was convinced that the man's alibi was false.
2 I'm sure he's guilty, but I can't pr_____ it.
3 Jack the Ripper's v_____ were all women.
4 The police are convinced they will be able to s_____ the mystery.
5 Walter Sickert was a s_____ in the Jack the Ripper case.

PRONUNCIATION

a Circle the word with a different sound.

1	daughter	bought	caught	through
2	luck	tough	although	enough
3	charge	plug	gadget	programme
4	keyboard	speaker	headphones	screen
5	murder	turn	perfect	careful

b Under<u>line</u> the stressed syllable.

1 comfor|ta|ble   2 a|dap|tor   3 ca|ble   4 wit|ness   5 e|vi|dence

CAN YOU UNDERSTAND THIS TEXT?

a Read the article once. The read it again with the glossary and mark the sentences **T** (true), **F** (false), or **DS** (doesn't say).

1 The boy was on the Isle of Wight to attend the festival.
2 Bob Dylan and the boy had communication problems.
3 There was a beautiful view from the kitchen.
4 The boy liked the song which the American sang to him.
5 Some years later the boy committed a crime.
6 He was very moved when he heard *North Country Blues*.
7 Bob Dylan taught him to read and write.

b Choose five new words or phrases from the text. Check their meaning and pronunciation and try to learn them.

The ICON and the GYPSY

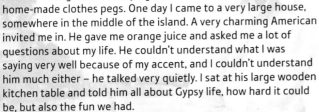

I was a young Gypsy boy trying to grow up in the 1960s in a country which was very hostile to our lifestyle, and with no access to education, and no chance to listen to music, or to attend festivals.

By chance my family were on the Isle of Wight during the famous 1969 music festival. I was knocking on doors, trying to sell our home-made clothes pegs. One day I came to a very large house, somewhere in the middle of the island. A very charming American invited me in. He gave me orange juice and asked me a lot of questions about my life. He couldn't understand what I was saying very well because of my accent, and I couldn't understand him much either – he talked very quietly. I sat at his large wooden kitchen table and told him all about Gypsy life, how hard it could be, but also the fun we had.

I must have been there for most of the morning and he got me to sing a couple of the Gypsy songs I knew. Before I left he played me a song on his guitar and gave me a record, which he said was his, and had the song on. But I didn't have a record player, and I soon lost the record.

I had no idea who he was and I forgot about him until I was in my early twenties. Unfortunately I had got into some trouble and was in Brixton prison for burglary. My sentence was for two years. We had a vicar who used to visit twice a week and because we were bored we would sometimes attend his sessions. At one of the sessions he played some music on an old record player and as soon as I heard it I recognized the singer. He told me it was a man called Bob Dylan and said that if I liked it, he would bring more of his records to the next meeting. The following week I spent hours transfixed as I listened to the records. One song stood out – *North Country Blues* – it was the song he had sung to me in the kitchen on the Isle of Wight all those years ago. When the song had finished, I cried – all the troubles and hardship I had lived with just poured out of me.

Those sessions with the vicar became my education. With his guidance and Dylan's poetry a world opened up to me. He taught me to read and write, and by the time my prison sentence came to an end I had started a journey that transformed my life. With the vicar's support I went to college and became a carpenter – I didn't look back.

Gypsy a member of a race of people who spend their lives travelling around from place to place, living in caravans
Isle of Wight a small island off the south coast of England
vicar an Anglican priest

Adapted from The Times

CAN YOU UNDERSTAND THESE PEOPLE?

5 44)) **In the street** Watch or listen to five people and answer the questions.

Lizzie   Harry   Sean   Isobel   Giles

1 Lizzie helped someone who _____.
   a wasn't feeling well
   b didn't have enough money for a taxi
   c couldn't find the right platform

2 Harry couldn't live without her mobile phone because _____.
   a she uses the maps on it
   b it has a lot of apps
   c it's useful in an emergency

3 Sean _____ guess who the murderer is.
   a can usually   b likes to try to   c doesn't try to

4 Isobel's favourite thing about Alexander McQueen's clothes is _____.
   a they are reasonably priced
   b the different designs and materials
   c that they are based on designs from the past

5 Giles thinks he's lucky because he _____.
   a caught a flight from Australia at the last minute
   b is generally happy
   c once won some money on the lottery

CAN YOU SAY THIS IN ENGLISH?

Do the tasks with a partner. Tick (✓) the box if you can do them.

Can you…?

1 ☐ complete these three sentences:
    If you had told me about the party earlier,…
    I would have bought those shoes if…
    I wouldn't have been so angry if…

2 ☐ describe something that you do too much, and something that you don't do enough

3 ☐ talk about a gadget that you use and why it is useful

4 ☐ describe a person that you admire (who they are / what you know about them / why you admire them)

5 ☐ check five things you think you know about your partner using questions tags

Short films The Hound of the Baskervilles
VIDEO   Watch and enjoy a film on iTutor.

Communication

1B PERSONALITY Students A+B

Read the explanation and compare with a partner. Do you agree with your results?

> The activity you have just done is a personality test. The first adjective you wrote down is how you see yourself, the second is how other people see you, and the third is what you are really like.

PE1 HOW AWFUL! HOW FANTASTIC! Student A

a Read your sentences 1–9 to **B**. **B** must react with a phrase, e.g. *You're kidding, Oh no!* etc.

1 I collect old English tea cups.
2 I spilled some coffee on my laptop last night and now it doesn't work.
3 I'm going to New York next weekend.
4 Someone stole my bike yesterday.
5 My dog can open the kitchen door by himself.
6 My father's going to be interviewed on TV tomorrow.
7 My grandmother's just bought a sports car.
8 My parents met when they were only 15.
9 I've just won €2,000 in the lottery!

b Listen to **B**'s sentences and react with a phrase.

c Tell **B** some real (or invented) news about you for **B** to react. React to **B**'s news.

2A SPENDER OR SAVER? Students A+B

Check your results, then compare with a partner. Do you agree with your results?

Mostly 'a' answers
You can't be trusted with your own money! You definitely need someone to help you to manage your finances better. Why not speak to an organized friend about how to plan? This will help you to make your money go further and stop you getting into debt.

Mostly 'b' answers
Although you understand how to manage your money, sometimes you need to be a bit more organized. Try setting yourself a weekly or monthly budget, then keep to it. You will then know how much money you have, what you spend it on, and how much you can save.

Mostly 'c' answers
Congratulations! It sounds like you really know what you are doing when it comes to managing your money. You know how important it is to keep track of your spending and are responsible with your money.

2B ARE YOU HUNGRY? Student A

a Ask **B** your questions. He / she must respond with the phrase in brackets.

1 Is the water cold? (Yes, it's **freezing**.)
2 Was the film good? (Yes, it was **fantastic**.)
3 Were you tired after the exam? (Yes, I was **exhausted**.)
4 Was the room dirty? (Yes, it was **filthy**.)
5 Is it a big house? (Yes, it's **enormous**.)
6 Were you surprised? (Yes, I was **amazed**.)
7 Are you sure? (Yes, I'm **positive**.)

b Respond to **B**'s questions. Say *Yes, it's… / I'm…*, etc. + the strong form of the adjective which **B** used in the question. Remember to <u>stress</u> the strong adjective.

Are you afraid of flying? | *Yes, I'm terrified.*

c Repeat the exercise. Try to respond as quickly as possible.

3A I'M A TOURIST – CAN YOU HELP ME? Student A

a Think of the town / city where you are, or the nearest big town. You are a foreign tourist and you are planning to get around using public transport. Ask **B** questions 1–5. Get as much information from **B** as you can.

1 What kind of public transport is there?
2 What's the best way for me to get around the city?
3 Can I hire a bike? Are there any cycle lanes?
4 Is it easy to find taxis? How expensive are they?
5 What's the best way to get to the airport from the town centre? How long does it take?

b Swap roles. **B** is a foreign tourist in the town, who has hired a car. You live in the town. Answer **B**'s questions and give as much information as you can.

PE3 COULD YOU DO ME A FAVOUR?
Students A+B

a Look at the verb phrases below. Choose two things you would like somebody to do for you. Think about any details, e.g. what kind of dog it is, how much money you need, etc.

- **look after** (your children, your dog for the weekend, you flat while you're away, etc.)
- **lend you** (some money, their car, etc.)
- **give you a lift** (home, to the town centre, etc.)
- **help you** (with a problem, with your homework, to paint your flat, to choose some new clothes, etc.)

b Ask as many other students as possible. Be polite (*Could you do me a big favour? Would you mind...? Do you think you could...?*) and explain why you want the favour. How many people agree to help you?

4A GUESS THE SENTENCE   Student A

a Look at sentences 1–6 and think of the correct form of *be able to* + a verb. **Don't write anything yet!**

> **1** I'm sorry I won't _____ to your party next weekend.
> **2** It was August, but we _____ a hotel without any problems.
> **3** I used to _____ a little Japanese, but I can't now.
> **4** I love _____ in bed late at the weekend.
> **5** Will you _____ the work before Saturday?
> **6** I've never _____ fish well.

b Read your sentence 1 to **B**. If it isn't right, try again until **B** tells you, 'That's right'. Then write it in. Continue with 2–6.

c Now listen to **B** say sentence 7. If it's the same as your sentence 7 below, say 'That's right'. If not, say 'Try again' until **B** gets it right. Continue with 8–12.

> **7** It must be fantastic to **be able to speak** a lot of languages.
> **8** I won't **be able to see** you tonight. I'm too busy.
> **9** My grandmother can't walk very well, but luckily we **were able to park** just outside the restaurant.
> **10** They haven't **been able to find** a flat yet. They're still looking.
> **11** You should **be able to do** this exercise. It's very easy.
> **12** We really enjoy **being able to eat** outside in the summer.

4B THE BIG DAY   Students A+B

Read a newspaper article about what happened at Heidi and Freddie's wedding. Do you think they behaved well or badly? Why?

News online

Mother-in-law from hell...
What happened next...

By NEWS ONLINE Reporter

Yesterday Heidi Withers married Freddie Bourne in a £25,000 ceremony at St Mary the Virgin Church in Berkeley, Gloucestershire. It was followed by a reception at 900-year-old Berkeley Castle. However, there was no sign of Carolyn, Freddie's stepmother, the woman who was ridiculed for the email she sent Heidi. She and her husband Edward, Freddie's father, were not invited.

Heidi arrived almost 25 minutes late for the ceremony, which was due to begin at 2.45 p.m. Perhaps, as Carolyn suggested was her habit, she had been in bed until the last possible minute. She arrived at the church with security guards holding umbrellas to prevent onlookers from catching sight of her, and with her head covered. This is a well-known tactic for celebrities, but for a 29-year-old secretary it seemed, in the words of one onlooker, 'a bit ridiculous'.

Edward and Carolyn admitted being disappointed at not receiving an invitation. They spent the weekend on a walking holiday with friends. They have had no contact with the couple since the saga began, and did not even know the date of the wedding.

Communication

5A OTHER SPORTING SUPERSTITIONS Student A

a Read about Tiger Woods and Kolo Touré.

TIGER WOODS always wears a red shirt on the last day of a golf tournament. It's a routine he has followed since he was eight and he believes it makes him play more aggressively.

When **KOLO TOURÉ** played for Arsenal, he always insisted on being the last player to leave the dressing room after the half-time break. This was never usually a problem. However, in one match when William Gallas, his teammate, was injured and needed treatment at half-time during a match, Touré stayed in the dressing room until Gallas had been treated. This meant that Arsenal had to start the second half with only nine players.

b Now cover the text and tell **B** about their superstitions from memory.

c Listen to **B** telling you about Laurent Blanc and Alexander Wurz's superstitions.

d Together decide which superstition you think is a) the strangest b) the most impractical.

PE5 ASKING POLITELY FOR INFORMATION
Student A

a You are a tourist in **B**'s town. You want to ask **B**, who you have stopped in the street, questions 1–5 and you want to be very polite. Rewrite 2–5 as indirect questions.

1 Do shops open on Sundays?
Could you tell me *if shops open on Sundays*?
2 Is there a post office near here?
Do you know _____ ?
3 What time do banks close here?
Could you tell me _____ ?
4 Where's the railway station?
Do you know _____ ?
5 Does the number 21 bus go to the city centre?
Could you tell me _____ ?

b Ask **B** your indirect questions 1–5. Always begin *Excuse me.*

c Now **B** is a tourist, and is going to stop you in the street and ask you some questions. Answer politely with the necessary information.

6B JUDGING BY APPEARANCES
Students A+B

Dominic McVey, born in 1985, is a British entrepreneur from London, who set up a business at the age of 13 importing micro-scooters from the United States. He was a millionaire by the age of 15. His business interests now include website publishing and fashion.

Mira Sorvino is an American actress of Italian descent. She won an Oscar as best supporting actress in 1995 for her role in Woody Allen's *Mighty Aphrodite*. Before becoming an actress she studied Chinese at Harvard University, where she graduated *magna cum laude* (with great honour).

Olga Rutterschmidt, an 80-year-old California woman, and her friend Helen Golay were convicted in 2008 of murdering two homeless men. They committed the murders to collect millions of dollars from the men's life insurance policies.

7A THREE IN A ROW
Students A+B

Play the game in small groups.

One team is **X** and one is **O**. Choose a square in turn. Finish the sentence so that it is grammatically correct and makes sense. If you are right, put your **X** or **O** in the square. The first team to get 'three in a row' is the winner.

Unless we hurry...	I'll leave home when...	I won't get married until...
I'll give you the money as soon as...	If I see him...	When I can speak English fluently...
He'll lose his job if...	As soon as he gets here...	You'll never be rich unless...

7B GUESS THE SENTENCE
Student A

a Look at sentences 1–6 and think of the missing verb phrase (+ = positive, − = negative). **Don't write anything yet!**

1 I'd cook dinner every day if I _____ earlier from work. +

2 If we _____ this summer, maybe we could afford to get a new car. −

3 I think you _____ more if you saw the original version. +

4 I'd see my grandparents more often if they _____. +

5 I _____ the fish if I were you. It isn't usually very good here. −

6 I _____ if the water was a bit warmer. +

b Read your sentence 1 to **B**. If it isn't right, try again until **B** tells you 'That's right'. Then write it in. Continue with 2–6.

c Listen to **B** say sentence 7. If it's the same as your sentence 7 below, say 'That's right'. If not, say 'Try again' until **B** gets it right. Continue with 8–12.

7 The house would look better if you **painted it**.

8 If I met my ex in the street, I **wouldn't say hello** to him.

9 If it **wasn't so late**, I'd stay a bit longer.

10 The flight **would be more comfortable** if we were in business class.

11 I wouldn't mind the winter so much if it **didn't get dark** so early.

12 If I had more money, I'**d buy a house** with a beautiful garden.

8A I WANT TO SPEAK TO THE MANAGER
Student A

Look at the situations and role-play the conversations. Spend a few minutes preparing what you are going to say.

1 **You're a customer.** You bought something in a clothes shop in the sales yesterday (decide what) and there's a problem (decide what). Go back to the shop. **B** is the shop assistant. You'd like to change it for another identical one. If you can't, you'd like a refund.

You start. (*Excuse me. I bought...*

2 **You're the manager of a restaurant.** Your normal chef is off this week, and you have a temporary chef who is not very good. One of the waiters has had a problem with a customer, who would like to speak to you. When customers complain you usually offer them a free drink or a coffee. If it's absolutely necessary, you might give a 10% discount on their bill, but you would prefer not to. **B** is the customer.

B will start.

8B THE RIGHT JOB FOR YOU   Students A+B

In which group(s) do you have most ticks? Read the appropriate paragraph to find out which jobs would suit you. Would you like to do any of them?

If you have most ticks in 1-4, the best job for you would be in the 'caring professions'. If you are good at science, you could consider a career in medicine, for example becoming a doctor or nurse. Alternatively, teaching or social work are areas which would suit your personality.

If you have most ticks in 5-8, you should consider a job involving numbers, for example becoming an accountant or working in the stock market. The world of business would also probably appeal to you, especially sales or marketing.

If you have most ticks in 9-12, you need a creative job. Depending on your specific talents you might enjoy a job in the world of music, art, or literature. Areas that would suit you include publishing, journalism, graphic design, fashion, or the music industry.

If you have most ticks in 13-16, you have an analytical mind. You would suit a job in computer science or engineering. You also have good spatial sense which would make architecture and related jobs another possibility.

Communication

9A GUESS THE CONDITIONAL
Student A

a Look at sentences 1–6 and think of the missing verb or verb phrase (+ = positive, – = negative). **Don't write anything yet!**

1 We _____ the hotel if we hadn't had satnav. –

2 If I _____ that it was your birthday, I would have bought you something. +

3 If I _____ about the concert earlier, I would have been able to get a ticket. +

4 The cat wouldn't have got in if you _____ the window open. –

5 If our best player hadn't been sent off, we _____ the match. +

6 I wouldn't have recognized her if you _____ me who she was. –

b Read your sentence 1 to **B**. If it isn't right, try again until **B** tells you 'That's right'. Then write it in. Continue with 2–6.

c Listen to **B** say sentence 7. If it's the same as your sentence 7 below, say 'That's right'. If not, say 'Try again' until **B** gets it right. Continue with 8–12.

7 I **wouldn't have been** so angry if you had told me the truth right from the start.

8 If I hadn't gone to that party that night, I **wouldn't have met** my wife.

9 If we hadn't taken a taxi, we **would have missed** the train.

10 If I'd known that programme was on last night, I **would have watched** it.

11 I **would have gone out** with you last night if I hadn't had to work late.

12 If I **had listened** to my friends, I would never have married James.

10A RELATIVES QUIZ Student A

a Complete the questions with a relative clause to describe the **bold** words. Start the clause with *who*, *which*, *that*, *whose*, or *where*, or no relative pronoun when there is a new subject.

1 **a pedestrian** What do you call someone...?
2 **a loan** What do you call some money...?
3 **fans** What do you call people...?
4 **a boarding school** What do you call a place...?
5 **a coach** What do you call the person...?
6 **traffic lights** What do you call the things...?
7 **football pitch** What do you call the place...?
8 **selfish** What do you call somebody...?
9 **a cash machine** What do you call a thing...?

b Ask **B** your questions.

c Answer **B**'s questions.

10B JUST CHECKING Student A

a You are a police inspector. **B** is a suspect in a crime. Ask **B** the questions below, but **don't write anything down**. Try to remember **B**'s answers.

- What's your name?
- Where do you live?
- How old are you?
- Where were you born?
- Are you married?
- What do you do?
- What car do you drive?
- How long have you lived in this town?
- What did you do last night?
- Where were you at 7.00 this morning?

b Now check the information with **B** using a question tag.

> Your name is Tom Gibson, isn't it?
>
> You live in New York, don't you?

c Change roles. Now you are the suspect and **B** is the police inspector. Answer **B**'s questions. You can invent the information if you want to.

d **B** will now check the information he / she has. Just say, 'Yes, that's right' or 'No, that's wrong' and correct the wrong information.

PE1 HOW AWFUL! HOW FANTASTIC! Student B

a Listen to **A**'s sentences and react with a phrase, e.g. *You're kidding, Oh no!* etc.

b Read your sentences 1–9 for **A** to react.

1 I failed my driving test yesterday.
2 I lost my wallet on the way to class.
3 I met George Clooney at a party last week.
4 I think I saw a ghost last night.
5 I won a salsa competition last weekend.
6 I'm going to be on a new edition of Big Brother.
7 My dog died yesterday.
8 My grandfather has a black belt in karate.
9 My uncle is 104.

c Tell **A** some real (or invented) news about you for **A** to react. React to **A**'s news.

2B ARE YOU HUNGRY? Student B

a Respond to **A**'s questions. Say *Yes, it's… / I'm…*, etc. + the strong form of the adjective which **A** used in the question. Remember to <u>stress</u> the strong adjective.

Is the water cold?   *Yes, it's freezing.*

b Ask **A** your questions. He / she must respond with the phrase in brackets.

1 Are you afraid of flying? (Yes, I'm **terrified**.)
2 Is the soup hot? (Yes, it's **boiling**.)
3 Was the teacher angry? (Yes, he / she was **furious**.)
4 Is the bedroom small? (Yes, it's **tiny**.)
5 Are the children hungry? (Yes, they're **starving**.)
6 Is the chocolate cake nice? (Yes, it's **delicious**.)
7 Was she happy with the present? (Yes, she was **delighted**.)

c Repeat the exercise. Try to respond as quickly as possible.

3A I'M A TOURIST – CAN YOU HELP ME? Student B

a Think of the town / city where you are, or the nearest big town. **A** is a foreign tourist who is planning to get around using public transport. You live in the town. Answer **A**'s questions and give as much information as you can.

b Swap roles. You are a foreign tourist in the town. You have hired a car. Ask **A** questions 1–5. Get as much information from **A** as you can.

1 What time is the rush hour in this town?
2 Where are there often traffic jams?
3 What's the speed limit in the town? Are there speed cameras anywhere?
4 What will happen if I park somewhere illegal?
5 Where's the nearest tourist attraction outside the city? How long does it take to drive there from here?

4A GUESS THE SENTENCE Student B

a Look at sentences 7–12 and think of the correct form of *be able to* + a verb. **Don't write anything yet!**

7 It must be fantastic to _____ a lot of languages.
8 I won't _____ you tonight. I'm too busy.
9 My grandmother can't walk very well, but luckily we _____ just outside the restaurant.
10 They haven't _____ a flat yet. They're still looking.
11 You should _____ this exercise. It's very easy.
12 We really enjoy _____ outside in the summer.

b Now listen to **A** say sentence 1. If it's the same as your sentence 1 below, say 'That's right'. If not, say 'Try again' until **A** gets it right. Continue with 2–6.

1 I'm sorry I won't **be able to come** to your party next weekend.
2 It was August, but we **were able to find** a hotel without any problems.
3 I used to **be able to understand** a little Japanese, but I can't now.
4 I love **being able to stay** in bed late at the weekend.
5 Will you **be able to finish** the work before Saturday?
6 I've never **been able to cook** fish well.

c Read your sentence 7 to **A**. If it isn't right, try again until **A** tells you, 'That's right'. Then write it in. Continue with 8–12.

Communication

5A OTHER SPORTING SUPERSTITIONS
Student B

a Read about Laurent Blanc and Alexander Wurz.

LAURENT BLANC, the French football captain, kissed the head of the goalkeeper Fabien Barthez before each game at the 1998 World Cup. France won, but Blanc was suspended and didn't play in the final.

ALEXANDER WURZ, an Austrian racing driver, used to race with odd-coloured shoes, the left one red and the right one blue. It came about when he lost a shoe before a big race and had to borrow one of a different colour. After winning the race, he decided it was a lucky omen.

b Now listen to **A** telling you about Tiger Woods and Kolo Touré's superstitions.

c Cover the text and tell **B** about Laurent Blanc and Alexander Wurz's superstitions from memory.

d Together decide which superstition you think is a) the strangest b) the most impractical.

PE5 ASKING POLITELY FOR INFORMATION   Student B

a You are a tourist in **A**'s town. You want to ask **A**, who you have stopped in the street, questions 1–5 and you want to be very polite. Rewrite 2–5 as indirect questions.

1 Do shops close at lunchtime?
   Could you tell me *if shops close at lunchtime?*

2 Is there a cash machine near here?
   Do you know _____?

3 Where's the nearest chemist's?
   Could you tell me _____?

4 What time do the buses stop running at night?
   Do you know _____?

5 Do banks open on Saturday mornings?
   Could you tell me _____?

b **A** is a tourist, and is going to stop you in the street and ask you some questions. Answer politely with the necessary information.

c Ask **A** your indirect questions 1–5. Always begin *Excuse me*.

7B GUESS THE SENTENCE Student B

a Look at sentences 7–12 and think of the missing verb phrase (+ = positive, − = negative). **Don't write anything yet!**

7 The house would look better if you _____. +

8 If I met my ex in the street, I _____ to him. −

9 If it _____, I'd stay a bit longer. −

10 The flight _____ if we were in business class. +

11 I wouldn't mind the winter so much if it _____ so early. −

12 If I had more money, I _____ with a beautiful garden. +

b Now listen to **A** say sentence 1. If it's the same as your sentence 1 below, say 'That's right'. If not, say 'Try again' until **A** gets it right. Continue with 2–6.

1 I'd cook dinner every day if I **got home** earlier from work.

2 If we **didn't go on holiday** this summer, maybe we could afford to get a new car.

3 I think you **would enjoy the film** more if you saw the original version.

4 I'd see my grandparents more often if they **lived nearer**.

5 I **wouldn't have** the fish if I were you. It isn't usually very good here.

6 I**'d go swimming** if the water was a bit warmer.

c Read your sentence 7 to **A**. If it's not right, try again until **A** tells you 'That's right'. Then write it in. Continue with 8–12.

8A I WANT TO SPEAK TO THE MANAGER Student B

Look at the situations and role-play the conversations. Spend a few minutes preparing what you are going to say.

> **1** **You're a shop assistant in a clothes shop. A** is going to come to you with a problem with something he / she bought in the sales yesterday. You can't change it for an identical one because there are no more in his / her size.
>
> Try to persuade **A** to change it for something else, because you don't usually give refunds during the sales.

A will start.

> **2** **You're a customer in a restaurant.** You have just finished your meal and you didn't enjoy it at all (decide what was wrong with it). You complained to the waiter, but the waiter didn't solve the problem. You have asked the waiter to call the manager. Try to get at least a 50% discount on your meal. **A** is the manager.

You start. 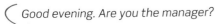 *Good evening. Are you the manager?*

9A GUESS THE CONDITIONAL Student B

a Look at sentences 7–12 and think of the missing verb or verb phrase (+ = positive, − = negative). **Don't write anything yet!**

7 I _____ so angry if you had told me the truth right from the start. −

8 If I hadn't gone to that party that night, I _____ my wife. −

9 If we hadn't taken a taxi, we _____ the train. +

10 If I'd known that programme was on last night, I _____ it. +

11 I _____ with you last night if I hadn't had to work late. +

12 If I _____ to my friends, I would never have married James. +

b Listen to **A** say sentence 1. If it's the same as your sentence 1 below, say 'That's right'. If not, say 'Try again' until **A** gets it right. Continue with 2–6.

1 We **wouldn't have found** the hotel if we hadn't had satnav.

2 If I **had remembered** that it was your birthday, I would have bought you something.

3 If I**'d known** about the concert earlier, I would have been able to get a ticket.

4 The cat wouldn't have got in if you **hadn't left** the window open.

5 If our best player hadn't been sent off, we **would have won** the match.

6 I wouldn't have recognized her if you **hadn't told me** who she was.

c Read your sentence 7 to **A**. If it isn't right, try again until **A** tells you 'That's right'. Then write it in. Continue with 8–12.

Communication

10A RELATIVES QUIZ Student B

a Complete the questions with a relative clause to describe the **bold** words. Start the clause with *who*, *which*, *that*, *whose*, or *where*, or no relative pronoun when there is a new subject.

1 **shy** What do you call somebody...?
2 **a memory stick** What do you call a thing...?
3 **a referee** What do you call the person...?
4 **a cycle lane** What do you call the place...?
5 **a murderer** What do you call somebody...?
6 **a receipt** What do you call the piece of paper...?
7 **a taxi rank** What do you call the place...?
8 **a colleague** What do you call a person...?
9 **a scooter** What do you call a thing...?

b Answer **A**'s questions.

c Ask **A** your questions.

10B JUST CHECKING Student B

a You are a suspect in a crime. **A** is a police inspector. Answer **A**'s questions. You can invent the information if you want to.

b **A** will now check the information he / she has. Just say, 'Yes, that's right' or 'No, that's wrong' and correct the wrong information.

c Change roles. Now you are a police inspector and **A** is a suspect. Ask **A** the questions below, but **don't write anything down**. Try to remember **A**'s answers.

- What's your name?
- Where do you live?
- How old are you?
- Where were you born?
- Are you married?
- What do you do?
- What car do you drive?
- How long have you lived in this town?
- What did you do last night?
- Where were you at 7.00 this morning?

d Now check the information with **A** using a question tag.

Your name is John Hatton, isn't it?

You live in New York, don't you?

Writing

1 A DESCRIPTION OF A PERSON

a Read the two *Facebook* messages once and answer the questions.

  1 Why has Angela written to Sofia?

  2 Does Sofia recommend her friend to Angela?

📨 Messages   + New Message

Angela Vernon

Hi Sofia,

I hope you're well.

I'm looking for an au pair to look after Mike and Sally, and I remembered your Polish friend Kasia, who I met last summer. She said she might be interested in working in England as an au pair, so I thought I would write and ask her. The thing is, I don't really know her, so before I write and suggest it, could you tell me a bit about her (age, personality, etc., and what she likes doing) so that I can see if she would fit in with the family? Please be honest!

Angela

Sofia Lugo

Hi Angela,

Kasia is one of my best friends, so of course I know her very well. She's 22 and she's just finished economics at university, but she doesn't have a job yet and I'm sure she would be interrested in going to the UK. Her parents are both doctors, and she has two younger brothers. She gets on very well with them and they are a very close family.

Kasia's an intelligent girl and very hard-working. She can be quite shy at first, but when she gets to know you she's incredibly friendly. She loves children – she often looks after her brothers – so she has a lot of experience, and she's also very responsable.

In her free time she likes going to the cinema, listening to music, and she's also very good at fotography – she always has her camera with her. She's really independant and happy to do things on her own, so you won't have to worry about taking her to places.

The only problem with Kasia is that she's a bit forgetfull... she sometimes loses things, like her keys, or her phone. Also, to be honest her English isn't fantastic, but I'm sure she'll improve very quickly. I think Mike and Sally will love her.

I hope this helps! Let me know if you need anything else.

Love,

Sofia

b The computer has found five spelling mistakes in Sofia's email. Can you correct them?

c Read both emails again. Then cover them and answer the questions from memory.

  1 What five ⊞ adjectives describe Kasia's personality?

  2 What does she like doing in her free time?

  3 What negative things does Sofia say about Kasia?

  4 Does Sofia think Kasia will get on with Angela's family?

d Look at the **highlighted** expressions we use to modify adjectives. Put them in the correct place in the chart.

Kasia is   *very*   forgetful.

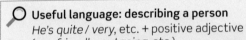

> 🔍 **Useful language: describing a person**
> *He's quite / very*, etc. + positive adjective
> (e.g. *friendly, outgoing*, etc.)
> *She's a bit* + negative adjective (e.g. *untidy, shy*, etc.)
> *He likes / loves / doesn't mind* + verb + *-ing*
> *She's happy to* + infinitive
> *He's good* | **with** *children*
> | **at** *making new friends*

e Imagine you received Angela's message asking about a friend of yours. **Write** an email to answer it. **Plan** what you're going to write using the paragraph headings below. Use the **Useful language** box and **Vocabulary Bank** *Personality p.153* to help you.

Paragraph 1	age, family, work / study
Paragraph 2	personality (good side)
Paragraph 3	hobbies and interests
Paragraph 4	any negative things?

f **Check** your email for mistakes (grammar, vocabulary, punctuation, and spelling).

◀ *p.11*

Writing

2 AN INFORMAL EMAIL

a Kasia went to Britain and stayed for six months with a couple, Angela and Matt, working as an au pair. After going back to Poland, she sent them an email. Look at the list of things she says in her email. Number them in a logical order 1–6.

- ☐ She promises to send some photos.
- ☐ She thanks them for her stay and says how much she enjoyed it.
- ☐ She talks about what she's been doing recently.
- ☐ She apologizes for not writing before.
- ☐ She thanks them again and invites them to stay.
- ☐ She talks about the nice things that happened when she was with them.

b Now read Kasia's email and check your answers to **a**.

c Correct eight mistakes in the email (grammar, vocabulary, punctuation, and spelling.)

> 🔍 **Useful language: informal emails**
>
> **Beginnings**
> *Hi* + name (or *Dear* + name if you want to be a bit more formal)
> *Sorry for not writing earlier, but…*
> *Thank you / Thanks* (so much) for (*your letter, having me to stay*, etc.)…
> *It was great to hear from you…*
>
> **Endings**
> *That's all for now.*
> *Hope to hear from you soon. / Looking forward to hearing from you soon.*
> *(Give my) regards / love to…*
> *Best wishes / Love (from)*
> *PS* (when you want to add a short message at the end of an email) *I've attached a photo…*

d Imagine you have some British friends in the UK, and you stayed with them for a week last month. **Write** an email to say thank you. **Plan** what you're going to say. Use 1–6 in **a** and the **Useful language** box to help you.

e **Check** your email for mistakes (grammar, vocabulary, punctuation, and spelling).

◀ *p.21*

From: Kasia [kasia_new@redmail.com]
To: Angela [angelav1970@yahoo.com]
Subject: Thanks

Hi Angela,

I'm really sorry for not writing earlier, but I am very busy since I got back!

Thanks for a wonderful six months. I loved being in Chichester, and I had a great time. I also think my english got a bit better… dont you think?

It was so nice to look after Mike and Sally. I thought they were adorable, and I think we had a fantastic time together. I have really good memories – for example our travel to the Isle of Wight and the zoo there!

I've been a bit stressed these last few weeks, because I've started working at a restaurant, while I look for a proper job. Be a waitress is very hard work, but I can now afford to rent a flat with Sofia and two other friends, and I'm saving for to buy a car! I've also spent a lot of time with my family – my brothers have changed so much over the past six months!

I've had several mesages from Mike and Sally since I've been back! Please tell them from me that I miss them and that I send them some photos very soon.

That's all for now. Thanks again for everything. And I hope you know you're welcome in Gdansk at any time – my family would love to meet you. Summer here is usually lovely.

Hope to hear from you soon. Give my regards to Matt!

Best wishes,

Kasia

PS I've attached a photo I took of me with the kids. I hope you like it!

3 AN ARTICLE FOR A MAGAZINE

a Look at the four forms of public transport in London. Which one do you think is probably…?

- the most expensive
- the healthiest
- the best if you want to see the sights of London
- the safest to use late at night

the Tube

double-decker bus

Boris Bike

black taxi

b Read an article from an online magazine for foreign students about public transport in London and check your answers to **a**. Then answer these questions from memory.

1 What can you use an Oyster card for?
2 Why are the bikes you can hire called 'Boris Bikes'?
3 What's the difference between a black taxi and a mini-cab?

c Read the article again and complete the gaps with a preposition from the list.

~~around~~   at   in   next to   off   on (x2)   on the top of   with
---

> 🔍 **Useful language: transport in your town**
> *You can buy Oyster cards at tube stations.*
> *You must have a ticket or card before you get on a bus.*
> (*You* = people in general)
>
> **Comparatives and superlatives**
> *Buses aren't as quick as trams.*
> *Cycling is the cheapest way to get around.*

d Write an article about transport in your nearest town or city for foreign students. **Plan** what headings you're going to use, and what to say about each form of transport.

e Check your article for mistakes (grammar, vocabulary, punctuation, and spelling).

 p.27

🔵 Transport in London

London Underground (The Tube)

This is the quickest way to get [1]*around* the city and there are many underground stations all over London. The cheapest way to use the underground is to get an Oyster card. This is like a phone card. You put money on it, and then top it up when you need to, and then you use it every time you get [2]_____ or [3]_____ the Tube. You can buy Oyster cards at tube stations and in newsagents.

Buses

They can be quicker than the underground if there isn't too much traffic. The easiest way to use the buses, like the underground, is to just use your Oyster card. You can also buy tickets from machines [4]_____ bus stops. On some buses you can buy a ticket with cash when you get [5]_____ the bus. Some of the buses operate 24 hours a day, so you can also use them late at night. Travelling [6]_____ a double-decker bus is also a good way to see London.

Bikes

Bikes are now more popular than ever in London, especially [7]_____ tourists and people who want to be fit. There are quite a lot of cycle lanes, and bikes that you can hire, nicknamed 'Boris Bikes' after Boris Johnson, the mayor of London. You can use your credit card to hire a bike, and the first 30 minutes are free.

Taxis and Mini-cabs

London's black taxis are expensive, but they are comfortable and the taxi drivers know London very well. You normally tell the driver where you want to go before you get [8]_____ the taxi. Mini-cabs are normal cars which work for a company, and which you have to phone. They are much cheaper, but make sure you use a licensed company. Taxis or mini-cabs are probably the safest way to travel late [9]_____ night.

Writing

4 TELLING A STORY

a A magazine asked its readers to send in stories of a time they got lost. Read the story once. Why did Begoña and her husband get lost? What else went wrong?

b Read the story again and complete it with a connecting word or phrase from the list.

> although   as soon as   because   but
> instead of   so   ~~then~~   when

> **Useful language: getting lost**
> *We were going in the wrong direction.*
> *We took the wrong exit / turning.*
> *We turned right instead of left.*
> *We didn't know where we were.*
> *We had to turn round and go back in the opposite direction.*

c **Write** about a journey where you got lost (or invent one) to send to the magazine. **Plan** what you're going to write using the paragraph headings below. Use the **Useful language** to help you.

Paragraph 1	When was the journey? Where were you going? Who with? Why?
Paragraph 2	How did you get lost? What happened?
Paragraph 3	What happened in the end?

d **Check** your story for mistakes (grammar, vocabulary, punctuation, and spelling).

◀ *p.47*

DISASTROUS JOURNEYS!

We asked you to tell us about a time you got lost.
Begoña from Spain wrote to us...

This happened a few years ago. I live in Alicante, in Spain and my husband and I had rented a house in Galicia for the summer holiday. We were going to first drive to Tarragona, to stay for a few days with some friends, and ¹ *then* drive from Tarragona to Galicia.

The first part of the journey was fine. We were using our new satnav for the first time, and it took us right to the door of our friends' house. Three days later, ² _____ we continued our journey, we put in the name of the small town in Galicia, Nigrán, which was our final destination. We started off, obediently following the instructions, but after a while we realized that ³ _____ driving west towards Lérida, we were going north. In fact, soon we were quite near Andorra. I was sure we were going in the wrong direction, ⁴ _____ my husband wanted to do what the satnav was telling us – it was his new toy! It was only when we started seeing mountains that even he admitted this couldn't be the right way. ⁵ __ we stopped, got out an old map, and then turned round! We had wasted nearly two hours going in the wrong direction!

It was an awful journey ⁶ _____ as well as getting lost, when we were nearly at our destination we had another problem. We stopped for a coffee at a little bar, but ⁷ _____ we got back onto the motorway we realized that we had left our dog under the table in the café! For the second time that day we had to turn round and go back. Luckily, the dog was still there! However, ⁸ _____ the beginning of our trip was a disaster, we had a wonderful holiday!

116

5 A FILM REVIEW

CLASSIC FILMS YOU <u>MUST</u> SEE
PLEASE POST YOUR SUGGESTIONS

The Godfather (1972)

The film *The Godfather* is ¹*based* on the book by Mario Puzo. The film was ²_____ by Francis Ford Coppola. It ³_____ Marlon Brando as Vito Corleone and Al Pacino as his son, Michael. The film won three Oscars in 1973 for Best Actor (Marlon Brando), Best Movie, and Best Screenplay.

The film is ⁴_____ in New York in the 1940s and 50s. It was filmed on ⁵_____ in New York and in Sicily.

The film is about the Corleone family. Vito, 'The Godfather', is head of one of the most powerful criminal families in America. Don Vito is a fair but ruthless man, who runs his business by doing favours and expecting favours in return. The Corleones get involved in a war with other criminal families, because they don't want to sell drugs. Don Vito is shot and he is seriously injured. While Don Vito is in hospital, control of the family passes to his eldest son, Sonny. Sonny is a hot-head, and with him in charge, the war between the various families becomes more violent. Don Vito's youngest son, Michael, has always stayed outside the family business, but when Don Vito is shot, he returns home to do what he can to help the family. He also takes his revenge against the people who are trying to kill his father. In the end, Sonny is shot and Michael becomes the new Godfather.

I strongly ⁶_____ *The Godfather*. It has ⁷_____, drama, an unforgettable ⁸_____, and an important message: that violence never really solves anything. The two ⁹_____, *The Godfather II* and *The Godfather III* are also good, but the first film is definitely my favourite.

a Read the film review and complete it with the words in the list.

action ~~based~~ directed location recommend sequels set soundtrack stars

b Read the review again and number the paragraphs in order 1–4.

Paragraph ☐	The plot
Paragraph ☐	The name of the film, the director, the stars, and any prizes it won
Paragraph ☐	Why you recommend the film
Paragraph ☐	Where and when it is set Where it was filmed

c Look at paragraph three again. What tense do we use to tell the story of a film or book?

d Have you seen *The Godfather*? If yes, do you agree with the review? If no, does the review make you want to see it?

> 🔍 **Useful language: describing a film**
> *It was directed / written by...*   *In the end...*
> *It is set in...*   *My favourite scene is...*
> *It is based on the book...*   *I strongly recommend*
> *It's about...*   *(the film) because...*
> *It stars...*

e **Write** a film review about a film you would recommend people to buy on DVD or see at the cinema. **Plan** what you are going to write in the four paragraphs. Use the **Useful language** and **Vocabulary Bank** *Cinema p.159* to help you.

f **Check** your review for mistakes (grammar, vocabulary, punctuation, and spelling).

◄ p.57

Writing

6 DESCRIBING A HOUSE OR FLAT

a The website Homerent.com is for people who want to rent out their houses while they are away on holiday. Read two posts from the website. Which one would you prefer to stay in for a two-week holiday? Why?

b Read about the flat in Budapest again. <u>Underline</u> any adjectives which help to 'sell' the flat? What do they mean?

c Now read about the Turkish villa again. Improve the description by replacing the word *nice* with one of the adjectives below. Often there is more than one possibility.

amazing   beautiful   breathtaking   lovely   ideal
luxurious   magnificent   perfect   spacious   superb

> **🔍 Useful language: describing location**
> *It is* | *perfectly situated in...*
> | *walking distance from...*
> | *a (fifteen-minute) walk from...*
> | *a short drive from...*
> *The neighbourhood is (safe, friendly, etc.)...*
> *It's a (beautiful) area...*

d **Write** a description of your house or flat for the website. **Plan** what you're going to write. Use the **Useful language** and **Vocabulary Bank** *Houses p.162* to help you.

Paragraph 1	A brief introduction. What kind of house / flat is it? Where is it exactly?
Paragraph 2	Describe the house / flat. What rooms does it have? Does it have any special characteristics?
Paragraph 3	Describe the neighbourhood. How far is it from places of interest, public transport, etc.?
Paragraph 4	Say who the house flat is suitable for. Are there any restrictions?

e **Check** your description for mistakes (grammar, vocabulary, punctuation, and spelling).

◀ *p.71*

🏠 Homerent.com

| Home | Search | Join our community | Help |

Beautiful one-bedroom flat in Budapest

The flat is perfectly situated in the heart of Budapest's 5th district.

It's a cosy 55-square-metre flat on the 11th floor of a new building, with a lift. It has one large double bedroom, a spacious living / dining room with a balcony, a modern, well-equipped kitchen, and a bathroom. There's a spectacular view of the Danube from the windows. The living room has a big table, which is ideal for having a meal with friends, and there is also a large TV. The flat has wooden floors, cable television, and Wi-fi internet.

The 5th district is a lively neighbourhood in central Budapest, with plenty of shops and cafés. The flat is walking distance from Váci utca, Budapest's main shopping street. It's five minutes away from a subway station, so you can visit the city very easily.

The house is ideal for a couple who would like to go sightseeing in this beautiful town. It's a no-smoking house and no pets are allowed.

Beach villa in Kuşadası, Turkey

Kuşadası is a ~~nice~~ *beautiful* holiday resort on the west coast of Turkey, 90 km south of Izmir.

Our house is *nice*. It has three double bedrooms, a living room, a *nice* kitchen, and two bathrooms. All the rooms have air conditioning, and the bedrooms have their own balconies. There is a *nice* terrace with table and chairs, so you can eat outside. There are *nice* views of the beach and the mountains. There is a *nice* garden and a communal swimming pool, which we share with the other nearby houses.

The house is near several *nice* beaches, where you can do lots of water sports. It's also a short drive from the mountains, where you can go hiking.

This house is perfect for a family with children or for two couples. The house is not suitable for pets.

118

7 A LETTER OF COMPLAINT

a Read the letter of complaint. Then answer the questions.

1 Who is Chris Mason complaining to?
2 What item is he complaining about? Why?
3 Who did he contact first?
4 What problem did he have when he phoned to complain?
5 In which paragraph does Chris use flattery? How?

b Read it again and complete the gaps with a word from the list.

~~Dear~~ delivered forward However in stock
reference service unhelpful Yours

> 🔍 **Useful language: a formal letter (or email)**
>
> **You don't know the person's name**
> Start: *Dear Sir / Madam,*
> Finish: *Yours faithfully,*
>
> **You know the person's name**
> Start: *Dear + Mr / Ms / Mrs Garcia,*
> Finish: *Yours sincerely,*
>
> **Style**
> • Don't use contractions
> • Write *I look forward to hearing from you.* as the final sentence
> • Write your full name under your signature
>
> **Note:** a formal email is exactly the same as a formal letter, except in an email we don't write the address or date.

c Write a letter (or an email) of complaint about something you bought online. **Plan** what you're going to write. Use the **Useful language** to help you.

d Check your letter or email for mistakes (grammar, vocabulary, punctuation, and spelling).

◀ *p.77*

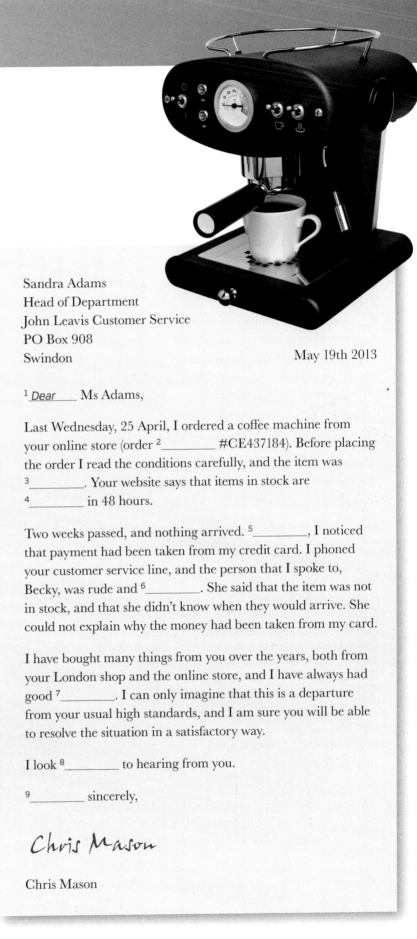

Sandra Adams
Head of Department
John Leavis Customer Service
PO Box 908
Swindon   May 19th 2013

¹ *Dear*_____ Ms Adams,

Last Wednesday, 25 April, I ordered a coffee machine from your online store (order ²_____ #CE437184). Before placing the order I read the conditions carefully, and the item was ³_____. Your website says that items in stock are ⁴_____ in 48 hours.

Two weeks passed, and nothing arrived. ⁵_____, I noticed that payment had been taken from my credit card. I phoned your customer service line, and the person that I spoke to, Becky, was rude and ⁶_____. She said that the item was not in stock, and that she didn't know when they would arrive. She could not explain why the money had been taken from my card.

I have bought many things from you over the years, both from your London shop and the online store, and I have always had good ⁷_____. I can only imagine that this is a departure from your usual high standards, and I am sure you will be able to resolve the situation in a satisfactory way.

I look ⁸_____ to hearing from you.

⁹_____ sincerely,

Chris Mason

Chris Mason

Writing

8 A COVERING EMAIL WITH YOUR CV

a Look at the job advertisement. Which job could *you* apply for?

We are looking for dedicated, enthusiastic, and energetic people to work at the forthcoming Olympic Games.

There are vacancies in the following areas:

- *Administration*
- *Hospitality and catering*
- *Translation and language services*
- *Medical support*

All applicants must be appropriately qualified and a B2 level of English is essential. Send your CV and a covering email (in English) to:

recruitment@theolympicgames.com

b Ricardo Suarez wants to apply for a job, and is submitting his CV. Read the covering email to go with it. Circle the best phrase in each pair.

> **From:** Ricardo Suarez [Suarezr@chatchat.com]
> **To:** recruitment@theolympicgames.com
> **Subject:** Job application
>
> Dear Sir / Madam,
>
> ¹*I am writing / I'm writing* to apply for a job with the medical support staff at the forthcoming Olympic Games.
>
> I am a qualified physiotherapist and ²*I've been working / I have been working* at a Rehabilitation Centre here since January 2006. ³*My English is great / I speak English fluently (level C1)*.
>
> ⁴*I enclose / I attach* my CV.
>
> ⁵*Hope to hear from you soon! / I look forward to hearing from you.*
>
> ⁶*Yours sincerely, / Yours faithfully,*
>
> Ricardo Suarez

c **Write** a covering email (to go with your CV) to apply for a job in the next Olympics. **Plan** what you're going to write. Use the **Useful language** on *p.119* to help you.

d **Check** your email for mistakes (grammar, vocabulary, punctuation, and spelling).

◀ *p.81*

9 A MAGAZINE ARTICLE – ADVANTAGES AND DISADVANTAGES

a Read an article for a student magazine about the advantages and disadvantages of living without a TV. The computer has found ten mistakes (grammar, vocabulary, punctuation, and spelling). Can you correct them?

Living without a TV

Almost every family today ¹have a TV, in fact probably more than one, and people everywhere spend hours watching it. But a few families choose to live without a TV because they think there are advantages.

The first advantage is that families spend more time ²talk to each other. Secondly, they spend more time doing more creative things like reading or painting. Thirdly, they spend more time outdoors, and are usually ³more fit.

But on the other hand, there are also disadvantages. For example, children who don't have a TV may feel ⁴differents from ⁵there school friends, and often won't know what they are talking about. Also, it is not true that all TV ⁶programes are bad. There are good ones, like ⁷documentarys, and people who live without a TV may know less about ⁸whats happening in the world.

In conclusion, ⁹althought living without a TV has some advantages, I think today it's unrealistic and that we should just try to turn the TV ¹⁰out when there's nothing good on.

b Read the article again. Then cover it and in pairs answer the questions from memory.

1 What are the three advantages?

2 What are the two disadvantages?

3 Is the writer for or against having a TV?

c You are going to write a similar article about smartphones. First with a partner, make a list of the advantages and disadvantages.

Advantages	Disadvantages

d Now decide which are the three biggest advantages and number them 1–3 (1 = the biggest). Do the same with the disadvantages.

> 🔍 **Useful language: writing about advantages and disadvantages**
>
> **Listing advantages**
> *First / Firstly,...* *Secondly,...* *Thirdly,...*
>
> **Listing disadvantages**
> *On the other hand, there are also (some) disadvantages...*
> *For instance / For example...*
> *Also,...*
>
> Conclusion
> *In conclusion / To sum up, I think...*

e **Write** an article called 'Smartphones – A great invention?' Start the article with this introduction.

> Many people today don't just have a mobile phone, they have a smartphone like an iPhone or a Blackberry. But is it a great invention? I think there are both advantages and disadvantages.

Write three more paragraphs. **Plan** what you're going to write. Use the **Useful language** to help you.

Paragraph 2	Write two or three advantages.
Paragraph 3	Write two or three disadvantages.
Paragraph 4	Conclusion – decide if you think smartphones are a great invention or not.

f **Check** your article for mistakes (grammar, vocabulary, punctuation, and spelling).

◀ *p.91*

10 A BIOGRAPHY

a Read a text about Mark Zuckerberg. Then re-write the text with the extra information (sentences A–F) as relative clauses.

> **Mark Zuckerberg,** the American computer programmer, was one of the founders of *Facebook*.
>
> In his teens he began to write software programs as a hobby. After school he went to Harvard. While he was there he created a website called *Facemash*. It was shut down by the university, but it inspired him to create *Facebook*.
>
> He left Harvard and moved to California with Dustin Moskovitz, and together they made *Facebook* an international success.
>
> In 2012 Zuckerberg married Priscilla Chan.

Paragraph 1	**A** Mark Zuckerberg was born in New York in 1984
Paragraph 2	**B** He studied computer science and sociology at Harvard
	C *Facemash* allowed students to share photos
	D He launched *Facebook* from his room in 2004
Paragraph 3	**E** Dustin Moskovitz had been his roommate
Paragraph 4	**F** He had dated Priscilla Chan for nine years

1 *Mark Zuckerberg, the American computer programmer,* **who was born in New York in 1984**, *was one of the founders of* Facebook.

b Cover **A–F**. Read the text again and try to remember the extra information.

c **Write** a short biography of an interesting or successful person you know about. **Plan** what you're going to write, and try to use some relative clauses.

d **Check** your biography for mistakes (grammar, vocabulary, punctuation, and spelling).

◀ *p.95*

Listening

1 6))

A I usually have meat or seafood. Usually prawns or something as a starter and then maybe lamb for the main course.
B I quite often have ready-made vegetable soups that you only have to heat up – in fact they're the only vegetables I ever eat! And I usually have a couple of frozen pizzas in the freezer for emergencies. I don't really order take-away when I'm on my own, but if I'm with friends in the evening, we sometimes order Chinese food for dinner.
C Eggs and Coke. I have eggs for breakfast at least twice a week and I drink a couple of cans of Coke every day.
D If I'm feeling down, chicken soup, with nice big pieces of chicken in it. It's warm and comforting. I usually have a banana before going to the gym. If I know I'm going to have a really long meeting, I usually have a coffee and a cake because I think it will keep me awake and give me energy.
E Fruit – cherries, strawberries, raspberries and apples. Vegetables – peppers, tomatoes, and cucumbers. The only thing I really don't like is beetroot. I can't even stand the smell of it.

1 7))

Part 1

Interviewer What was your favourite food when you were a child?
Steve Well, I always liked unusual things, at least things that most English children at the time didn't like. For instance, when I was six or seven my favourite things were snails, oh and prawns with garlic.
Interviewer Funny things for a six-year-old English boy to like!
Steve Well, the thing is my parents liked travelling and eating out a lot, and I first tried snails in France, and the prawns, my first prawns I had at a Spanish restaurant in the town where we lived.
Interviewer So you were keen on Spanish food right from the start. Is that why you decided to come to Spain?
Steve Partly, but of course, I suppose like a lot of British people I wanted to see the sun! The other thing that attracted me when I got here were all the fantastic ingredients. I remember going into the market for the first time and saying 'Wow!'
Interviewer When you opened your restaurant, how did you want it to be different from typical Spanish restaurants?
Steve Well, when I came to Spain, all the good restaurants were very formal, very traditional. In London then, the fashion was for informal places where the waiters wore jeans, but the food was amazing. So I wanted a restaurant a bit like that. I also wanted a restaurant where you could try more international food, but made with some of these fantastic local ingredients. For example, Spain's got wonderful seafood, but usually here it's just grilled or fried. I started doing things in my restaurant like cooking Valencian mussels in Thai green curry paste.
Interviewer What do you most enjoy cooking?
Steve What I most enjoy cooking, I think, are those traditional dishes which use quite cheap ingredients, but they need very long and careful cooking, and then you turn it into something really special... like a really good casserole, for example.
Interviewer And is there anything you don't like cooking?

Steve Maybe desserts. You have to be very very precise when you're making desserts. And that's not the way I am.

1 8))

Part 2

Interviewer What's the best thing about running a restaurant?
Steve I think the best thing is making people happy. That's why even after all this time I still enjoy it so much.
Interviewer And the worst thing?
Steve That's easy, it has to be the long hours. This week for example I'm cooking nearly every day. We usually close on Sundays and Mondays, but this Monday is a public holiday, when lots of people want to eat out, so we're open.
Interviewer Seu Xerea is in all the British restaurant guides now. Does that mean you get a lot of British customers?
Steve Yes, we get a lot of British people, especially at the weekends, but then we get people from other countries too.
Interviewer And are the British customers and the Spanish customers very different?
Steve Yes, I think they are. The British always say that everything is lovely, even if they've only eaten half of it. The Spanish, on the other hand, are absolutely honest about everything. They tell you what they like, they tell you what they don't like. I remember when I first opened, I had sushi on the menu, which was very unusual at that time, and I went into the dining room and I said to people, 'So what do you think of the sushi?' And the customers, who were all Spanish, said 'Oh, it was awful! It was raw fish!' Actually, I think I prefer that honesty, because it helps us to know what people like.
Interviewer What kind of customers do you find difficult?
Steve I think customers who want me to cook something in a way that I don't think is very good. Let's see, a person who asks for a really well-done steak, for instance. For me that's a difficult customer. You know, they'll say 'I want a really really well-done steak' so I give them a really really well-done steak and then they say 'It's tough'. And I think well, of course it's tough. It's well done! Well-done steak is always tough.
Interviewer People say that the Mediterranean diet is very healthy. Do you think people's eating habits in Spain are changing?
Steve Well, I think they are changing – unfortunately I think they're getting worse. People are eating more unhealthily.
Interviewer How do you notice that?
Steve I see it with, especially with younger friends. They often eat in fast food restaurants, they don't cook... and actually the younger ones come from a generation where their mothers don't cook either. That's what's happening now, and it's a real pity.

1 27))

Interviewer This morning we're talking about family and family life and now Danielle Barnes is going to tell us about a book she has just read called *Birth Order* by Linda Blair. So what's the book about Danielle?
Danielle Well, it's all about how our position in the family influences the kind of person we are. I mean whether we're first born, a middle child, a youngest child or an only child. Linda Blair argues that our position in the family is possibly the strongest influence on our character and personality.

Interviewer So tell us more about this, Danielle. What about the oldest children in a family, the first-born?
Danielle Well first-born children often have to look after their younger brothers and sisters, so they're usually sensible and responsible as adults. They also tend to be ambitious and they make good leaders. Many US Presidents and British Prime Ministers, including for example Winston Churchill were oldest children.
On the negative side oldest children can be insecure and anxious. This is because when the second child was born they lost some of their parents' attention and maybe they felt rejected.
Interviewer That's all very interesting. What about the middle child?
Danielle Middle children are usually more relaxed than oldest children. That's probably because the parents are more relaxed themselves by the time the second child arrives. They're usually very sociable – the kind of people who get on with everybody and they're also usually sensitive to what other people need. Now this is because they grew up between older and younger brothers and sisters. For the same reason they are quite good at sorting out arguments, and they're always sympathetic to the ones on the losing side, or in general to people who are having problems. On the other hand, middle children can sometimes be unambitious, and they can lack direction in life.
Interviewer And youngest children?
Danielle I was very interested in this part of the book as I'm a youngest child myself. It seems that youngest children are often very outgoing and charming. This is the way they try to get the attention of both their parents and their older brothers and sisters. They are often more rebellious, and this is probably because it's easier for the youngest children to break the rules – by this time their parents are more relaxed about discipline. On the negative side, youngest children can be immature, and disorganized, and they often depend too much on other people. This is because they have always been the baby of the family.
Interviewer Fascinating. And finally, what about only children?
Danielle Only children usually do very well at school because they have a lot of contact with adults. They get a lot of love and attention from their parents so they're typically self-confident. They're also independent, as they're used to being by themselves. And because they spend a lot of time with adults they're often very organized.
Interviewer I'm an only child myself and people always think that I must be spoilt. Is that true, according to Linda Blair?
Danielle Well, it's true that only children can sometimes be spoilt by their parents because they're given everything they ask for. Also, on the negative side, only children can be quite selfish, and they can also be impatient, especially when things go wrong. This is because they're not used to sorting out problems with other brothers and sisters.

1 28))

Jenny My name's Jenny Zielinski. And New York is my city. I live here and I work for a magazine, *NewYork24seven*.
Rob My name's Rob Walker. I'm a writer on *NewYork24seven*. You can probably tell from my accent that I'm not actually from New York. I'm British, and I came over to the States a few months ago.

Jenny I met Rob in London when I was visiting the UK on a work trip. He was writing for the London edition of *24seven*. We got along well right away. I really liked him.

Rob So why am I in New York? Because of Jenny, of course. When they gave me the opportunity to work here for a month, I took it immediately. It gave us the chance to get to know each other better. When they offered me a permanent job I couldn't believe it!

Jenny I helped Rob find an apartment. And now here we are. Together in New York. I'm so happy. I just hope Rob's happy here, too.

Rob I really loved living in London. A lot of my friends and family are there, so of course I still miss it. But New York's a fantastic city. I've got a great job and Jenny's here too.

Jenny Things are changing pretty fast in the office. We have a new boss, Don Taylor. And things are changing in my personal life, too. This evening's kind of important. I'm taking Rob to meet my parents for the very first time. I just hope it goes well!

🔵1 29))

Jenny I can't believe we got here so late.

Rob I'm sorry, Jenny. I had to finish that article for Don.

Jenny Don't forget the chocolates.

Rob OK.

Rob Oh no!

Jenny I don't believe it. Don't tell me you forgot them!?

Rob I think they're still on my desk.

Jenny You're kidding.

Rob You know what my desk's like.

Jenny Yeah, it's a complete mess. Why don't you ever tidy it?

Rob We could go and buy some more.

Jenny How can we get some more? We're already late!

Jenny Hi there!

Harry You made it!

Jenny Sorry we're late. So, this is my mom and dad, Harry and Sally. And this, of course, is Rob.

Rob Hello.

Sally It's so nice to meet you at last.

Harry Yes, Jenny's finally decided to introduce you to us.

Sally Come in, come in!

Jenny Mom, I'm really sorry – we bought you some chocolates but we left them at the office.

Sally What a pity. Never mind.

Harry Yeah, don't worry about it. We know what a busy young woman you are. And your mom has made way too much food for this evening anyway.

Sally Oh Harry.

Jenny But I also have some good news.

Sally Really? What's that?

Jenny Well, you know we have a new boss? He's still new to the job and needs support, so today he made me the managing editor of the magazine.

Sally So you've got a promotion? How fantastic!

Harry That's great news! Hey, does that mean Jenny's going to be your boss, Rob?

Rob Er... yes, I guess so.

Jenny Well, not exactly. I'm a manager, but I'm not Rob's manager.

Sally Let's go and have dinner.

Jenny What a great idea!

🔵1 32))

Harry You know, our Jenny has done incredibly well, Rob. She's the first member of our family to study at Harvard. She's a very capable and ambitious young woman.

Jenny Oh Dad.

Rob No, it's true, Jenny.

Harry But what about you, Rob? How do you see your career? Do you see yourself going into management?

Rob Me? No. Not really. I'm more of a... a writer.

Harry Really? What kind of things do you write?

Rob Oh... you know, interviews, reviews... things like that... and I'm doing a lot of work for the online magazine...

Jenny Rob's a very talented writer, Dad. He's very creative.

Harry That's great but being creative doesn't always pay the bills.

Jenny You know, my dad's a very keen photographer. He took all of these photos.

Harry Oh, Rob won't be interested in those.

Rob But I am interested. I mean, I like photography. And I think I recognize some of these people...

Harry That's because most of them are of Jenny.

Rob But there are some great jazz musicians, too. That's Miles Davis... and isn't that John Coltrane? And that's Wynton Marsalis.

Harry You know about Wynton Marsalis?

Rob Know about him? I've interviewed him!

Harry How incredible! I love that guy. He's a hero of mine.

Rob Well, he's a really nice guy. I spent a whole day with him, chatting and watching him rehearse.

Harry Really? I want to hear all about it.

Sally Have a cookie, Rob.

Harry Go ahead, son! Sally makes the best cookies in New York!

🔵1 40))

1 I'm a spender, I think. I try to save, but something always seems to come along that I need to buy and I finish up broke. I can get by with very little money for myself when I need to, but I don't seem to be good at holding on to it. Also, if my kids ask to borrow some money, I always say yes.

2 I would say that I'm spender. I spend money on things like concerts, or on trips because I like having the experience and the memories. I know that I should spend my money on things that last, or save for the future, but I don't want to miss all those good things that are happening right now.

3 I consider myself a spender. I don't have much money, but when I do have some there's always something I need or want to spend it on. I love computers and computer games, so I often buy things to make sure my computer is always up to date. I know it's not very sensible, but it's important to me.

4 That's difficult to say. I can save money if there's something I really, really want, but usually my money disappears as soon as I get it. I get some money from my parents every week so I have just enough money to go to the cinema with my friends and to buy something for myself, maybe a book or a DVD or some makeup... I usually end up buying something. But for example if I want to go on a trip with my friends, then I can make an effort and save some money for a few weeks.

5 Since I was very small, I've always saved about a third of the money I get. I would never think of spending all the money I have. You could say that I'm careful about money. When I want to buy something which is expensive I don't use a credit card, I take the money out of the bank and so I never have to worry about getting into debt.

6 I'd say a saver, definitely. I like having some money saved in case I have an emergency. I also think very carefully before I buy something and I always make sure it's the best I can buy for that price. But I wouldn't describe myself as mean. I love buying presents for people, and when I do spend my money I like to buy nice things, even if they're more expensive.

🔵1 45))

Part 1

Interviewer Jane, you're a primary school teacher, and a writer. What kind of books do you write?

Jane Well, I write books for children who are learning English as a foreign language.

Interviewer How long have you been a writer?

Jane Er, let me see, since 1990. So for about 22 years.

Interviewer Tell us about the trip that changed your life. Where were you going?

Jane Well, it was in the summer of 2008, and my family – my husband and I and our three children,

decided to have a holiday of a lifetime, and to go to Africa. We went to Uganda and Ruanda, to see the mountain gorillas. It was something we'd always wanted to do. Anyway about half way through the trip we were in Uganda, and we were travelling in a lorry when the lorry broke down. So the driver had to find a mechanic to come and help fix it.

Interviewer And then what happened?

Jane Well, as soon as we stopped, lots of children appeared and surrounded us. I could see some long buildings quite near, so I asked the children what they were, and they said in English 'That's our school.' And I was very curious to see what a Ugandan school was like, so I asked them to show it to me.

Interviewer What was it like?

Jane I was shocked when I first saw it. The walls were falling down, the blackboards were broken, and there weren't many desks. But the children were so friendly, and I asked them if they would like to learn a song in English. They said yes, and I started teaching them some songs, like 'Heads, shoulders, knees and toes', a song I've used all over the world to teach children parts of the body. Almost immediately the classroom filled up with children of all ages and they all wanted to learn. I was just amazed by how quickly they learned the song!

Interviewer Did you meet the teachers?

Jane Yes, we did, and the headmaster too. He explained that the school was called St Josephs, and it was a community school for orphans, very poor children and refugees. I asked him what the school needed. I thought that he might say 'we need books, or paper,' and then later we could send them to him. But actually he said 'What we need is a new school'. And I thought yes, of course he's right. These children deserve to have better conditions than this to learn in. So when I got back home, my husband and I, and other people who were with us on the trip decided to set up an organization to get money to build a new school.

🔵1 46))

Part 2

Interviewer So Adelante África was born. Why did you decide to call it that?

Jane Well, we wanted a name that gave the idea of Africa moving forward, and my husband is Spanish, and he suggested Adelante África, because in Spanish Adalante means 'go forward', and Adelante África sort of sounded better than 'Go forward, Africa'.

Interviewer How long did it take to raise the money for the new school?

Jane Amazingly enough, not long really, only about two years. The school opened on the 14th March 2010 with 75 children. Today it has nearly 500 children.

Interviewer That's great! I understand that since the new school opened you've been working on other projects for these children.

Jane Yes. When we opened the school we realised that although the children now had a beautiful new school, they couldn't really make much progress because they were suffering from malnutrition, malaria, things like that. So we've been working to improve their diet and health, and at the moment we're building a house where children who don't have families can live.

Interviewer And are your children involved in Adelante Africa too?

Jane Yes, absolutely! They all go out to Uganda at least once a year. My daughter Tessie runs the Facebook page, and my other daughter Ana runs a project to help children to go to secondary school, and Georgie, my son, organizes a football tournament there every year.

Interviewer And how do you think you have most changed the children's lives?

Jane I think the school has changed the children's lives because it has given them hope. People from outside came and listened to them and cared about them. But it's not only the children whose lives have changed. Adelante África has also changed me and my family. We have been very lucky in life. I feel that life has given me a lot. Now I want to give something back. But it's not all giving. I feel that I get more from them than I give! I love being there. I love their smiles and how they have such a strong sense of community, and I love feeling that my family and the other members of Adelante África are accepted as part of that community.

Interviewer And do you have a website?

Jane Yes, we do. www.adelanteafrica.com. We've had the website for about four years. It was one of the first things we set up. If you'd like to find out more about Adelante África, please go there and have a look. There are lots of photos and even a video my son took of me teaching the children to sing on that first day. Maybe it will change your life too, who knows?

(1) 52)))

Phone call 4
I haven't had any music for the last three days, because my iPod broke, so paddling has been getting more boring. To pass the time I count or I name countries in my head and sometimes I just look up at the sky. Sometimes the sky is pink with clouds that look like cotton wool, other times it's dark like the smoke from a fire and sometimes it's bright blue. The day that I reached the half way point in my trip the sky was bright blue. I'm superstitious so I didn't celebrate – there's still a very long way to go.

Phone call 5
This week the mosquitoes have been driving me mad. They obviously think I'm easy food! They especially like my feet. I wake up in the night when they bite me and I can't stop scratching my feet.

But I'm feeling happier now than I've been feeling for weeks. I've seen a lot of amazing wildlife this week. One day I found myself in the middle of a group of dolphins. There were about six pairs jumping out of the water. I've also seen enormous butterflies, iguanas, and vultures which fly above me in big groups. Yesterday a fish jumped into my kayak. Maybe it means I'm going to be lucky. I am starting to feel a bit sad that this adventure is coming to an end.

And finally on the news, BBC presenter Helen Skelton has successfully completed her 3,200 kilometre journey down the Amazon River in a kayak. She set off from Nauta in Peru six weeks ago on a journey which many people said would be impossible. But yesterday she crossed the finish line at Almeirim in Brazil to become the first woman to paddle down the Amazon. Here's Helen: 'It's been hard but I've had an amazing time. The only thing I've really missed is my dog Barney. So the first thing I'm going to do will be to pick him up and take him for a nice long walk.'

(2) 9)))

The Stig was using public transport, for the first time in his life! He saw a big red thing coming towards him. A bus! He got on it, and used his Oyster Card to pay. Ten minutes later he got off and got the tube at Acton Town to take the District line to Monument. 18 stops!

The train now approaching is a District line train to West Ham. Please mind the gap between the train and the platform.

The Stig noticed that everyone was reading a newspaper, so he picked up a free one that was on a seat and started reading.

The next station is Monument. Change here for the Central line and the Docklands Light Railway.

He got off the tube and ran to the platform for the Docklands Light Railway. After a few minutes a train arrived. Now it was just ten stops and he would be there!

(2) 15)))

Host And on tonight's programme we talk to Tom Dixon, who is an expert on road safety. Tom, new technology like satnav has meant new distractions for drivers, hasn't it?

Tom That's right, Nicky, but it isn't just technology that's the problem. Car drivers do a lot of other things while they're driving which are dangerous and which can cause accidents. Remember, driver distraction is the number one cause of road accidents.

Host Now I know you've been doing a lot of tests with simulators. According to your tests, what's the most dangerous thing to do when you're driving?

Tom The tests we did in a simulator showed that the most dangerous thing to do while you're driving is to send or receive a text message. This is incredibly dangerous and it is of course illegal. In fact, research done by the police shows that this is more dangerous than drinking and driving.

Host Why is that?

Tom Well, the reason is obvious – many people use two hands to text, one to hold the phone and the other to type. Which means that they don't have their hands on the wheel, and they are looking at the phone, not at the road. Even for people who can text with one hand, it is still extremely dangerous. In the tests we did in the simulator two of the drivers crashed while texting.

Host And which is the next most dangerous?

Tom The next most dangerous thing is to set or adjust your sat nav. This is extremely hazardous too because although you can do it with one hand, you still have to take your eyes off the road for a few seconds.

Host And number three?

Tom Number three was putting on make-up or doing your hair. In fact this is something that people often do, especially women of course, when they stop at traffic lights, but if they haven't finished when the lights change, they often carry on when they start driving again. It's that fatal combination of just having one hand on the steering wheel, and looking in the mirror, not at the road.

Host And number four?

Tom In fourth place, there are two activities which are equally dangerous. One of them is making a phone call on a mobile. Our research showed that when people talk on the phone they drive more slowly (which can be just as dangerous as driving fast) but their control of the car gets worse, because they're concentrating on the phone call and not on what's happening on the road. But the other thing, which is just as dangerous as talking on your mobile, is eating and drinking. In fact if you do this, you double your chance of having an accident because eating and drinking always involves taking at least one hand off the steering wheel. And the worrying thing here is that people don't think of this as a dangerous activity at all and it isn't even illegal.

Host And in fifth, well actually sixth place. It must be listening to music, but which one?

Tom Well, it's listening to music you know.

Host Oh, that's interesting.

Tom We found in our tests that when drivers were listening to music they knew and liked, they drove either faster or slower depending on whether the music was fast or slow.

Host So fast music made drivers drive faster.

Tom Exactly. And a study in Canada also found that if the music was very loud then drivers' reaction time was 20% slower. If you're listening to very loud music you're twice as likely to go through a red light.

Host So the safest of all of the things in the list is to listen to music we don't know.

Tom Exactly. If we don't know the music then it doesn't distract us. In this part of the tests all drivers drove safely.

(2) 23)))

A Excuse me, is this seat free?

B Yes, sure sit down. Ah, he's lovely. Is he yours?

A Yes, yes. He's a she actually. Miranda.

B Oh. Three months?

A Three and a half. How about yours?

B Stephen. He's four months. Did you have a bad night?

A Yes, Miranda was crying all night. You know, that noise gets to you. It drives me mad.

B Do you know what you need? These.

A What are they? Earplugs?

B Yes. Earplugs! When the baby starts crying you just put these in. You can still hear the crying, but the noise isn't so bad and it's not so stressful.

A That's a great idea! Who told you to do that?

B It's all in this book I've read. You should get it.

A Yeah? What's it called?

B It's called 'Commando Dad'. It was written by an ex-soldier. He was a commando in the army and it's especially for men with babies or small children. It's brilliant.

A Really? So what's so good about it?

B Well, it's like a military manual. It tells you exactly what to do with a baby in any situation. It makes everything easier. There's a website too that you can go to – commandodad.com. It has lots of advice about looking after babies and small kids and I really like the forums where men can write in with their problems, or their experiences.

A What sort of things does it help you with?

B All sorts of things. How to change nappies – he has a really good system, how to dress the baby, how to get the baby to sleep, the best way to feed the baby, how to know if the baby is ill. It's really useful and it's quite funny too, I mean he uses sort of military language, so for example he calls the baby a BT which means a baby trooper, and the baby's bedroom is base camp, and taking the baby for a walk is manoeuvres, and taking the nappies to the rubbish is called bomb disposal.

A What else does it say?

A And what does he think about men looking after children? Does he think we do it well?

B He thinks that men are just as good as women at looking after children in almost everything.

A Almost everything?

B Yeah, he says the one time when women are better than men is when the kids are ill. Women sort of understand better what to do. They have an instinct. Oh. Now it's my turn. Right, I know exactly what that cry means. It means he's hungry.

A Wow! What was that book called?

(2) 28)))

Kerri You work hard but your money's all spent
Haven't got enough to pay the rent
You know it's not right and it makes no sense
To go chasing, chasing those dollars and cents
Chasing, chasing those dollars and cents...

Rob That was great, Kerri.

Kerri Thanks.

Rob Kerri, you used to be in a band, now you play solo. Why did you change?

Kerri What happened with the band is private. I've already said I don't want to talk about it in interviews. All I'll say is that I have a lot more freedom this way. I can play – and say – what I want.

Rob Did your relationship with the band's lead guitarist affect the break up?

Kerri No comment. I never talk about my private life.

Rob Your Dad was in a famous punk band and your Mum's a classical pianist, have they influenced your music?

Kerri Of course they have – what do you think? Isn't everyone influenced by their parents?

Rob When did you start playing?

Kerri I started playing the guitar when I was about four.

Rob Four? That's pretty young.

Kerri Yeah, the guitar was nearly as big as me!

Rob I think that your new album is your best yet. It's a lot quieter and more experimental than your earlier albums.

Kerri Thank you! I think it's my best work.

Rob So what have you been doing recently?

Kerri Well, I've been writing and recording some new songs. And I've played at some of the summer festivals in the UK.

Rob And what are you doing while you're in the States?

Kerri I'm going to play at some clubs here in New York, then I'm doing some small gigs in other places. I just want to get to know the country and the people. It's all very new to me.

Jenny Good job, Rob. She isn't the easiest person to interview.

Rob She's OK. And this video clip will work great online.

Don Well, thank you for coming in today, Kerri. Now I suggest we have some lunch. Rob, could you call a taxi?

Rob Er, sure.

2 29))

Don So when will you be coming back to New York, Kerri?

Kerri Oh, I don't know.

Waitress Hi guys, is everything OK?

Don Yes, it's delicious, thank you.

Waitress That's great!

Kerri New York waiters never leave you alone! I really don't like all this 'Hi guys! Is everything OK?' stuff.

Don What? You mean waiters aren't friendly in London?

Rob Oh, they're very friendly!

Kerri Yes, they're friendly but not too friendly. They don't bother you all the time.

Waitress Can I get you anything else? More drinks, maybe?

Don No thanks. We're fine.

Waitress Fantastic.

Kerri See what I mean? Personally, I think people in London are a lot more easy-going. London's just not as hectic as New York.

Don Sure, we all like peace and quiet. But in my opinion, New York is possibly... well, no, is definitely the greatest city in the world. Don't you agree?

Kerri To be honest, I definitely prefer London.

Don Come on, Rob. You've lived in both. What do you think?

Rob Erm, well, I have to say, London's very special. It's more relaxed, it's got great parks and you can cycle everywhere. It's dangerous to cycle in New York!

Don Why would you cycle when you can drive a car?

Kerri You can't be serious.

Don OK, I agree, London has its own peculiar charm. But if you ask me, nothing compares with a city like New York. The whole world is here!

Kerri But that's the problem. It's too big. There are too many people. Everybody's so stressed out. And nobody has any time for you.

Jenny I don't think that's right, Kerri. New Yorkers are very friendly...

Kerri Oh sure, they can sound friendly with all that 'Have a nice day' stuff. But I always think it's a little bit... fake.

Don You've got to be kidding me!

Rob I'm sorry. I'll just have to take this... Hello?... Yes... You're who?... The taxi driver?... What did she leave? ... Her cell phone... right. OK. Yes, we're still at the restaurant. See you in about five minutes.

2 32))

Kerri Thank you for a nice lunch, Don.

Don You're welcome.

Waitress Thanks for coming, guys! Have a nice day.

Don See? Nice, friendly service.

Kerri Maybe. But I think she saw the big tip you left on the table!

Jenny Did you mean what you said in the restaurant, Rob?

Rob Did I mean what?

Jenny About missing London?

Rob Sure, I miss it, Jenny.

Jenny Really?

Rob But hey, not that much! It's just that moving to a new place is always difficult.

Jenny But you don't regret coming here, do you?

Rob No ... no ... not at all.

Jenny It's just that... you seemed homesick in there. For the parks, the cycling ...

Rob Well there are some things I miss but – Oh, hang on a minute. Look over there. Our taxi driver's back.

Taxi driver Excuse me, Ma'am.

Kerri Who me? What is it?

Taxi driver I believe this is your cell phone. You left it in my cab.

Kerri What?... Oh, wow... thank you!

Taxi driver Have a nice day!

Kerri That was so kind of him!

Don See? New Yorkers are really friendly people.

2 40))

1 One very easy thing you can do is just change the language to English on all the gadgets you have, for example on your phone, or laptop, or tablet. That way you're reading English every day and without really noticing you just learn a whole lot of vocabulary, for example the things you see on your screen like *Are you sure you want to shut down now*, things like that.

2 My tip is to do things that you like doing, but in English. So for example, if you like reading, then read in English, if you like the cinema, watch films in English with subtitles, if you like computer games, play them in English. But don't do things you don't enjoy in your language, I mean if you don't like reading in your language, you'll enjoy it even less in English, and so you probably won't learn anything.

3 What really helped me to improve my English was having an Australian boyfriend. He didn't speak any Hungarian – well, not many foreigners do – so we spoke English all the time, and my English improved really quickly. We broke up when he went back to Australia but by then I could speak pretty fluently. We didn't exactly finish as friends, but I'll always be grateful to him for the English I learned. So my tip is try to find an English-speaking boyfriend or girlfriend.

4 I've always thought that learning vocabulary is very important, so I bought a vocabulary flash card app for my phone. I write down all the new words and phrases I want to remember in Polish and in English and then when I get a quiet moment I test myself. It really helps me remember new vocabulary. So that's my tip. Get a vocabulary learning app for your phone.

5 I think one of the big problems when you're learning something new is motivation, something to make you carry on and not give up. So my tip is to book yourself a holiday in an English-speaking country or a country where people speak very good English, like Holland, as a little reward for yourself and so you can actually practise your English. It's really motivating when you go somewhere and find that people understand you and you can communicate! Last year I went to Amsterdam for a weekend and I had a great time and I spoke a lot of English.

6 If you love music, which I do, my tip is to listen to as many songs as possible in English and then learn to sing them. It's so easy nowadays with YouTube. First I download the lyrics and try to understand them. Then I sing along with the singer and try to copy the way he or she sings – this is fantastic for your pronunciation. Then once I can do it well, I go back to YouTube and get a karaoke version of the song, and then I sing it. It's fun and your English will really improve as a result.

2 48))

I always thought that good manners were always good manners, wherever you were in the world. But that was until I married Alexander. We met in Russia, when I was a student there, and I always remember when I first met him. He came to my flat one afternoon, and as soon as he came in he said to me, in Russian, *Nalei mnye chai* – which means 'pour me some tea'. Well, I got quite angry and I said, 'Pour it yourself.' I couldn't believe that he hadn't used a 'Could you...?' or a 'please'. To me it sounded really rude. But Alexander explained that in Russian it was fine – you don't have to add any polite words.

Some months later I took Alexander home to meet my parents in the UK. But before we went I had to give him an intensive course in 'pleases' and 'thank yous'. He thought they were completely unnecessary. I also told him how important it was to smile all the time.

Poor Alexander – he complained that when he was in England he felt really stupid, 'like the village idiot' he said, because in Russia if you smile all the time people think that you're mad. And in fact, this is exactly what my husband's friends thought of me the first time I went to Russia because I smiled at everyone, and translated every 'please' and 'thank you' from English into Russian!

Another thing that Alexander just couldn't understand was why people said things like, 'Would you mind passing me the salt, please?' He said, 'It's only the salt, for goodness sake! What do you say in English if you want a real favour?'

He was also amazed when we went to a dinner party in England, and some of the food was…well, it wasn't very nice, but everybody – including me – said, 'Mmm…this is delicious'.

In Russia, people are much more direct. The first time Alexander's mother came to our house for dinner in Moscow, she told me that my soup needed more salt and pepper, that it didn't really taste of anything. I was really annoyed, and later after she left Alexander and I argued about it. Alexander just couldn't see my point. He said, 'Do you prefer your dinner guests to lie?' Actually you know, I think I do. I'd prefer them to say 'that was lovely' even if they didn't mean it.

Anyway, at home we now have an agreement. If we're speaking Russian, he can say 'Pour me some tea', and not say 'thank you' when I give it to him. But when we're speaking English, he has to add a 'please', a 'thank you', and... a smile.

3 8))

Part 1

Interviewer What made you want to become a referee?

Juan My father was a referee but that didn't influence me – in fact the opposite because I saw all the problems that he had as a referee. But as a child I was always attracted by the idea of being a referee and at school I used to referee all kinds of sports, basketball, handball, volleyball and of course football. I was invited to join the Referee's Federation when I was only 14 years old.

Interviewer Were you good at sport yourself?

Juan Yes, I was a very good handball player. People often think that referees become referees because they are frustrated sportsmen, but this is just not true in most cases in my experience.

Interviewer What was the most exciting match you ever refereed?

Juan It's difficult to choose one match as the most exciting. I remember some of the Real Madrid–Barcelona matches, for example the first one I ever refereed. The atmosphere was incredible in the stadium. But really it's impossible to pick just one – there have been so many.

Interviewer What was the worst experience you ever had as a referee?

Juan The worst? Well, that was something that happened very early in my career. I was only 16 and I was refereeing a match in a town in Spain and the home team lost. After the match, I was attacked and injured by the players of the home team and by the spectators. After all these years I can still remember a mother, who had a little baby in her arms, who was trying to hit me. She was so angry with me that she nearly dropped her baby. That was my worst moment, and it nearly made me stop being a referee.

Interviewer Do you think that there's more cheating in football than in the past?

Juan Yes, I think so.

Interviewer Why?

Juan I think it's because there's so much money in football today that it's become much more important to win. Also football is much faster than it used to be, so it's much more difficult for referees to detect cheating.

Interviewer How do footballers cheat?

Juan Oh, there are many ways, but for me the worst thing in football today is what we call 'simulation'. Simulation is when a player pretends to have been fouled when in fact he hasn't. For example, sometimes a player falls over in the penalty area when, in fact, nobody has touched him and this can result in the referee giving a penalty when it wasn't a penalty. In my opinion, when a player does this he's cheating not only the referee, not only the players of the other team, but also the spectators, because spectators pay money to see a fair contest.

(3 9)))

Part 2

Interviewer What's the most difficult thing about being a referee?

Juan The most difficult thing is to make the right decisions during a match. It's difficult because you have to make decisions when everything's happening so quickly – football today is very fast. You must remember that everything is happening at 100 kilometres an hour. Also important decisions often depend on the referee's interpretation of the rules. Things aren't black and white. And of course making decisions would be much easier if players didn't cheat.

Interviewer Do you think that the idea of fair play doesn't exist any more.

Juan Not at all. I think fair play does exist – the players who cheat are the exceptions.

Interviewer Finally, who do you think is the best player in the world at the moment?

Juan I think most people agree that the best footballer today is Leo Messi.

Interviewer Why do you think he's so good?

Juan It's hard to say what makes him so special, but a study was done on him which showed that Messi can run faster with the ball than many footballers can do without the ball. Apart from his great ability, what I also like about him is that he isn't the typical superstar footballer. You can see that he enjoys playing football and he behaves in public and in his personal life in a very normal way. That's unusual when you think how famous he is. And what's more he doesn't cheat – he doesn't need to!

(3 23)))

Presenter Hello and welcome to Forum, the programme that asks you what you think about current topics. Today Martha Park will be talking about the social networking site Facebook, how we use it, how much we like it – or dislike it. So get ready to call us or text us and tell us what you think. The number as always is 5674318. Martha.

Martha Hello. Since Facebook was first launched in 2004, a lot of research has been done to find out what kind of people use it, what they use it for, and what effect it has on their lives. According to a recent study by consumer research specialist Intersperience the average 22 year old in Britain has over 1,000 online friends. In fact, 22 seems to be the age at which the number of friends peaks.

It also appears that women have slightly more online friends than men. And another study from an American university shows that people who spend a lot of time on Facebook reading other people's posts tend to feel more dissatisfied with their own lives, because they feel that everyone else is having a better time than they are. So, over to you. Do you use Facebook? How do you feel about it? Can you really have 1,000 friends? Are social networking sites making us unhappy? Phone in and share your experiences…

(3 24)))

Presenter And our first caller is George. Go ahead George.

George Hi. Er yeah, I use Facebook a lot, every day really. I think it's a great way to, er, organize your social life and keep in touch with your friends. I have loads of friends.

Martha How many friends do you have George?

George At the moment I have 1,042.

Martha And how many of them do you know personally?

George About half maybe?

Martha And what do you use Facebook for?

George For me, it's a good way to get in touch with my friends without having to use the phone all the time. When I'm having a busy week at university, I can change my status so I can let my friends know I can't go out. That's much easier than wasting time telling people 'sorry I'm too busy to meet up'. It's just easier and quicker than using the phone.

Presenter Thanks George. We have another caller. It's Beth. Hello, Beth.

Beth Hi. Er, I don't use Facebook or any other social networking site.

Martha Why's that Beth?

Beth Two reasons really. First, I don't spend much time online anyway. I do a lot of sport – I'm in a hockey team, so I meet my teammates almost every day, and we don't need to communicate on Facebook.

Martha And the other reason?

Beth I just don't really like the whole idea of social networking sites. I mean, why would I want to tell the whole world everything that I'm doing? I don't want to share my personal information with the world, and become friends with people I don't even know. And I don't want to read what other people had for breakfast or lunch or dinner or what they're planning to do this weekend.

Presenter Thanks for that Beth. Our next caller is Caitlin. It's your turn Caitlin.

Martha Hi Caitlin

Caitlin Hi Martha.

Martha And do you use Facebook Caitlin?

Caitlin I use it from time to time but not very much. I only really use it to keep up with friends who have moved abroad or live too far away for us to meet regularly. For example, one of my best friends recently moved to Canada and we often chat on Facebook. But I never add 'friends' who are people I hardly know. I just can't understand those people who collect hundreds or even thousands of Facebook friends! I think it's just competition, people who want to make out that they're more popular than everybody else.

Martha So you think the Facebook world is a bit unreal?

Caitlin Absolutely. I think people write things and post photos of themselves just to show everyone they know what a fantastic time they're having and what exciting lives they lead. But they're probably just sitting at home in front of the computer all the time.

Presenter Thanks for that Caitlin. We've just got time for one more caller before the news and it's Ned. Hi Ned. You'll have to be quick.

Martha Hi Ned.

Ned Hi. When I started off with Facebook I thought it was great, and I used it to communicate with close friends and with family, and I got back in touch old friends from school. It was good because

all the people I was friends with on Facebook were people I knew, and I was interested in what they were doing. But then I started adding friends, people I hardly knew who were friends of friends, people like that – in the end I had more than a 1,000 – and it just became too much. There were just too many people leaving updates, writing messages on my wall. So last month I decided to delete most of them. It took me about half an hour to delete and in the end the only people I left were actual, real-life friends and family, and old school friends. I got it down to 99. It was really liberating.

Presenter Thanks Ned and we'll be back after the news, so keep those calls coming.

(3 25)))

Jenny Monica!

Monica Jenny!

Jenny Wow! How are you? You look great!

Monica Thanks, Jenny! You look really good, too.

Jenny Hey, why don't we get some coffee?

Monica I'd love to, but I'm on the way to meet… oh, come on. Five minutes!

Jenny So, how is everything?

Monica Oh great. Things couldn't be better actually. Scott and I … we're getting married!

Jenny You're what? Congratulations!

Monica Thank you!

Jenny When did you get engaged?

Monica Only a few days ago. I'm glad I saw you actually. I was going to call you. We've only told family so far.

Jenny I can't believe it. Monica the wife! And to think you used to go clubbing every night!

Monica Well, that was a few years ago! All I want to do now is stay in and read wedding magazines.

Jenny And how are the plans coming along?

Monica I haven't done anything yet. My mom and Scott's mom want to organize the whole thing themselves!

Jenny That's what mothers are for!

Monica True. But what about you? You look fantastic.

Jenny Well, I guess I'm kind of happy, too.

Monica Uh huh. What's his name?

Jenny Rob.

Monica You've been keeping him very quiet! Is it serious?

Jenny Erm, it's kind of, you know…

Monica So it is!

Jenny It's still early. We haven't been together for long. He only moved here from London a few months ago…

Monica What? He's British? And you think you can persuade him to stay in New York? That won't be easy!

Jenny I think he likes it here. You know how guys are, you never know what they're thinking.

Monica When can I meet him?

Jenny Er… that's him now.

(3 26)))

Rob Do you mind if I join you?

Monica Of course not. Come on, sit down.

Rob Thank you.

Monica I have to leave in a minute anyway.

Rob Could I have a large latte, please?

Waiter Of course.

Jenny Rob, this is Monica.

Monica Nice to meet you, Rob.

Rob You too, Monica. You know, Jenny talks about you a lot. And I've seen college photos of you two together. At Jenny's parents' house.

Jenny Of course you have. My dad's photos.

Rob You've hardly changed at all.

Monica What a nice man! I can see why you like him, Jenny. The perfect English gentleman.

Waiter Your latte.

Rob Oh, thanks. Can you pass the sugar?

Jenny Sure.

Monica Sorry guys, but I have to go.

Rob You're sure I haven't interrupted anything?

Monica Not at all. It's just that I have to meet someone. But let's get together very soon.

Jenny We will!

Monica Bye, Rob. Nice meeting you.

Rob Bye.

Jenny Bye. Talk soon.

Rob She seems like a happy person.

Jenny She is, especially right now - she's getting married.

Rob That's fantastic news!

Jenny Yeah, it is. I guess we're at that age now. When most of our friends are settling down and getting married.

Rob Yeah… Oh, speaking of friends, I want to ask you a favour. Is it OK if we change our plans a bit this week?

Jenny Er… sure. What's up?

Rob I've just had a call from an old friend of mine, Paul. I haven't seen him since we were at university and he's travelling around the States at the moment. Anyway, he's arriving in New York this evening and, er… I've invited him to stay for the week.

Jenny Cool! It'll be fun to meet one of your old friends! What's he like?

Rob Oh, Paul's a laugh. He used to be a bit wild, but that was a long time ago. He's probably changed completely.

Jenny Well, I'm looking forward to meeting him.

Rob Just one other thing. Could you do me a big favour? I have to work late this evening so… would you mind meeting him at the airport?

Jenny Not at all. I'd like to meet him.

Rob And do you think you could take him to my flat? I'll give you the keys.

Jenny No problem, Rob.

Rob Thanks so much, Jenny. You're a real star.

3 29))

Paul Hey man!

Rob Paul!

Paul It's great to see you, mate.

Rob You too, Paul. It's been years. You haven't changed at all.

Paul Just got better looking!

Rob How come you're so late?

Jenny Paul's flight from LA was delayed. And then the traffic coming back was just awful.

Paul But that gave us time to get to know each other.

Jenny Yeah. Paul told me all about his travels. Every detail.

Paul And look at this. Your own New York flat. How cool is that?

Rob It's good. Really good. But – do you want something to eat? I got some things on my way home.

Paul Stay in? It's my first night in the Big Apple! Let's go out and have a pizza or something.

Rob I thought you'd be tired after the flight.

Paul No way, man! I'm ready for action.

Rob Great! I'll get my jacket…

Jenny Rob, I think I'll go home if you don't mind. I, uh, I'm exhausted.

Rob Oh, OK then.

Paul So it's a boys' night out!

Rob Just like the old days!

Paul And after the pizza we can go on somewhere else. Rob, we've got a lot to talk about!

3 36))

Interviewer So tell me, how did you get involved in the film, Dagmara?

Dagmara Well, as you probably know, *Schindler's List* was shot in Krakow, in Poland, which is where I live. I was a university student at the time studying English. The film company set up their production office here three months before they started shooting the film and I got a job there as a production assistant, preparing and translating documents and the script.

Interviewer But how did you get the job as Steven Spielberg's interpreter?

Dagmara Well, it was a complete coincidence. Just before the shooting started, there was a big party

in one of the hotels in Krakow for all the actors and the film crew, and I was invited too. When I arrived at the party the Polish producer of the film came up to me and said, 'The woman who was going to interpret for Steven Spielberg can't come, so we need you to interpret his opening speech.'

Interviewer How did you feel about that?

Dagmara I couldn't believe it! I was just a student – I had no experience of interpreting – and now I was going to speak in front of hundreds of people. I was so nervous that I drank a couple of glasses of champagne to give myself courage. I must have done a pretty good job though, because soon afterwards Spielberg came up to me to say thank you and then he said, 'I'd like you to be my interpreter for the whole film.' I was so stunned I had to pinch myself to believe that this was happening to me.

3 37))

Interviewer So what exactly did you have to do?

Dagmara I had to go to the film set every day and translate Spielberg's instructions to the Polish actors, and also to the extras. I had to make them understand what he wanted them to do. It was really exciting and I often felt as if I was a director myself.

Interviewer So, was it a difficult job?

Dagmara Sometimes it was really hard. The worst thing was when we had to shoot a scene again and again because Spielberg thought it wasn't exactly right. Some scenes were repeated as many as 16 times – and then sometimes I would think that maybe it was my fault – that I hadn't translated properly what he wanted, so I'd get really nervous. I remember one scene with lots of actors in it which we just couldn't get right and Spielberg started shouting at me because he was stressed. Eventually we got it right and then he apologized, and I cried a little, because I was also very stressed – and after that it was all right again.

Interviewer So, was Spielberg difficult to work with?

Dagmara Not at all. I mean he was very demanding, I had to do my best every day, but he was really nice to me. I felt he treated me like a daughter. For instance, he was always making sure that I wasn't cold – it was freezing on the set most of the time – and he would make sure that I had a warm coat and gloves and things.

Interviewer Did you ever get to be an extra?

Dagmara Yes, twice! I was going to be in two party scenes, and I got to wear beautiful long dresses and high heels. Unfortunately, one scene didn't make it to the final cut of the film, and before we started shooting the other one I tripped walking down some stairs and twisted my ankle really badly. I was in so much pain that I couldn't take part in the filming. And that was the end of my 'acting career'. I still have the photos of me looking like a girl from the 40s, though!

Interviewer Have you ever worked with Spielberg again?

Dagmara Yes. A year later he invited me to interpret for him again, this time during the premiere of *Schindler's List* in Poland, which was broadcast live on national television! Before that, he had also asked me come to work as a production assistant on his next movie in Hollywood. I was very tempted and thought really hard about it, but I hadn't finished my studies yet, and all my family and friends were in Poland – so in the end I decided not to go.

Interviewer Do you regret it?

Dagmara Not at all. I had my moment, and it was unforgettable, but that was it!

3 47))

A few years ago I was with an Italian friend of mine called Adriana in London, and we went for a walk in Hampstead Heath, which is a big park in North London. It was a nice day, and the park was full of people, parents with children, people walking their

dogs. Anyway, we sat down on a bench to have a rest. While we were sitting there we saw an old man walking towards us. He was walking very slowly, and he looked a real mess – he had long white hair and he was wearing a jacket with a hole in it and old looking shoes. And my friend said 'Oh, look at that poor man. He must be a tramp. He looks like he hasn't had a good meal for some time – shall I give him some money?' She started to look in her bag for some money, but I looked at him again and just said 'Don't!' She couldn't understand why I didn't want her to give the old man some money and she thought I was being very mean and unfriendly.

3 48))

When the old man had gone past I said 'Adriana, that man isn't a tramp. He's Michael Foot, an ex-politician. He used to be the leader of the Labour Party and he's a very brilliant and intelligent man. And he definitely *isn't* homeless – he lives in one of the most expensive parts of London and he certainly doesn't need any money! He just doesn't believe in dressing very smartly. Even when he was a politician he used to look a bit of a mess.' Adriana was really surprised. She said that in Italy no politician or ex-politician would ever look like that. But I told her that in Britain you can't always judge people by their appearance because a lot of people, even rich people don't worry too much about the way they dress…

4 8))

Part 1

Gareth had only eight weeks for the experiment, during which time he would be teaching three days a week. His aim was to try to improve the boys' reading age by six months. On the other two days the boys would have normal lessons with the girls.

His plan was based on his own experience of being a learner, and from talking to educational experts. He had three main principles:

First, that it was essential to make the work feel like play. 'If I can do that, the boys will learn,' said Gareth. The second principle was competition. Gareth says 'Boys absolutely love competition! It has gone out of fashion in British schools, but I think it's really important. Boys have to learn to lose and to fail and to come back from that. If you've never done that until you fail your A levels, or until you go for your first job interview and don't get the job, then you've got a problem.'

The third thing Gareth thought was important was to allow boys to take risks. All kinds of risks. Not just physical risks like climbing trees, but doing things like acting in front of other people. Doing things which are a bit scary, but which are very motivating if you manage to do them.

4 9))

Part 2

When Gareth started, he made some changes to the way the children were learning. The boys spent a lot of time outside, and they did PE (physical education) every day before normal lessons began. They even made their own outdoor classroom. Gareth also tried to involve the boy's parents as much as possible in their education and he visited them at their homes on several occasions.

Gareth set up three major activities for the boys, to help improve their language skills. The first activity was a school debating competition against the girls. The topic that the children had to debate was 'Computer games should be banned'.

When they started to prepare for the debate, the boys weren't very enthusiastic, but soon they started to get more involved. In the end the girls won the debate, but the boys had learned to argue and make points, to express themselves better. They were disappointed not to have won, but they wanted to do it again.

Next, Gareth organised a Reading World Cup, where the boys had to read in teams. Some of the boys couldn't read very well, but they all got very excited about the World Cup, and became much more enthusiastic readers! There was a prize for the winners, and this really motivated the boys.

Finally, the boys (working with the girls) had to write their own play and perform it at the local theatre. The play they wrote was about Romans and aliens. All the children, boys and girls, worked really hard and although some of them felt very nervous before they performed the play, it was a great success and the boys especially were thrilled. Gareth said afterwards, 'It was a risk, and it was scary – but it was good scary.'

4 10)))
Part 3
The boys had a great time with Gareth as their teacher. But at the end of the eight weeks, had their reading really improved? In the last week of the term, they had to do their national reading exams. The exams were independently marked, and when the results were announced the boys had made great progress – all of them had improved by six months and some of them had advanced the equivalent of two years in just eight weeks!

4 23)))
1   My dream house would be in one of our national parks like Yellowstone or Redwood. It would be totally green – I'd have solar panels and wind turbines, and I'd collect rainwater. The house would be made of wood and would be heated by wood fires. I would try to live off the land as much as possible and I'd plant vegetables and fruit, and maybe have chickens. It would all be organic, with no pesticides or anything like that.
2   My dream house would be in Paris. It'd be on the top floor of an old apartment building and I'd have a view of the Eiffel tower or Notre Dame. It would be full of furniture that I'd found in antiques markets, places like that, and amazing paintings, one of which would turn out to be an undiscovered Picasso or Matisse. There would be a beautiful old dining table and chairs for candlelit dinners… then all I'd need would be the right person to share it with.
3   My dream house would be a flat in Soho in New York. It wouldn't be too big – it'd just have a couple of bedrooms, and a huge living room with a home cinema. It would be very modern and incredibly practical, with things like automatic temperature control, a kitchen with all the latest gadgets – if possible a stove that would produce amazing meals on its own – I'm a lazy kind of guy.
4   If I had to choose where to live, I'd choose Hawaii. So my dream house would be made of glass with the most amazing view of the beach from every room in the house, and it'd have indoor and outdoor pools, and maybe a tennis court – I'm quite sporty. It would also have a big indoor aquarium. There's something so peaceful about looking at fish. And fabulous bathrooms of course.

4 26)))
Paul   Bad luck, mate.
Rob   Nice shot.
Paul   I've had years of practice.
Rob   You used to play pool a lot at university.
Paul   You did, too.
Rob   Yeah. I don't really have the time any more.
Paul   Or anybody to play with.

Paul   So what do you do in your free time?
Rob   The magazine keeps me pretty busy. And when I'm free, I'm usually with Jenny.
Paul   Ah. Your turn. Don't blow it.
Rob   What is it?
Paul   I was just thinking about you.
Rob   What about me?
Paul   Do you remember the great times we had at uni? You had such crazy hair – the last time I saw you it was blond!
Rob   Don't remind me.
Paul   Those were the days. But look at you now with your girlfriend and your 9 to 5 job. If you don't

come back to London soon, you'll become an all American boy!
Rob   Come off it.
Paul   It's true! I mean, just look at that shirt.
Rob   What's wrong with my shirt?
Paul   You look like a businessman! Did you buy it?
Rob   Me? No. It was… it was a present from Jenny.
Paul   I thought so.
Rob   What does that mean?
Paul   Well, it's Jenny's taste.
Rob   Yes, and I really like it.
Paul   Jenny seems to know what she wants – and she probably gets it.
Rob   That's one of the things I like about her. Terrible.
Paul   You said it.
Rob   Sorry, Paul. We've got to go.
Paul   Oh come on, Rob. We haven't even finished the game.
Rob   Another time. Jenny's waiting for us.
Paul   Jenny. Right.

4 27)))
Paul   Oh, yeah. That was good. So! What shall we do now?
Rob   What do you want to do?
Paul   Well… I haven't been on a dance floor for weeks now. I've got to move my body. Let's go dancing!
Jenny   I'm going running in the morning. Why don't you join me?
Paul   No, thanks. I'm not very keen on running. But I've read about this place called Deep Space, where they play great music. We could go there.
Jenny   A club?
Paul   Don't you feel like dancing?
Jenny   Not on a Wednesday night. How about going to the late show at MOMA?
Paul   'MOMA'? What's that?
Jenny   MOMA. It's the Museum of Modern Art. There's a Kandinsky exhibition.
Paul   That isn't exactly my idea of a great night out.
Jenny   What about staying in and watching a movie on TV?
Paul   I'm in New York. I can watch TV anywhere.
Jenny   Who's that?
Rob   It's a text from Kerri. She's doing a gig at the Bowery Ballroom.
Paul   Kerri who?
Rob   Kerri Johnson. I interviewed her last week.
Paul   Kerri Johnson? I've seen her play live. She's cool. Do you like her Jenny?
Jenny   I have to admit I'm not crazy about her music … or her for that matter.
Paul   I didn't think so. So shall we go there?
Rob   Why not? Actually Kerri's staying very near here and she doesn't know New York very well. We could meet her outside and go together.
Paul   That's a great idea!
Rob   I'll send her a text.
Jenny   I think I might have an early night. You two can go on your own.
Rob   Are you sure you don't mind?
Paul   Of course she doesn't mind!
Jenny   No, Rob, it's fine. I have another busy day tomorrow. You do too, actually.
Rob   I know, we're meeting Don. I haven't forgotten.
Rob   It's Kerri. She's on her way now.
Paul   What are we waiting for? Let's go!

Monica   Hello?
Jenny   Hi Monica – it's not too late to call is it?
Monica   Jenny! No, why? Are you OK?
Jenny   I need to talk.
Monica   Can you come over? Why don't you take a cab?
Jenny   OK, thanks.

4 30)))
Jenny   Rob?
Rob   Hi, Jenny.
Jenny   Are you OK? Where are you anyway?
Rob   I'm at home. I'm feeling terrible. We got back really late last night.

Jenny   Now why doesn't that surprise me? You know, you're not a student anymore.
Rob   I know. There was a party after the gig – Kerri invited us – and of course Paul said yes.
Jenny   And this morning's meeting? In… ten minutes?
Rob   That's why I'm calling. I'm not going to make it. I'm really sorry.
Jenny   Rob! It's a very important meeting! I'll cover for you this time, but I won't be able to do it again.
Rob   It won't happen again. I promise. Anyway, Paul's leaving.
Jenny   He's leaving?
Rob   That's right. He's off to Boston this afternoon.
Jenny   Maybe that's a good thing. I mean, it's not that I don't like Paul, but…
Rob   I know, I know.
Jenny   I have to go. Talk to you later.
Don   Jenny, have you seen Rob? I wanted to have a word with him before the meeting and he isn't even here.
Jenny   I know. He just called to say he can't make it.
Don   He what?
Jenny   I was with him last night. He wasn't feeling very well. But it's OK. He told me everything I need to know for the meeting.
Don   Oh. OK then.
Jenny   You know Rob. He's such a professional.

4 32)))
Presenter   We're talking about great new shopping websites and I think we have time for one more. Janice, can you tell us about it?
Janice   Well, it's called *Never liked it anyway dot com*. It's a very clever name for a website, as you'll hear. This site was the idea of an American woman called Annabel Acton. She was living in New York with her boyfriend, who was English. He had invited her to travel to London with him at Christmas to meet his family. But five days before Christmas, they broke up. Now, unlike some of us, Annabel didn't want to sit around crying and eating ice cream, she wanted to do something positive.
Presenter   So what gave her the idea for the website?
Janice   Well, after the break up Annabel was left with a plane ticket to London that she didn't need. She also had jewellery that she didn't want anymore, and she had tickets to a concert that she didn't want to go to without her boyfriend. She also had paintings which they had bought together, which she didn't want on her wall anymore. She didn't want any of these things herself, but she thought someone somewhere would probably like to buy them, and that's what gave her the idea to set up the website.
Presenter   What exactly is it?
Janice   Well, it's a website where people who have just broken up with a partner can sell presents, and other things that they don't want any more, maybe because they remind them of their ex, or maybe, as the name suggests because they never liked these things anyway! And the idea, which I think is brilliant, is that they also tell the personal story behind the thing they're selling. Annabel calls it 'sell and tell'!
Presenter   What kind of things do people sell on the website?
Janice   Oh, everything – from something as small as a teddy bear to really expensive things like an engagement ring or a holiday. To give you an idea, today on the site one seller is offering a three-day honeymoon package at a luxury hotel in New York and a woman is selling her ex-boyfriend's car. And they're selling all these things at very good prices. So on *neverlikeditanyway* you can get a bargain, and also help someone who's going through a break-up.
Presenter   Thanks Janice, and that's all we've got time for today …

4 40))

1 I was in Sydney airport, in Australia, and I got a taxi to take me to the hotel. A few minutes after he'd left the airport, the taxi driver said that his meter was broken, but that he would charge me $50, which was what he said the journey normally cost. It was my first time in Sydney and of course I didn't have a clue what the normal fare was, so I just said OK. But later when I was checking in to the hotel I asked the receptionist what the normal taxi fare was from the airport, and she said about $35. I was really annoyed and I sent an email to the taxi company but I never got a reply.

2 I was travelling in the UK. It was a work trip and I knew that I was going to have to answer a lot of emails during that time, so I booked a hotel in Liverpool where they advertised Wi-fi in all the bedrooms. When I arrived it turned out the hotel charged £16 for 24 hours Wi-fi, which is about the same as I pay for a month's internet at home! I complained to the man at reception, but all he said was that I could use the Wi-fi in the lobby, which was free. I wasn't very happy about it. Hotels used to make a lot of money out of customers by charging a ridiculous amount for phone calls. Now that everybody uses their mobile to make phone calls, some hotels now charge a ridiculous amount for Wi-fi.

3 I was in an Italian restaurant in New York recently and I ordered manicotti, which is a kind of pasta, a bit like cannelloni , and it's filled with cheese and served with tomato sauce. Well, when it arrived, the tomato sauce was really hot, but the pasta and the filling were cold, it was like they were still frozen. Anyway, I called the waitress and she said that it couldn't be cold. So I said 'Sorry, it is cold. Do you want to try it?' So she took it back to the kitchen, and later the manager came out and apologized, and when I finally got the dish, it was good, hot all the way through. But I'd had to wait a long time for it. But later the manager came out again and offered me a free dessert. So I had a very good tiramisu for free.

4 49))

Guy Jeremiah presented Aquatina. He argued that bottled water is bad for the planet, because each person throws away at least 85 empty plastic bottles a year. His invention is a bottle that you can compress and keep in your pocket. Then you take it out of your pocket and fill it up when you are somewhere that has drinking water, for example a gym, a school, or your workplace, or even a café which can give you tap water. He tried to convince the Dragons by showing that in the UK more and more people are asking for tap water in bars and restaurants, and are not buying bottled mineral water. He also had the idea of a phone app which could tell people where the nearest place is where they can fill up their bottle.

Kirsty Henshaw's idea was for a frozen dessert, which is a healthy alternative to ice cream. These desserts are low fat, low in calories, and don't contain any sugar, milk, or gluten, or anything that could be a problem for people with allergies. The desserts come in different flavours, chocolate, strawberry and vanilla. Kirsty came up with the idea because her son is allergic to milk, and in the summer he got very sad when all the other children were eating ice creams and he couldn't have one. Kirsty's products are currently sold in a few health food shops, but she would like to increase production and sell her desserts in big supermarkets. The desserts are called Kirsty's Freedom.

4 50))

The Dragons asked Guy a lot of questions, for example they asked him how much he was going to sell the bottle for (which was £4.99) and how much it cost him to make. Guy explained that at the moment it was costing him a pound to make

each bottle, but that if he could make them in bigger quantities, it would only cost 50p. The Dragons also asked how many he had sold so far, to which he answered 340.

In the end they decided that they weren't interested. Their main reason was that they thought that you could always use any empty water bottle and refill it, you don't need to buy one specially, so they couldn't believe that it would ever make any money.

The Dragons were impressed by Kirsty's presentation, and they immediately asked to try the dessert. They liked it, although one of them thought it didn't really taste like ice cream, more like frozen yoghurt. Kirsty explained that her dessert wasn't supposed to taste like ice cream, and that was why she had called it a frozen dessert. They also asked her how much fat there was in it, and she said less than 3%. In the end, to Kirsty's delight they decided to invest £65,000 in Kirsty's business, because they thought that there was definitely a market for her product.

And since then?

Kirsty's frozen desserts are now sold in two of the biggest UK supermarket chains, Waitrose and Sainsbury's. She also has a website with recipes, interviews, and all sorts of information about nutrition.

Although the Dragons didn't invest in it, Guy's Aquatina is also doing well. It has its own website, and it's on sale in several UK shops and online.

5 6))

Apart from the hockey players, he also gives the examples of the Beatles, the most famous rock band of all time and Bill Gates, the founder of Microsoft. The Beatles were really lucky to be invited to play in Hamburg in 1960. The club owner who invited them normally only invited bands from London, but on one trip to the UK he met an entrepreneur from Liverpool who told him that there were some really good bands in that city. When the Beatles arrived in Hamburg, they had to work incredibly hard. They had to play for up to eight hours a night in the club seven nights a week. As John Lennon said later, 'We got better and we got more confidence. We couldn't have got it, with all the experience we got from playing all night long in the club.' By 1964, when they became really successful, the Beatles had been to Hamburg four times, and had already performed live an estimated 1,200 times, far more than many bands today perform in their entire careers.

Bill Gates's huge stroke of good luck came in 1968, when the high school he was at decided to spend some money they had been given on a computer. This computer was kept in a little room that then became the computer club. In 1968, most *universities* didn't have a computer club, let alone schools. From that time on Gates spent most of his time in the computer room, as he and his friends taught themselves how to use it. 'It was my obsession,' Gates says of those early high school years. 'I skipped athletics. I went up there at night. We were programming at weekends. It would be a rare week that we wouldn't get 20 or 30 hours in.' So Gates was unbelievably lucky to have access to a computer, but of course he also put in all those hours of practice too.

Talent, Gladwell concludes, is obviously important, but there are many talented people out there. What makes just a few of them special is that they are lucky, and that they put in far more hours of practice than the rest.

5 19))

Part 1

Presenter And now it's time for our book of the week, which is *The Winter of our Disconnect* by Susan Maushart. Jenny, to start with, it's a good title, isn't it?

Jenny Yes, brilliant. And it was a fascinating experiment and a good read.

Presenter Tell us about it.

Jenny Well, Susan Maushart is a journalist who's bringing up three teenage children. She decided

to do the experiment after reaching a point where she felt that the whole family, especially her children, were all living in their own little worlds, with headphones on, plugged into their laptops or their iPods or their smart phones and that they weren't relating to the other people in the family.

Andrew So it wasn't just her children who were permanently plugged into an electrical device?

Jenny Well, she admits that she herself was quite addicted to her phone and to her iPod and her laptop and that she was constantly reading news sites and googling information, but it was really her children who were totally dependent on new technology. In the book she makes the interesting distinction between 'digital immigrants' and 'digital natives'.

Nick What does that mean?

Jenny She describes herself as a digital immigrant, that's to say someone who didn't grow up with digital technology, which is really anyone who was born before 1980. Her children are digital natives, which means that they were born *after* computers and the internet were already part of life.

Nick Well, that's me then.

Jenny Yes, well, the main difference, she says, is that digital immigrants use the technology, to find information or to listen to music, but digital natives live and breathe the technology. So for them living without it is like living without water, without electricity...in the dark ages.

Nick What were the rules of the experiment?

Jenny The family had to live for six months without using any electrical gadgets in the house with a screen. So no smartphones, no TVs, no laptops or computers, no video consoles and no iPods. They *were* allowed to use technology at school or at friends' houses, or in internet cafés, and they were allowed to use landline phones. But everything else was switched off for the whole six months.

Sally Six months? How on earth did she get the children to agree?

Jenny She bribed them. She told them she was going to write a book about the experiment, and that they would share in any profits that she made from the book!

Sally Wow, that was very clever of her...

5 20))

Part 2

Presenter So what were the results? Was it a positive experience?

Jenny At the end of the book Susan says that it was a positive experience in every way. At first, of course, the kids complained bitterly, they kept saying they were bored. But then they they started to talk to each other again, to go and sit in each other's rooms and chat. They got interested in cooking and reading, they went to the cinema together. They played CDs on the CD player and they actually sat and listened to the music instead of just having music on their headphones all the time as background music. And Susan's 15-year-old son started playing the saxophone again. He had stopped playing a few years before, but then he started having lessons again and even started giving concerts... Oh and the children said that they slept better!

Sally Oh, well, that's good. What about the children's schoolwork? I mean, nowadays we sort of assume that everyone needs the internet to do research for homework and so on.

Jenny In fact, the children's school reports showed that they all improved. When they needed the internet they used the computers at school or at university (the eldest daughter was at university), or they went to friends' houses. But when they did their homework they did it better than before because they weren't multi-tasking – they weren't doing homework and listening to music and sending messages all at the same time. So they concentrated better, and their schoolwork improved.

Andrew What about, Susan, the mother? Did she find it difficult to live without modern technology?

Jenny What she found most difficult was writing her weekly article for the newspaper because she had to do it by hand, and not on her laptop. She says that at the beginning her hand used to really ache, she just wasn't used to writing by hand anymore. But that was just a small problem.

Nick Any other negatives?

Jenny Well, of course the phone bill for their landline was enormous!

Nick Has the experiment had a lasting effect?

Jenny Susan says that it has. She thinks that they all get on much better as a family, her son is still playing the saxophone and he sold his video console. They've all realised that we live in a digital world, but that we need to disconnect from time to time and to re-connect to the people around us. So they have new rules in the house, like no TVs in bedrooms and no TV in the kitchen where they eat. And no wasted hours on the internet.

Sally That would be a good rule for me too!

5 21))

Part 3

Presenter OK, so imagine you all did the experiment. What would you miss the most? Sally?

Sally Well, I already live without the internet many weekends because we have a house in the country in the middle of nowhere where there's no internet coverage. So I know that what I would miss most is being able to google information, like the phone number of a restaurant, or what time a film starts. Or even, dare I say it, the football results. I don't have a TV, so I wouldn't miss that, but I would miss not having the internet.

Presenter Andrew?

Andrew Well, I simply couldn't live without a computer or a laptop because I work from home so I don't have an office to go to, and I absolutely need the internet too. I couldn't do the experiment – I just wouldn't be prepared to go to an internet café all day to work. Susan, the journalist who did the experiment, only had to write one column a week, but I work from home eight hours a day.

Presenter Jenny.

Jenny I think I could do it, I think I could easily live without any of these electrical gadgets at home. I mean, I have my office so I could use the internet there. I don't use an iPod, I still prefer to listen to CDs…

Nick You old dinosaur.

Jenny Yes, yes I know… and I don't watch much TV. I am quite attached to my Blackberry, but I wouldn't mind using a normal phone for six months. I don't think there's anything I'd miss too much…

Presenter And finally Nick, our only digital native.

Nick Well, I'm sorry, but I just wouldn't be prepared to even try the experiment, not even for a week let alone six months. I wouldn't be prepared to live without my phone. I use it for everything, phoning, music, the internet. So, no, I wouldn't do it.

Presenter Not even if you were offered money?

Nick It would have to be a huge amount of money. No, I'm definitely not going to do it!

5 22))

Paul Yeah?

Jenny Hi there. It's me. Should I come up?

Jenny Paul!

Paul That's right.

Jenny Er… hi.

Paul Hi. Are you OK?

Jenny Yes, fine. Thanks. It's just that I erm…

Paul What?

Jenny I wasn't expecting to see you.

Paul Really? Well, as you can see, I'm still here. It seems Rob just can't live without me. Yeah, he's

going to miss me when I'm gone. But not for long. We'll meet up again when he goes back to London.

Jenny Goes back…?

Paul Yeah, he told me last night that he was planning to leave New York pretty soon.

Jenny He what?

Rob Hi Jenny. Do you want some breakfast? I've got bagels.

Jenny No thank you, Rob. Why don't you two enjoy them?

Rob What's wrong?

Paul No idea. I just said you were planning to leave New York soon and she …

Rob You what? I didn't say that!

Paul You didn't have to. This New York life isn't you, Rob and you know it.

Rob No, I don't! I like New York and Jenny's here.

Paul Oh come on! What's the big deal? It's not like you want to marry her.

Rob Well …

Paul What? You do?!

Rob Look Paul. I'm serious about New York and I'm serious about Jenny. And I want you to leave. Today.

Paul You're joking, mate.

Rob No, I'm not. I'll even buy the ticket.

5 23))

Rob Hi, Jenny

Jenny Rob.

Rob Paul told me what he said to you and it's not true. I'm not planning to leave New York.

Jenny Oh really? Could you tell me why Paul is still in your apartment?

Rob Well, he couldn't get a ticket to Boston.

Jenny But you told me he was going a few days ago. Or was that another lie?

Rob No, of course it wasn't! He couldn't get a ticket. The buses to Boston were all full.

Jenny So do you know if he's got one now?

Rob I bought it! He's leaving this evening. But that isn't really the issue here, is it? You have to believe me – I don't want to leave New York!

Jenny How can I believe you? I know you're missing London because you said the same thing to Kerri at the restaurant. Look Rob, I'd like to know what you really want.

Rob What do you mean?

Jenny When you and Paul were together, it was like you were a different person.

Rob You know what Paul's like. What was I meant to do? But that isn't the kind of life I want anymore. I'm not like that.

Jenny I know you're not, but I wonder if you really want to be here. I wonder if …

Rob Jenny, what is it?

Jenny Forget it.

Rob Jenny… what are you worrying about?

Jenny I don't know if this is going to work out.

Rob You're not serious.

Jenny I'm just not sure if we want the same things anymore.

Rob That's crazy…

Don Jenny – oh, good morning, Rob.

Rob Don.

Don I need a word. Can you tell me what you decided at the last meeting?

Jenny Right away, Don. Rob was just leaving.

5 26))

Rob But what can I do, Jenny? What can I say to convince you I'm serious?

Jenny I don't know, Rob.

Rob Wait! What Paul said just isn't true.

Jenny It isn't just what Paul said. It's obvious you want to go back.

Rob Of course I miss London, but I love my life here. What proof do you want of my commitment to New York, to you, to everything!

Jenny I don't know.

Rob There must be something I can do.

Jenny Look, we're going to see my parents later. I don't want us to be late.

Rob We won't be late. And I won't forget the chocolates this time either.

Jenny Well, that's a start, I guess.

Rob But Jenny – we need to talk about this.

Jenny We don't have time to discuss it now.

Rob Jenny!

Jenny What is it?

Rob What if I proposed to you?

Jenny 'Proposed'?

Rob That's right. Proposed.

Jenny Like, 'Will you marry me?'

Rob Exactly.

Jenny On one knee?

Rob I can do that. So what would you say?

Jenny Rob, stop it. It's embarrassing.

Rob Tell me.

Jenny Are you for real?

Rob Yes, I am actually. What about you?

Jenny Yes!

5 31))

The London Tube map

By the 1930s, the London Underground had become very large. This made it difficult to show the new lines and the new stations on a traditional kind of map, and passengers complained that the existing map was confusing. In 1931 a designer, called Harry Beck, was asked to design a map which was easier to read. His map, which was based on an electrical circuit, represented each line in a different colour. This map, which is still used today by thousands of people, both Londoners and tourists, is perhaps one of the most practical design icons ever.

However, the London Tube map doesn't represent distances correctly. People sometimes think if a place is one stop away, then it must very near, but in fact there's a big difference in distance between different stations. So for example, Covent Garden station is only 260 metres from Leicester Square, whereas the distance between Marble Arch and Bond Street (which looks the same distance on the map) is over a kilometre.

The London Eye

The London Eye has become an iconic London landmark since it was opened in 2000, to celebrate the new millennium. It is a symbol of modern Britain, and it has been called London's Eiffel Tower.

However, when it was originally designed, by husband and wife team Julia Barfield and David Marks, people thought it would only be used during the year 2000, the Millennium year, or perhaps just for a few years more. Nobody expected it to be so successful.

Today it is one of the UK's most popular tourist attractions and is visited by over three and a half million people a year. The wheel has 32 capsules which each carry up to 25 people, and they give visitors views of up to 40 kilometres from the top.

Penguin books

Penguin Books was founded by a publisher called Allen Lane in 1935. He was at a bookstall on a railway platform looking for something to read, but he could only find magazines. He decided that people needed to be able to buy books that were good quality fiction, but cheap, and not just in traditional book shops but also on railway stations and in chain stores.

Lane wanted a dignified but amusing symbol for the new books. His secretary suggested a penguin, and an employee was sent to London Zoo to make drawings of penguins. The first penguin paperbacks appeared in the summer of 1935. They included the works of Agatha Christie and the American writer Ernest Hemingway. The classic cover was invented in 1946. The books were colour coded – orange for fiction, blue for biography, and green for crime. The way people thought about books had changed forever – the paperback revolution had begun.

The cover designs have changed a lot over the years, but the original 1946 cover, which is considered a design icon, was recently brought back and is also used on mugs, notebooks, and other items.

Sgt Pepper's Lonely Hearts Club Band album cover

Sgt Pepper's Lonely Hearts Club Band album was the Beatles' eighth studio album and it was released in June 1967. It includes songs like *Lucy in the Sky with Diamonds*, and *A Day in the Life* and it became one of the best-selling albums of all time.

The iconic album cover was designed by the English Pop artist Peter Blake. It shows the band posing in front of a collage of some of their favourite celebrities. The celebrities include the actors Marlon Brando, James Dean and Marilyn Monroe, the writer Oscar Wilde, the psychiatrist Sigmund Freud, the singer Bob Dylan and the comedians Laurel and Hardy. Peter Blake later complained that he was only paid £200 for what became one of the most famous album covers ever.

5 35))

Interviewer Good morning and thank you for coming, Mr Morton – or should it be Inspector Morton – you were a detective with Scotland Yard, weren't you?

Inspector Morton Yes, that's right. For twenty-five years. I retired last year.

Interviewer People today are still fascinated by the identity of Jack the Ripper, around 125 years after the crimes were committed. It's incredible, isn't it?

Inspector Morton Well, it's not really that surprising. People are always interested in unsolved murders – and Jack the Ripper has become a sort of cult horror figure.

Interviewer Who are the main suspects?

Inspector Morton Well, there are a lot of them. But probably the best known are Prince Albert, Queen Victoria's grandson, the artist Walter Sickert, and a Liverpool cotton merchant called James Maybrick. And recently we've heard about another possible suspect, a German sailor called Carl Feigenbaum.

5 36))

Interviewer Patricia Cornwell in her book 'Jack the Ripper – case closed' said that she had identified the murderer and that she was convinced that Jack the Ripper was in fact Walter Sickert, the painter. What evidence did she put forward to support this claim?

Inspector Morton Well, she mainly used DNA analysis. She actually bought a painting by Sickert at great expense and she cut it up to get the DNA from it – people in the art world were furious.

Interviewer I can imagine.

Inspector Morton And then she compared the DNA from the painting with DNA taken from the letters that Jack the Ripper sent to the police. Patricia Cornwell says that she's 99% certain that Walter Sickert was Jack the Ripper.

Interviewer But you don't think she's right, do you?

Inspector Morton No, I don't. I don't think her scientific evidence is completely reliable and there's a lot of evidence which says that Sickert was in France not London when some of the women were killed.

Interviewer What about James Maybrick? Do you think he was the murderer?

Inspector Morton Well, somebody found a diary which is supposed to be his, where he admits to being Jack the Ripper. But nobody has been able to prove that the diary is genuine and, personally, I don't think he was the murderer.

Interviewer And Prince Albert, the Queen's grandson?

Inspector Morton This for me is the most ridiculous theory. I can't seriously believe that a member of the royal family could be a serial murderer. In any case, Prince Albert was in Scotland when at least two of the murders were committed.

Interviewer There's been another recent theory, hasn't there? That Jack the Ripper was German.

Inspector Morton Yes. This is a new theory, based on new research by a Jack the Ripper expert called Trevor Marriot, who's in fact another retired detective, like me. He believes that Carl Feigenbaum, a German sailor, was responsible for some if not all the five murders. Feigenbaum was executed in the electric chair in New York in 1894 for the brutal murder of a woman, and after his death his lawyer said that he was convinced that his client was Jack the Ripper. Marriot has discovered that Feigenbaum was a member of the crew of a ship that was in London at the time of the murders. So it's perfectly possible that he could have been the Ripper.

Interviewer Do we know what he looked like?

Inspector Morton Well, there are no photos of Feigenbaum, but Marriot has made a computer image of him based on descriptions from when he was in prison.

Interviewer So, who do you think the murderer was?

Inspector Morton I can't tell you because I don't know.

Interviewer So you don't think we'll ever solve the mystery?

Inspector Morton No, I wouldn't say that. I think one day the mystery will be solved. Some new evidence will appear and we'll be able to say that the case of Jack the Ripper is finally closed. But at the moment it's still a mystery, and people like a good mystery.

1A

present simple and continuous, action and non-action verbs

present simple: *I live, he works, etc.*

> 1 I **work** in a bank. She **studies** Russian.　　　(1 10))
> We **don't have** any pets. Jack **doesn't wear** glasses.
> Where **do** you **live**? **Does** your brother **have** a car?
> 2 She usually **has** cereal for breakfast.
> **I'm** never late for work.
> We only **eat out** about once a month.

1 We use the present simple for things that are always true or happen regularly.
  - Remember the spelling rules for third person singular, e.g. *lives, studies, watches.*
  - Use **ASI** (**A**uxiliary, **S**ubject, **I**nfinitive) or **QUASI** (**Q**uestion word, **A**uxiliary, **S**ubject, **I**nfinitive) to help you with word order in questions. *Do you know David? What time does the film start?*
2 We often use the present simple with adverbs of frequency, e.g. *usually, never,* or expressions of frequency, e.g. *every day, once a week.*
  - Adverbs of frequency go <u>before</u> the main verb, and <u>after</u> be.
  - Expressions of frequency usually go at the end of the sentence or verb phrase.

present continuous: *be + verb + -ing*

> A Who **are** you **waiting** for?　　　(1 11))
> B **I'm waiting** for a friend.
>
> A **Is** your sister still **going out** with Adam?
> B No, they broke up. She **isn't going out** with anyone at the moment.

- We use the present continuous (not the present simple) for actions in progress at the time of speaking, e.g. things that are happening now or around now. These are normally temporary, not habitual actions.
- Remember the spelling rules, e.g. *living, studying, getting.*
- We also use the present continuous for future arrangements (see **1B**).

action and non-action verbs

> A What **are** you **cooking**?　　　(1 12))
> B **I'm making** pasta.
> A Great! I **love** pasta.
>
> A What **are** you **looking** for?
> B My car keys.
> A I'll help you in a moment.
> B But I **need** them now!

- Verbs which describe **actions**, e.g. *cook, make,* can be used in the present simple or continuous. *I'm making the lunch. I usually make the lunch at the weekend.*
- Verbs which describe **states** or **feelings** (not actions), e.g. *love, need, be,* are **non-action verbs**. They are not usually used in the present continuous, even if we mean 'now'.
- Common non-action verbs are *agree, be, believe, belong, depend, forget, hate, hear, know, like, love, matter, mean, need, prefer, realize, recognize, remember, seem, suppose.*

> 🔍 **Verbs that can be both action and non-action**
> A few verbs have an action and a non-action meaning, e.g. *have* and *think.*
> *I have a cat now.* = possession (non-action)
> *I can't talk now. I'm having lunch.* = an action
> *I think this music's great.* = opinion (non-action)
> *What are you thinking about?* = an action

a Complete the sentences with the present simple or present continuous forms of the verbs in brackets.

> We *don't go* to Chinese restaurants very often. (not go)

1 These days, most children _____ too many fizzy drinks. (have)
2 _____ you _____ any vitamins at the moment? (take)
3 Don't eat that spinach if you _____ it. (not like)
4 _____ your boyfriend _____ how to cook fish? (know)
5 We _____ takeaway pizzas during the week. (not get)
6 What _____ your mother _____? It smells great! (make)
7 You look sad. What _____ you _____ about? (think)
8 The diet in my country _____ worse. (get)
9 How often _____ you _____ seafood? (eat)
10 I _____ usually _____ fish. (not cook)

b (Circle) the correct form, present simple or continuous.

> (I don't believe) / I'm not believing that you cooked this meal yourself.

1 Come on, let's order. The waiter *comes | is coming.*
2 Kate *doesn't want | isn't wanting* to have dinner now. She isn't hungry.
3 The head chef is ill, so he *doesn't work | isn't working* today.
4 The bill *seems | is seeming* very high to me.
5 We've had an argument, so we *don't speak | aren't speaking* to each other at the moment.
6 My mum *thinks | is thinking* my diet is awful these days.
7 *Do we need | Are we needing* to go shopping today?
8 Can I call you back? *I have | I'm having* lunch right now.
9 I didn't use to like oily fish, but now *I love | I'm loving* it!
10 What *do you cook | are you cooking*? It smells delicious!

◀ p.7

1B

future forms

be going to + infinitive

future plans and intentions (1) 17))

My sister**'s going to adopt** a child.
Are you **going to buy** a new car or a second-hand one?
I'm not going to go to New York tomorrow. The meeting is cancelled.

predictions (1) 18))

Barcelona **are going to win**. They're playing really well.
Look at those black clouds. I think it**'s going to rain**.

• We use *going to* (NOT *will | won't*) when we have already decided to do something. NOT ~~My sister will adopt a child.~~
• We also use *going to* to make a prediction about the future, especially when you can see or have some evidence (e.g. black clouds).

present continuous: be + verb + -ing

future arrangements (1) 19))

Lorna and Jamie **are getting** married in October.
We**'re meeting** at 10.00 tomorrow in Jack's office.
Jane**'s leaving** on Friday and **coming back** next Tuesday.

• We often use the present continuous for future arrangements.
• There is very little difference between the present continuous and *going to* for future plans / arrangements, and often you can use either.
  – *going to* shows that you have made a decision. *We're going to get married next year.*

– the present continuous emphasizes that you have made the arrangements. *We're getting married on October 12th.* (= we've booked the church, etc.)

• We often use the present continuous with verbs relating to travel arrangements, e.g. *go, come, arrive, leave*, etc. *I'm going to Paris tomorrow and coming back on Tuesday.*

will / shall + infinitive

instant decisions, promises, offers, predictions, (1) 20))
future facts, suggestions

1 **I'll have** the steak. (instant decision)
   I **won't tell** anybody where you are. (promise)
   I'll carry that bag for you. (offer)
   You**'ll love** New York! (prediction)
   I'll be at home all afternoon. (future fact)
2 **Shall I help** you with your homework? (offer)
   Shall we **eat** out tonight? (suggestion)

I'll have the steak.

1 We use *will | won't* (NOT the present simple) for instant decisions, promises, offers, and suggestions. NOT ~~I carry that bag for you.~~
   • We can also use *will | won't* for predictions, e.g. *I think Barcelona will win,* and to talk about future facts, e.g. *The election will be on 1st March.*
2 We use *shall* (NOT *will*) with *I* and *we* for offers and suggestions when they are questions.

---

a (Circle) the correct form. Tick ✓ the sentence if both are possible.

My grandparents *are going to retire | will retire* next year. ✓

1 *Will we | Shall we* invite your parents for Sunday lunch?
2 *I'm going to make | I'll make* a cake for your mum's birthday, if you want.
3 *I'm not having | I'm not going to have* dinner with my family tonight.
4 The exam *will be | is being* on the last Friday of term.
5 You can trust me. *I'm not telling | I won't tell* anyone what you told me.
6 My cousin *is arriving | will arrive* at 5.30 p.m.
7 I think the birth rate *will go down | shall go down* in my country in the next few years.
8 *I'm not going to go | I won't go* to my brother-in-law's party next weekend.
9 *Shall I | Will I* help you with the washing-up?

b Complete **B**'s replies with a correct future form.

A What's your stepmother going to do about her car?
B She*'s going to buy* a second-hand one. (buy)
1 **A** I'm going to miss you.
   B Don't worry. I promise I _____ every day. (write)
2 **A** What are Alan's plans for the future?
   B He _____ a degree in engineering. (do)
3 **A** Can I see you tonight?
   B No, I _____ late. How about Saturday? (work)
4 **A** What would you like for starters?
   B I _____ the prawns, please. (have)
5 **A** There's nothing in the fridge.
   B OK. _____ we _____ a takeaway? (get)
6 **A** I don't have any money, so I can't go out.
   B No problem, I _____ you some. (lend)
7 **A** Shall we have a barbecue tomorrow?
   B I don't think so. On the radio they said that it _____. (rain)
8 **A** We land at about eight o'clock.
   B _____ I _____ you _____ from the airport? (pick up)

2A

present perfect and past simple

present perfect simple: *have / has* + past participle (*worked, seen, etc.*)

> 1 **past experiences**   **1 42))**
>   I've **been** to London, but I **haven't been** to Oxford.
>   **Have** you ever **lost** your credit card?
>   Sally **has** never **met** Bill's ex-wife.
>
> 2 **recent past actions**
>   I've **cut** my finger!
>   Too late! Our train **has** just **left**!
>
> 3 **with *yet* and *already* (for emphasis)**
>   I've **already seen** this film twice. Can't we watch another one?
>   My brother **hasn't found** a new job yet. He's still looking.
>   **Have** you **finished** your homework yet? No, not yet.

1 We use the present perfect for past experiences, when we don't say exactly when they happened.
  • We often use *ever* and *never* when we ask or talk about past experiences. They go <u>before</u> the main verb.
2 We use the present perfect for recent past actions, often with *just*.
  • *just* goes <u>before</u> the main verb.
3 We also use the present perfect with *yet* and *already*.
  • *already* is used in ⊞ sentences and goes <u>before</u> the main verb.
  • *yet* is used with ⊟ sentences and ⍰. It goes <u>at the end</u> of the phrase.
  • For irregular past participles see **Irregular verbs** *p.165*.

past simple (*worked, stopped, went, had, etc.*)

> They **got** married last year.   **1 43))**
> What time **did** you **wake up** this morning?
> I **didn't have** time to do my homework.

• Use the past simple for finished past actions (when we say, ask, or know when they happened).

present perfect or past simple?

> I've **been** to Madrid twice.   **1 44))**
> (= in my life up to now)
> I **went** there in 1998 and 2002.
> (= on two specific occasions)
> I've **bought** a new computer.
> (= I don't say exactly when, where, etc.)
> I **bought** it last Saturday. (= I say when)

• Use the present perfect (NOT the past simple) to talk about past experiences and recent past actions **when we don't specify a time**.
• Use the past simple (NOT the present perfect) to ask or talk about finished actions in the past, **when the time is mentioned or understood**. We often use a past time expression, e.g. *yesterday, last week,* etc.

---

a Complete the mini dialogues with the present perfect form of the verb in brackets and an adverb from the list. You can use the adverbs more than once.

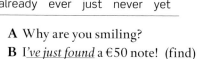
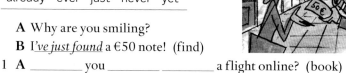

| already ever just never yet |

  A Why are you smiling?
  B I've *just found* a €50 note! (find)
1 **A** _____ you _____ _____ a flight online? (book)
  B Yes, of course. I've done it loads of times.
2 **A** When are you going to buy a motorbike?
  B Soon. I _____ _____ _____ nearly €1,000. (save)
3 **A** _____ you _____ the electricity bill _____? (pay)
  B No, sorry. I forgot.
4 **A** _____ your parents _____ _____ you money? (lend)
  B Yes, but I paid it back as soon as I could.
5 **A** How does eBay work?
  B I don't know. I _____ _____ _____ it. (use)
6 **A** What are you celebrating?
  B We _____ _____ _____ a prize in the lottery! (win)
7 **A** Why haven't you got any money?
  B I _____ _____ _____ my salary. I bought a new tablet last week. (spend)
8 **A** Would you like a coffee?
  B No, thanks. I _____ _____ _____ one. (have)

b Right or wrong? Tick ✓ or cross ✗ the sentences. Correct the wrong sentences.

  I've never been in debt. ✓
  How much has your new camera cost? ✗
  How much did your new camera cost?

1 Dean has just inherited €5,000 from a relative.
2 Did your sister pay you back yet?
3 We booked our holiday online a month ago.
4 When have you bought that leather jacket?
5 They've finished paying back the loan last month.
6 We haven't paid the gas bill yet.
7 Have you ever wasted a lot of money on something?
8 I'm sure I haven't borrowed any money from you last week.
9 I spent my salary really quickly last month.
10 Have you seen the Batman film on TV yesterday?

◀ *p.16*

present perfect + *for* / *since*, present perfect continuous

present perfect + *for* / *since*

They**'ve known** each other for ten years. **1 47**)))

Julia **has had** that bag since she was at university.

A How long **have** you **worked** here?
B Since 1996.

A How long **has** your brother **had** his motorbike?
B For about a year.

- We use the present perfect + *for* or *since* with **non-action verbs** (e.g. *like, have, know,* etc.) to talk about something which started in the past and is still true now.
  They've known each other for ten years. (= they met ten years ago and they still know each other today)
- We use *How long…?* + present perfect to ask about an unfinished period of time (from the past until now).
- We use *for* + a period of time, e.g. *for two weeks,* or *since* + a point of time, e.g. *since 1990.*
- Don't use the present simple with *for* / *since,* NOT ~~They know each other for a long time.~~

present perfect continuous: *have / has been* + verb + *-ing*

1 How long **have** you **been learning** English? **1 48**)))
  Nick **has been working** here since April.
  They**'ve been going out** together for about three years.
2 Your eyes are red. **Have** you **been crying?**
  No, I**'ve been cutting** onions.

1 We use the present perfect continuous with *for* and *since* with **action verbs** (e.g. *learn, work, go,* etc.) to talk about actions which started in the past and are still true now.
  - Don't use the present continuous with *for* / *since,* NOT ~~I am working here for two years.~~
2 We can also use the present perfect continuous for continuous or repeated actions which have been happening very recently. The actions have usually just finished.

I**'ve** (I **have**) You**'ve** (You **have**) He / She / It**'s** (He **has**) We**'ve** (We **have**) They**'ve** (They **have**)	**been working** here for two years.
I **haven't** (I **have not**) You **haven't** He / She / It **hasn't** We **haven't** They **haven't**	**been working** here for two years.

Have you **been working** here for two years?	Yes, I **have.**	No, I **haven't.**
Has she **been working** here for two years?	Yes, she **has.**	No, she **hasn't.**

> 🔍 **work** and **live**
> *Work* and *live* are often used in either present perfect simple or present perfect continuous with the same meaning.
> I**'ve lived** here since 1980.
> I**'ve been living** here since 1980.

---

a Correct the mistakes.

  Harry is unemployed since last year.
  Harry has been unemployed since last year.

1 We've had our new flat since six months.
2 Hi Jackie! How are you? I don't see you for ages!
3 How long are you knowing your husband?
4 Emily has been a volunteer for ten years ago.
5 Paul doesn't eat anything since yesterday because he's ill.
6 It hasn't rained since two months.
7 How long has your parents been married?
8 They're having their dog since they got married.
9 I haven't had any emails from my brother for last Christmas.
10 My grandmother lives in the same house all her life.

b Make sentences with the present perfect simple or present perfect continuous (and *for* / *since* if necessary). Use the present perfect continuous if possible.

  I / work for a charity / eight years
  I've been working for a charity for eight years.

1 we / know each other / we were children
2 the children / play computer games / two hours
3 your sister / have that hairstyle / a long time?
4 I / love her / the first day we met
5 my internet connection / not work / yesterday
6 how long / you / wait?
7 I / be a teacher / three years
8 it / snow / five o'clock this morning
9 Sam / not study enough / recently
10 you / live in London / a long time?

◀ *p.19*

3A

comparatives and superlatives: adjectives and adverbs

comparing two people, places, things, etc.

> 1 My sister is a bit **taller than** me. **2 11**))
>   London is **more expensive than** Edinburgh.
>   This test is **less difficult than** the last one.
>   Olive oil is **better** for you **than** butter.
> 2 The new sofa isn't **as comfortable as** the old one.
>   I don't have **as many** books **as** I used to.

1 We use comparative **adjectives** to compare two people, places, things, etc.
   • Regular comparative adjectives: spelling rules
     old > *old**er***   *big* > *big**ger***   *easy* > *eas**ier***
     modern > **more** *modern*   *difficult* > **more** *difficult*
   • Irregular comparative adjectives:
     good > *better*   *bad* > *worse*   *far* > *further*
   • One-syllable adjectives ending in -*ed*:
     bored > **more** *bored*   *stressed* > **more** *stressed*
     tired > **more** *tired*
2 We can also use (*not*) *as* + adjective + *as* to make comparisons.

> 🔍 **Object pronouns (*me, him*, etc.) after *than* and *as***
>
> After *than* or *as* we can use an object pronoun (*me, him, her*, etc.) or a subject pronoun (*I, he, she*, etc.) + auxiliary verb.
> *She's taller than me.* OR *She's taller than I am.* NOT ~~She's taller than I.~~
>
> *They're not as busy as us.* OR *They're not as busy as we are.* NOT ~~They're not as busy as we.~~
>
> **the same as**
> We use *the same as* to say that two people, places, things, etc. are identical.
> *Her dress is the same as mine.*

comparing two actions

> 1 My father drives **faster than** me. **2 12**))
>   You walk **more quickly** than I do.
>   Liverpool played worse today **than** last week.
> 2 Max doesn't speak English **as well as** his wife does.
>   I don't earn **as much as** my boss.

1 We use comparative **adverbs** to compare two actions.
   • Regular comparative adverbs: spelling rules
     fast > *fast**er***   *slowly* > **more** *slowly*   *carefully* > **more** *carefully*
   • Irregular comparatives:
     well > *better*   *badly* > *worse*
2 We can also use (*not*) *as* + adverb + *as* to make comparisons.

superlatives

> Kevin is **the tallest** player in the team. **2 13**))
> Oslo is **the most expensive** capital city in Europe.
> The small bag is **the least expensive**.
> Lucy is **the best student** in the class.
> Who dresses **the most stylishly** in your family?
> That's **the worst** we've ever played.

• We use superlative **adjectives** and **adverbs** to compare people, things, or actions with all of their group.
• Form superlatives like comparatives, but use -*est* instead of -*er* and *most* / *least* instead of *more* / *less*.
• We normally use *the* before superlatives, but you can also use possessive adjectives, e.g. **my** *best friend*, **their** *most famous song*.
• We often use a superlative with present perfect + *ever*, e.g. *It's the best book I've ever read.*

> 🔍 ***in* after superlatives**
> Use *in* (NOT *of*) before places after a superlative.
> *It's the longest bridge **in** the world.* NOT ~~of the world~~
> *It's the best beach **in** England.* NOT ~~of England~~

---

a Complete with the comparative or superlative of the **bold** word (and *than* if necessary).

What's <u>the fastest</u> way to get across London? **fast**
1 I think skiing is _____ horse-riding. **easy**
2 A motorbike is _____ a scooter. **powerful**
3 I think that travelling by train is _____ form of transport. **relaxing**
4 You walk _____ I do. **slowly**
5 _____ time to travel is on holiday weekends. **bad**
6 _____ I've ever driven is from London to Edinburgh. **far**
7 The London Underground is _____ the subway in New York. **old**
8 This is _____ coach I've ever been on. **hot**
9 Of all my family, my mum is _____ driver. **good**

b Complete with one word.

Going by motorboat is <u>more</u> exciting than travelling by ferry.
1 A coach isn't as comfortable _____ a train.
2 It's _____ most expensive car we've ever bought.
3 The traffic was worse _____ we expected.
4 This is the longest journey I've _____ been on.
5 He gets home late, but his wife arrives later than _____.
6 The _____ interesting place I've ever visited is Venice.
7 I leave home at the same time _____ my brother.
8 He drives _____ carefully than his girlfriend – he's never had an accident.
9 We don't go abroad _____ often as we used to.
10 What's the longest motorway _____ the UK?

◀ p.26

3B

articles: *a / an, the*, no article

a / an

1 I saw **an old man** with **a dog**.　　(2) 17))
2 It's **a nice house**. She's **a lawyer**.
3 What **an awful day**!
4 I have classes three times **a week**.

- We use *a / an* with singular countable nouns:
  1 the first time you mention a thing / person.
  2 when you say what something is or what somebody does.
  3 in exclamations with *What…!*
  4 in expressions of frequency.

the

1 I saw an old man with **a dog**.　　(2) 18))
  The dog was barking.
2 My father opened **the door**.
  The children are at school.
3 **The moon** goes round **the Earth**.
4 I'm going to **the cinema** tonight.
5 It's **the best** restaurant in town.

- We use *the*:
  1 when we talk about something we've already mentioned.
  2 when it's clear what you're referring to.
  3 when there's only one of something.
  4 with places in a town, e.g. *cinema* and *theatre*.
  5 with superlatives.

no article

1 **Women** usually talk more than **men**.　　(2) 19))
  Love is more important than **money**.
2 She's not **at home** today.
  I get back **from work** at 5.30.
3 I never have **breakfast**.
4 See you **next Friday**.

- We don't use an article:
  1 when we are speaking in general (with plural and uncountable nouns). Compare:
    I love **flowers**. (= flowers in general)
    I love **the flowers** in my garden. (= the specific flowers in my garden)
  2 with some nouns, (e.g. *home, work, school, church*) after *at | to | from*.
  3 before meals, days, and months.
  4 before *next | last* + day, week, etc.

---

a (Circle) the correct answers.

I love (weddings)/ *the weddings*!

1 Jess is *nurse | a nurse* in a hospital. *A hospital | The hospital* is a long way from her house.

2 What *a horrible day | horrible day*! We'll have to eat our picnic in *the car | a car*.

3 My wife likes *love stories | the love stories*, but I prefer *the war films | war films*.

4 We go to *theatre | the theatre* about *once a month | once the month*.

5 I'm having *dinner | the dinner* with some friends *the next Friday | next Friday*.

6 My boyfriend is *chef | a chef*. I think he's *the best cook | best cook* in the world.

7 I'm not sure if I closed *the windows | windows* before I left *the home | home* this morning.

8 In general, I like *dogs | the dogs*, but I don't like *dogs | the dogs* that live next door to me.

9 I got to *the school | school* late every day *the last week | last week*.

10 I think *happiness | the happiness* is more important than *success | the success*.

b Complete with *a | an, the*, or – (= no article).

A We're lost. Let's stop and buy <u>a</u> map.
B No need. I'll put <u>the</u> address in <u>the</u> satnav.

1 A How often do you go to _____ gym?
  B About three times _____ week. But I never go on _____ Fridays.

2 A What time does _____ train leave?
  B In ten minutes. Can you give me _____ lift to _____ station?

3 A What _____ lovely dress!
  B Thanks. I bought it in _____ sales _____ last month.

4 A What's _____ most interesting place to visit in your town?
  B Probably _____ castle. It's _____ oldest building in town.

5 A What shall we do _____ next weekend?
  B Let's invite some friends for _____ lunch. We could eat outside in _____ garden.

6 A Do you like _____ dogs?
  B Not really. I prefer _____ cats. I think they're _____ best pets.

7 A Is your mum _____ housewife?
  B No, she's _____ teacher. She's always tired when she finishes _____ work.

8 A Have you ever had _____ problem in your relationship?
  B Yes, but we got over _____ problem and we got married _____ last year.

9 A When is _____ meeting?
  B They've changed _____ date. It's _____ next Tuesday now.

◀ p.29

4A

can, could, be able to (ability and possibility)

can / could

> I **can** speak three languages fluently. 2 34))
> Jenny **can't** come tonight. She's ill.
> My cousin **could** play the violin when she was three.
> They **couldn't** wait because they were in a hurry.
> **Could** you open the door for me, please?

Could you open the door for me, please?

- *can* is a modal verb. It only has a present form (which can be used with future meaning) and a past or conditional form (*could*).
- For all other tenses and forms, we use *be able to* + infinitive.

be able to + infinitive

> 1 Luke **has been able to** swim since he was three. 2 35))
>   I'd like **to be able to** ski.
>   I love **being able to** stay in bed late on Sunday morning.
>   You**'ll be able to** practise your English in London.
> 2 Fortunately, I **am able to** accept your invitation.
>   My colleagues **weren't able to** come to yesterday's meeting.

1 We use *be able to* + infinitive for ability and possibility, especially where there is no form of *can*, e.g. future, present perfect, infinitive and gerund, etc.
2 We sometimes use *be able to* in the present and past (instead of *can* / *could*), usually if we want to be more formal.

---

a Complete with the correct form of *be able to* (+, –, or ?).

I**'ve** never *been able to* scuba dive.

1 Her mobile has been switched off all morning, so I _____ talk to her yet.
2 I don't like noisy bars. I like _____ have a conversation without shouting.
3 I _____ leave home when I get a job.
4 We're having a party next Saturday. _____ you _____ come?
5 You need _____ swim before you can go in a canoe.
6 I'm going to France next week, but I don't speak French. I hate _____ communicate with people.
7 Fortunately, firefighters _____ rescue all of the people trapped inside the burning house.
8 I'm very sorry, but we _____ go to your wedding next month. We'll be on holiday.
9 I'm feeling a bit worse. _____ you _____ contact the doctor yet?
10 The manager _____ see you right now because he's in a meeting.

b Circle the correct form. Tick ✓ if both are possible.

I've always wanted to *can* / *be able to* dance salsa.

1 My little boy *couldn't* / *wasn't able to* speak until he was nearly two years old.
2 She's much better after her operation. She'll *can* / *be able to* walk again in a few months.
3 He hasn't *could* / *been able to* mend my bike yet. He'll do it tomorrow.
4 It's the weekend at last! I love *can* / *being able to* go out with my friends.
5 When we lived on the coast, we used to *can* / *be able to* go to the beach every day.
6 I *can't* / *'m not able to* send any emails at the moment. My computer isn't working.
7 I *could* / *was able to* read before I started school.
8 We won't *can* / *be able to* go on holiday this year because we need to spend a lot of money on the house.
9 Linda's really pleased because she's finally *could* / *been able to* find a part-time job.
10 Alex *can* / *is able to* speak Portuguese fluently after living in Lisbon for ten years.

◀ p.34

4B

have to, must, should

have to / must (+ infinitive)

1 You **have to** wear a seatbelt in a car.   ② 42))
  Do you **have to** work on Saturdays?
  I **had to** wear a uniform at my primary school.
  I'**ll have to** get up early tomorrow. My interview is at 9.00.
2 You **must** be on time tomorrow because there's a test.
  You **must** remember to phone Emily – it's her birthday.
3 I love the Louvre! You **have to** go when you're in Paris.
  You **must** see this film – it's amazing!

• *have to* and *must* are normally used to talk about obligation or something that it is necessary to do.
1 *have to* is a normal verb and it exists in all tenses and forms, e.g. also as a gerund or infinitive.
2 *must* is a modal verb. It only exists in the present, but it can be used with a future meaning.
3 You can also use *have to* or *must* for strong recommendations.

> 🔍 **have to or must?**
> *Have to* and *must* have a very similar meaning, and you can usually use either form.
> *Have to* is more common for general, external obligations, for example rules and laws.
> *Must* is more common for specific (i.e. on one occasion) or personal obligations. Compare:
> *I have to wear a shirt and tie at work.* (= It's the rule in this company.)
> *I must buy a new shirt – this one is too old now.* (= It's my own decision.)
>
> **have got to**
> *Have got to* is often used instead of *have to* or *must* in spoken English, e.g. *I've got to go now. It's very late.*

don't have to

You **don't have to** pay – this museum is free.   ② 43))
You **don't have to** go to the party if you don't want to.

mustn't

You **mustn't** park here.   ② 44))
You **mustn't** eat that cake – it's for the party.

• We use *don't have to* when there is no obligation to do something, and *mustn't* when something is prohibited.
• *don't have to* and *mustn't* are completely different. Compare:
  You don't have to drive – we can get a train. (= You can drive if you want to, but it's not necessary / obligatory.)
  You mustn't drive along this street. (= It's prohibited, against the law, NOT ~~You don't have to drive along this street.~~)
• You can often use *can't* or *not allowed to* instead of *mustn't*.
  You mustn't | can't | 're not allowed to park here.

should / shouldn't (+ infinitive)

You **should** take warm clothes with you to Dublin.   ② 45))
It might be cold at night.
You **shouldn't** drink so much coffee. It isn't good for you.
I think the government **should** do something about unemployment.

• *should* is not as strong as *must | have to*. We use it to give advice or an opinion – to say if we think something is the right or wrong thing to do.
• *should* is a modal verb. The only forms are *should | shouldn't*.
• You can use *ought to | ought not to* instead of *should | shouldn't*.
  You ought to take warm clothes with you to Dublin.
  You ought not to drink so much coffee.

a Complete with the correct form of *have to* (⊞, ⊟, or ?).

  I'*ll have to* call back later because the line's engaged. ⊞
1 Passengers _____ switch off their laptops during take-off. ⊞
2 _____ you _____ do a lot of homework when you were at school? ?
3 My sister is a nurse, so some weeks she _____ work nights. ⊞
4 _____ you ever _____ have an operation? ?
5 Saturdays are the best day of the week. I love _____ get up early. ⊟
6 I _____ leave a message on her voicemail because she wasn't in. ⊞
7 In the future, people _____ go to school; they'll all study at home. ⊟
8 With old mobile phones, you used to _____ charge the battery more often. ⊞
9 _____ your boyfriend _____ answer his work emails at weekends? ?
10 The exhibition was free, so I _____ pay. ⊟

b (Circle) the correct form. Tick ✓ if both are possible.

  You *don't have to* / (*mustn't*) use your phone in quiet zones.
1 Do you think we *should* / *ought to* text Dad to tell him we'll be late?
2 You *don't have to* / *mustn't* send text messages when you are driving.
3 A pilot *has to* / *must* wear a uniform when he's at work.
4 You *shouldn't* / *mustn't* talk on your mobile when you're filling up with petrol.
5 I *have to* / *must* speak to my phone company. My last bill was wrong.
6 We *don't have to* / *mustn't* hurry. We have plenty of time.

◄ p.39

5A

past tenses

past simple: *worked, stopped, went, had,* etc.

> She **was** born in Berlin. (3) 10))
> They **got** married last year.
> On the way to Rome we **stopped** in Florence for the night.
> The plane **didn't arrive** on time.
> What time **did** you **get up** this morning?

- We use the past simple for finished actions in the past (when we say, ask, or know when they happened).
- Remember **Irregular verbs** *p.165*.

past continuous: *was / were* + verb + *-ing*

> 1 What **were** you **doing** at six o'clock last night? (3) 11))
> 2 I **was driving** along the motorway when it started snowing.
> 3 While I **was doing** the housework the children **were playing** in the garden.
> 4 It was a cold night and it **was raining**. I **was watching** TV in the sitting room...

1 We use the past continuous to talk about an action in progress at a specific time in the past.
2 We often use the past continuous to describe a past action in progress which was interrupted by another action (expressed in the past simple).
3 We often use the past continuous with *while* for two actions happening at the same time.
4 We often use the past continuous to describe the beginning of a story or anecdote.

past perfect: *had* + past participle

> When they turned on the TV, the match **had** already **finished**. (3) 12))
> As soon as I shut the door, I realized that **I'd left** my keys on the table.
> We couldn't get a table in the restaurant because we **hadn't booked**.

- We use the past perfect when we are talking about the past and we want to talk about an earlier past action. Compare:
  When John arrived, they **went out**. (= first John arrived and then they went out)
  When John arrived, they **had gone out**. (= they went out <u>before</u> John arrived)

using narrative tenses together

> It was a cold night and it **was raining**. I was (3) 13))
> **watching** TV in the sitting room. Suddenly I **heard** a knock at the door. I **got up** and **opened** the door. But there was nobody there. The person who **had knocked** on the door **had disappeared**...

- Use the past continuous (*was raining, was watching*) to set the scene.
- Use the past simple (*heard, got up,* etc.) to say what happened.
- Use the past perfect (*had knocked, had disappeared*) to say what happened <u>before</u> the previous past action.

---

a (Circle) the correct form.

> The teacher gave Robbie a zero because he *cheated | had cheated* in the exam.

1 They didn't win the match although they *were training | had trained* every evening.
2 Mike had an accident while he *cycled | was cycling* to work.
3 I *cleaned | had cleaned* the house when I got home. It looked great.
4 When we arrived, the match *started | had started*. We got there just in time and saw the whole match!
5 The captain *didn't score | hadn't scored* any goals when the referee sent him off.
6 My son got injured while he *played | was playing* basketball last Saturday.
7 Luckily, we *stopped | had stopped* skiing when the snowstorm started. We were already back at the hotel.
8 England *weren't losing | hadn't lost* any of their games when they played in the quarter-finals.
9 The referee suspended the match because it *was raining | rained* too hard to play.

b Complete with the past simple, past continuous, or past perfect.

> The marathon runner *was sweating* when she *crossed* the finish line. (sweat, cross)

1 The accident _____ when they _____ home. (happen, drive)
2 The crowd _____ when the referee _____ the final whistle. (cheer, blow)
3 I _____ her at first because she _____ so much. (not recognize, change)
4 The police _____ her on the motorway because she _____ a seat belt. (stop, not wear)
5 Some of the players _____ while the coach _____ to them. (not listen, talk)
6 We _____ use the ski slope because it _____ enough. (not can, not snow)
7 They _____ play tennis because they _____ a court. (not able to, not book)
8 The player _____ a yellow card because he _____ his shirt. (get, take off)

◄ *p.46*

present and past habits and states: *usually* and *used to*

1 I **usually get up** at 8.00 during the week.　　　　　**3 17**))
  I **don't normally go out** during the week.
  English houses **usually have** gardens.
  Do you **normally walk** to work?
2 We **used to go** to France for our holidays when I was a child.
  He **didn't use to do** any exercise, but now he runs marathons.
  I **never used to like** football, but I watch it every week now.
  We **used to be** close friends, but we don't talk to each other any more.
  That building **used to be** a restaurant, but it closed down last year.
  Did they **use to live** in the city centre?
  Didn't you **use to have** long hair?

1 For present habits we can use *usually* or *normally* + present simple.
  NOT ~~I used to get up at 8.00~~.
2 For past habits we use *used to* / *didn't use to* + infinitive.
  • *used to* does not exist in the present tense. NOT ~~I use to get up at 8.00 during the week~~.
  • We use *used to* for things that were true over a period of time in the past. *Used to* often refers to something which is not true now.
    I used to do a lot of sport. (= I did a lot of sport for a period of time in the past, but now I don't.)
  • We often use *never used to* instead of *didn't use to*.
  • *used to* / *didn't use to* can be used with action verbs (e.g. *go, do*) and non-action verbs (e.g. *be, have*).
  • We can also use the past simple to describe past habits (often with an adverb of frequency).
    We (often) went to France for our holidays when I was a child.
    I lived in the city centre until I got married.

🔍 **used to or past simple?**
We can use *used to* or past simple for repeated actions or states, and the meaning is the same.
I used to live in Leeds as a child. / I lived in Leeds as a child.
But if the action happened only once, or we mention exact dates or number of times, we have to use past simple.
I went to Paris last year. NOT ~~I used to go to Paris last year~~.
Jack caught the train to London four times last week. NOT ~~Jack used to catch the train to London four times last week~~.

any more and any longer
We often use *not...any more / any longer* (= not now) with the present simple to contrast with *used to*.
I used to go to the gym, but I don't (go) any more / any longer.

be used to and get used to
Don't confuse *used to / didn't use to (do sth)* with *be used to* or *get used to (doing sth)*.
I am used to getting up early every day. (= I am accustomed to it. I always do it so it is not a problem for me.)
Lola can't get used to living in the UK. (= She can't get accustomed to it. It is a problem for her.)

---

a Complete with *used to* (⊞, ⊟, or ?) and a verb from the list.

argue	be	get on	go out	have	
like	~~live~~	speak	spend	wear	work

Sonya *used to live* in New York City, but later she moved to New Jersey. ⊞

1 We _____ a lot in common, but now we're completely different. ⊞
2 I _____ much time online, but now I'm addicted to *Facebook*. ⊟
3 _____ your fiancé _____ glasses? He looks different now. ?
4 I _____ with my classmates, but now I spend all my time with my boyfriend. ⊞
5 Where _____ your husband _____ before he got the job in the bank? ?
6 My sister has lost a lot of weight. She _____ so slim. ⊟
7 _____ you _____ a lot with your parents when you were a teenager? ?
8 I _____ Japanese food, but now I eat a lot of sushi. ⊟
9 Laura _____ well with her flatmate, but now they've fallen out. ⊞
10 My ex _____ to me, but now he calls me quite often. ⊟

b Are the highlighted verb forms right ✓ or wrong ✗? Correct the wrong ones.

Sonya **use to see** Michael every day. ✗ *used to see*

1 His parents **used to split up** after he was born.
2 Do you **usually tell** a close friend about your problems?
3 My sister **didn't use to want** children, but now she's got four!
4 I **didn't used to like** my maths teacher when I was at school.
5 They **used to go** on holiday every year.
6 That couple have three kids, so they **don't use to go** out at night.
7 Where **did your parents use to meet** when they first went out?
8 My husband **use to work** for a bank, but now he's unemployed.
9 We love the theatre. We **usually go** to a play at least once a month.

◀ *p.49*

6A

the passive: *be* + past participle

1 A lot of films **are shot** on location.   **3 31**)))
  Our car **is being repaired** today.
  Andy's bike **has been stolen**.
  The director died when the film **was being made**.
  You**'ll be picked up** at the airport by one of our staff.
  This bill **has to be paid** tomorrow.
2 *Batman Begins* **was directed by** Christopher Nolan.

A lot of films are shot on location.

1 We often use the passive when it's not said, known, or important who does an action.
Andy's bike has been stolen. (= Somebody has stolen Andy's bike. We don't know who.)

2 If you want to say who did the action, use *by*.
- We can often say things in two ways, in the active or in the passive. Compare:
Batman Begins was directed by Christopher Nolan. (= the focus is more on the film)
Christopher Nolan directed Batman Begins in 2005. (= the focus is more on Nolan)
- We form negatives and questions in the same way as in active sentences.
*Some films **aren't shot** on location.*
*Is your car **being** repaired today?*
- We often use the passive to talk about processes, for example scientific processes, and in formal writing, such as newspaper reports.
*Then the water **is heated** to 100 degrees…*
*Many buildings in the city **have been damaged** by the earthquake.*

---

a (Circle) the correct form, active or passive.

The college *built* | (*was built*) in the 16th century.

1 The costumes for the show *are making* | *are being made* by hand.
2 The landscape *inspired* | *was inspired* him to write a poem.
3 This castle *hasn't inhabited* | *hasn't been inhabited* for nearly a century.
4 The director's last film *set* | *is set* in the present.
5 The film *will shoot* | *will be shot* in the autumn.
6 The actors *aren't recording* | *aren't being recorded* the dialogue until next week.
7 The house *wasn't using* | *wasn't being used* by the owners during the winter.
8 The make-up artist *has transformed* | *has been transformed* the actor into a monster.
9 They *hadn't owned* | *hadn't been owned* the company for very long before they went bankrupt.
10 The photo *took* | *was taken* by my husband on the balcony of our hotel.

b Rewrite the sentences with the passive. Only use *by* if necessary.

People don't use this room very often. *This room isn't used very often.*

1 They subtitle a lot of foreign films.
A lot of foreign films _____ .
2 García Márquez wrote *Love in the Time of Cholera*.
Love in the Time of Cholera _____ .
3 Someone is repairing my laptop.
My laptop _____ .
4 They haven't released the DVD of the film yet.
The DVD of the film _____ .
5 They won't finish the film until the spring.
The film _____ .
6 You have to collect the tickets from the box office.
The tickets _____ .
7 They hadn't told the actor about the changes in the script.
The actor _____ .
8 James Cameron directed *Avatar*.
Avatar _____ .
9 They've already recorded the soundtrack.
The soundtrack _____ .
10 They were interviewing the director about the film.
The director _____ .

◀ *p.55*

6B

modals of deduction: *might, can't, must*

might / may (when you think something is possibly true)

Tony's phone is switched off. He **might** be on the **(3 44))**
plane now, or just boarding.
Laura **might not** like that skirt. It's not really her style.
I don't know where Kate is. She **may** be at work or at the gym.
I'm surprised that Ted isn't here. He **may not** know that the meeting is today.

can't (when you are sure something is impossible / not true)

Nigel **can't** earn much money in his job. He's still **(3 45))**
living with his parents.
That woman **can't** be Jack's wife. Jack's wife has dark hair.

must (when you are sure something is true)

The neighbours **must** be out. There aren't any **(3 46))**
lights on in the house.
Your sister **must** have a lot of money if she drives a Porsche.

- We often use *might | may*, *can't*, or *must* to say how sure or certain we are about something (based on the information we have).
- We don't use *can* instead of *might | may*, NOT ~~He can be on the plane now.~~
- In this context the opposite of *must* is *can't*.
  The neighbours must be out. There aren't any lights on in the house. | The neighbours can't be out. All the lights are on in the house. NOT ~~The neighbours mustn't be out.~~

The neighbours must be out. There aren't any lights on in the house.

The neighbours can't be out. All the lights are on in the house.

- We can use *could* instead of *might* in positive sentences.
  Jack could (or might) be at the party – I'm not sure.
- We often use *be + gerund* after *might | must | can't*.
  They must be having a party – the music is very loud.

---

a Match the sentences.

He might be American. `D`

1 He can't be a university student. ☐
2 He must be cold. ☐
3 He might be going to the gym. ☐
4 He could be lost. ☐
5 He must be married. ☐
6 He must be a tourist. ☐
7 He can't be enjoying the party. ☐
8 He may not have a job. ☐
9 He can't be a businessman. ☐

A He's carrying a sports bag.
B He's carrying a camera and a guide book.
C He's looking at a map.
D ~~He's wearing a baseball cap.~~
E He's looking at job adverts in the newspaper.
F He isn't talking to anybody.
G He isn't wearing a suit.
H He's wearing a wedding ring.
I He's not old enough.
J He isn't wearing a jumper.

b Cover 1–9 and look at A–J. Remember 1–9.

c Complete with *must, might (not)*, or *can't*.

A What does Pete's new girlfriend do?
B I'm not sure, but she <u>might</u> be a model. She's very pretty.

1 **A** Do you know anyone who drives a Ferrari?
  B Yes, my nephew. I don't know his salary, but he _____ earn a fortune!

2 **A** Why don't you buy this dress for your mum?
  B I'm not sure. She _____ like it. It's a bit short for her.

3 **A** My sister works as an interpreter for the EU.
  B She _____ speak a lot of languages to work there.

4 **A** Did you know that Andy's parents have split up?
  B Poor Andy. He _____ feel very happy about that.

5 **A** Are your neighbours away? All the windows are closed.
  B I'm not sure. I suppose they _____ be on holiday.

6 **A** Where's your colleague today?
  B She _____ be ill. She called to say that she's going to the doctor's.

7 **A** Jane is looking at you in a very strange way.
  B Yes. I've grown a beard since I saw her last, so she _____ recognize me.

8 **A** My daughter has failed all her exams again.
  B She _____ be working very hard if she gets such bad grades.

9 **A** Why is Tina so happy?
  B I'm not sure, but she _____ have a new partner.

10 **A** Where's the manager's house?
  B I don't know, but he _____ live near the office because he commutes every day by train.

◀ p.60

7A

first conditional and future time clauses + *when, until,* etc.

first conditional sentences: *if* + present simple, *will / won't* + infinitive

1 If you **work** hard, you**'ll pass** your exams.   4 15))
   The boss **won't be** very pleased if we**'re** late for the meeting.
2 **Come** and see us next week if you **have** time.
3 Alison **won't get** into university unless she **gets** good grades.
   I **won't go** unless you **go** too.

- We use first conditional sentences to talk about a possible future situation and its consequence.
  1 We use the present tense (NOT the future) after *if* in first conditional sentences. NOT ~~If you'll work hard you'll pass all your exams.~~
  2 We can also use an imperative instead of the *will* clause.
  3 We can use *unless* instead of *if…not* in conditional sentences.
     *She won't get into university **unless** she gets good grades | **if** she **doesn't** get good grades.*

future time clauses

As soon as you **get** your exam results,   4 16))
   call me.
We**'ll have** dinner when your father **gets** home.
I **won't go** to bed until you **come** home.
I**'ll have** a quick lunch before I **leave**.
After I **finish** university, I**'ll** probably **take** a year off and travel.

- Use the present tense (NOT the future) after *when, as soon as, until, before,* and *after* to talk about the future.

The boss won't be very pleased if we're late for the meeting.

a Complete with the present simple or future with *will*.

If I fail my exams, I*'ll take* them again next year. (take)

1 That girl _____ into trouble if she doesn't wear her uniform. (get)
2 If you give in your homework late, the teacher _____ it. (not mark)
3 Don't write anything unless you _____ sure of the answer. (be)
4 Gary will be expelled if his behaviour _____. (not improve)
5 They'll be late for school unless they _____. (hurry)
6 Ask me if you _____ what to do. (not know)
7 Johnny will be punished if he _____ at the teacher again. (shout)
8 My sister _____ university this year if she passes all her exams. (finish)
9 I _____ tonight unless I finish my homework quickly. (not go out)
10 Call me if you _____ some help with your project. (need)

b (Circle) the correct word or expression.

I won't go to university (*if*) | *unless* I don't get good results.

1 Don't turn over the exam *after* | *until* the teacher tells you to.
2 Please check the water's not too hot *before* | *after* the kids get in the bath.
3 Your parents will be really happy *when* | *unless* they hear your good news.
4 I'll look for a job in September *before* | *after* I come back from holiday.
5 The schools will close *unless* | *until* it stops snowing soon.
6 The job is very urgent, so please do it *after* | *as soon as* you can.
7 We'll stay in the library *as soon as* | *until* it closes. Then we'll go home.
8 Harry will probably learn to drive *when* | *until* he's 18.
9 You won't be able to speak to the head teacher *unless* | *if* you make an appointment.
10 Give Mummy a kiss *before* | *after* she goes to work.

◀ p.66

second conditional

second conditional sentences: *if* + past simple, *would / wouldn't* + infinitive

1 If I **had** a job, **I'd get** my own flat.
   If David **spoke** good English, he **could get** a job in that new hotel.
   I **would get on** better with my parents if I **didn't live** with them.
   I **wouldn't do** that job unless they **paid me** a really good salary.

2 If your sister **were** here, she**'d know** what to do.
   If it **was** warmer, we **could have** a swim.

3 If I **were** you, **I'd buy** a new computer.

(4 17)))

• We use the second conditional to talk about a hypothetical / imaginary present or future situation and its consequence.
   If I had a job… (= I don't have a job, I'm imagining it.)

1 We use the past simple after *if*, and *would / wouldn't* + infinitive in the other clause.

• We can also use *could* instead of *would* in the other clause.

2 After *if* we can use *was* or *were* with *I*, *he*, and *she*.

3 We often use second conditionals beginning *If I were you, I'd…* to give advice. Here we don't normally use *If I was you…*

🔍 **First or second conditional?**
If I have time, I'll help you. (= this is a real situation, it's possible that I'll have time – first conditional)
If I had time, I'd help you. (= this is a hypothetical / imaginary situation, I don't actually have time – second conditional)

***would / wouldn't* + infinitive**
We also often use *would / wouldn't* + infinitive (without an *if* clause) when we talk about imaginary situations.
*My ideal holiday **would be** a week in the Bahamas.*
***I'd** never **buy** a car as big as yours.*

---

a Write second conditional sentences.

   I (not live) with my parents if I (not have to)
   I wouldn't live with my parents if I didn't have to.

1 Nick (not have to commute) every day if he (work) from home
2 If they (not have) such a noisy dog, they (get on) better with their neighbours
3 I (not buy) that bike if I (be) you – it's too expensive
4 We (sell) our house if somebody (offer) us enough money
5 If my mother-in-law (live) with us, we (get) divorced
6 you (share) a flat with me if I (pay) half the rent?
7 If my sister (tidy) her room more often, it (not be) such a mess
8 You (not treat) me like this if you really (love) me
9 If we (paint) the kitchen white, it (look) bigger
10 you (think) about camping if you (not can afford) to stay in a hotel?

b First or second conditional? Complete with the correct form of the verb.

   I'll stay with my sister if I have to go to London for my job interview. (stay)
   I'd buy my own flat if I *had* enough money. (have)

1 My kids _____ earlier if they didn't go to bed so late. (get up)
2 Where _____ you _____ if you go to university? (live)
3 If you make dinner, I _____ the washing-up. (do)
4 If you _____ your job, what will you do? (lose)
5 We wouldn't have a dog if we _____ a garden. (not have)
6 How will you get to work if you _____ your car? (sell)
7 If we sit in the shade, we _____ sunburnt. (not get)
8 If you could change one thing in your life, what _____ it _____? (be)
9 He won't be able to pay next month's rent if he _____ a job soon. (not find)
10 If she had a job, she _____ so late every night. (not stay up)

◀ *p.68*

8A

reported speech: sentences and questions

reported sentences

direct statements	reported statements	4 33)))
'I like travelling.'	She said (that) she liked travelling.	
'I'm leaving tomorrow.'	He told her (that) he was leaving the next day.	
'I'll always love you.'	He said (that) he would always love me.	
'I passed the exam!'	She told me (that) she had passed the exam.	
'I've forgotten my keys.'	He said (that) he had forgotten his keys.	
'I can't come.'	She said (that) she couldn't come.	
'I may be late.'	He said (that) he might be late.	
'I must go.'	She said (that) she had to go.	

- We use reported speech to report (i.e. to tell another person) what someone said.
- When the reporting verb (*said, told*, etc.) is in the past tense, the tenses in the sentence which is being reported usually change like this:

present > past
will > *would*
past simple / present perfect > past perfect

> ### When tenses don't change
> When you report what someone said very soon after they said it, the tenses often stay the same as in the original sentence.
> **Adam** *'I can't come tonight.'*
> *I've just spoken to Adam and he said that he can't come tonight.*
> **Jack** *'I really enjoyed my trip.'*
> *Jack told me that he really enjoyed his trip.*

- Some modal verbs change, e.g. *can>could, may>might, must>had to*. Other modal verbs stay the same, e.g. *could, might, should*, etc.
- You usually have to change the pronouns, e.g. *'I like jazz.'* Jane said that **she** liked jazz.
- Using **that** after *said* and *told* is optional.

- If you report what someone said on a different day or in a different place, some other time and place words can change, e.g. *tomorrow>the next day, here>there, this>that*, etc.
*'I'll meet you **here tomorrow**.'* He said he'd meet me **there the next day**.

> ### say and tell
> Be careful – after *said* don't use a person or an object pronoun:
> *He said he was tired.* NOT *He said me...*
> After *told* you must use a person or pronoun:
> *Sarah told Cally that she would call her.* NOT *Sarah told that she...*
> *He told me he was tired.* NOT *He told he was...*

reported questions

direct questions	reported questions 4 34)))
'Are you married?'	She asked him if he was married.
'Did she phone?'	He asked me whether she had phoned.
'What's your name?'	I asked him what his name was.
'Where do you live?'	They asked me where I lived.

- When you report a question the tenses change as in reported statements.
- When a question doesn't begin with a question word, add *if* (or *whether*).
'Do you want a drink?' He asked me **if** / **whether** I wanted a drink.
- You also have to change the word order to subject + verb, and not use *do* / *did*.

---

a   Complete the sentences using reported speech.

'I'm in love with another woman.'
My boyfriend told me he was in love with another woman.

1 'I'm selling all my books.' My brother said _____.
2 'I've booked the flights.' Emma told me _____.
3 'Your new dress doesn't suit you.' My mother told me
   _____.
4 'I may not be able to go to the party.' Matt said
   _____.
5 'I won't wear these shoes again.' Jenny said _____.
6 'I didn't buy you a present.' My girlfriend told me
   _____.
7 'I must get a dress for the party.' Rachel said _____.
8 'I haven't been to the gym for a long time.' Kevin said
   _____.
9 'I found a bargain in the sales.' My sister told
   me _____.
10 'I can't find anywhere to park.' Luke told me _____.

b   Complete the sentences using reported speech.

'Why did you dump your girlfriend?' My friend asked
me *why I had dumped my girlfriend*.

1 'When are you leaving?' My parents asked me _____.
2 'Have you ever been engaged?' She asked him _____.
3 'Will you be home early?' Anna asked Liam _____.
4 'Where do you usually buy your clothes?' My sister
   asked me _____.
5 'Did you wear a suit to the job interview?' We asked
   him _____.
6 'Do you ever go to the theatre?' I asked Lisa _____.
7 'What time will you arrive?' He asked us _____.
8 'How much money did you spend in the sales?' I asked
   my girlfriend _____.
9 'Can you help me?' Sally asked the policeman _____.
10 'What size are you?' The shop assistant asked me
   _____.

◀ p.74

8B

gerunds and infinitives

gerund (verb + -ing)

1 I'm not very **good at remembering** names. **(4 46)))**
  Katie's **given up smoking**.
2 **Driving** at night is quite tiring.
  Shopping is my favourite thing to do at weekends.
3 I **hate not being** on time for things.
  I **don't mind getting up** early.

- We use the gerund (verb + -ing)
  1 after prepositions and phrasal verbs.
  2 as the subject of a sentence.
  3 after some verbs, e.g. *hate, spend, don't mind*.
- Common verbs which take the gerund include: **admit**, **avoid**, **deny**, **dislike**, **enjoy**, **feel like**, **finish**, **hate**, **keep**, **like**, **love**, **mind**, **miss**, **practise**, **prefer**, **recommend**, **spend time**, **stop**, **suggest**, and phrasal verbs, e.g. **give up**, **go on**, etc.
- The negative gerund = *not* + verb + -*ing*.

the infinitive with to

1 My flat is very **easy to find**. **(4 47)))**
2 Liam is saving money **to buy** a new car.
3 My sister has never **learned to drive**.   **Try not to make** a noise.

- We use the infinitive + *to*
  1 after adjectives.
  2 to express a reason or purpose.
  3 after some verbs, e.g. *want, need, learn*.
- Common verbs which take the infinitive include: **(can't) afford**, **agree**, **decide**, **expect**, **forget**, **help**, **hope**, **learn**, **need**, **offer**, **plan**, **pretend**, **promise**, **refuse**, **remember**, **seem**, **try**, **want**, **would like**.
- The negative infinitive = *not to* + verb.

GRAMMAR BANK

- More verbs take the infinitive than the gerund.
- These common verbs can take either the infinitive or gerund with no difference in meaning: **start**, **begin**, **continue**, e.g. *It started to rain. It started raining.*

> 🔍 **Verb + person + infinitive with to**
> We also use the infinitive with *to* after some verbs, e.g. *ask, tell, want, would like* + person.
> *Can you ask the manager to come?*
> *She told him not to worry.*
> *I want you to do this now.*
> *We'd really like you to come.*

the infinitive without to

1 I **can't drive**. **(4 48)))**
  We **must hurry**.
2 She always **makes** me **laugh**.
  My parents didn't **let** me **go** out last night.

- We use the infinitive without *to*
  1 after most modal and auxiliary verbs.
  2 after *make* and *let*.

> 🔍 **Verbs that can take a gerund or an infinitive, but the meaning is different**
> ***Try** to be on time.* (= make an effort to be on time)
> ***Try** doing yoga.* (= do it to see if you like it)
> ***Remember** to phone him.* (= don't forget to do it)
> *I **remember** meeting him years ago.* (= I have a memory of it)

---

a Circle the correct form.

  I'm in charge of *recruiting* | *to recruit* new staff.

1 It's important for me *spending* | *to spend* time with my family.
2 *Applying* | *Apply* for a job can be complicated.
3 The manager asked me *not saying* | *not to say* anything about the redundancies.
4 My boss wants me *start* | *to start* work earlier.
5 Be careful *not asking* | *not to ask* her about her boyfriend – they've split up.
6 We carried on *working* | *to work* until we finished.
7 Dave is very good at *solving* | *to solve* logic problems.
8 The best thing about weekends is *not going* | *not to go* to work.
9 Layla gave up *modelling* | *to model* when she had a baby.
10 I went on a training course *to learning* | *to learn* about the new software.

b Complete with a verb from the list in the correct form.

not buy commute do leave lock
not make retire ~~set up~~ wear not worry

  I'd like *to set up* my own company.

1 My parents are planning _____ before they are 65.
2 Rob spends three hours _____ to work and back every day.
3 Mark's wife told him _____ about the problems he had at work.
4 Did you remember _____ the door?
5 In the end I decided _____ the shoes because they were very expensive.
6 The manager lets us _____ early on Fridays.
7 All employees must _____ a jacket and tie at work.
8 Please try _____ any more mistakes in the report.
9 I don't mind _____ overtime during the week.

◀ p.79

9A

third conditional

If I**'d known** about the meeting, I **would have gone**. ((5 3))
If James **hadn't gone** on that training course, he **wouldn't have met** his wife.
You **wouldn't have lost** your job if you **hadn't been** late every day.
Would you **have gone** to the party if you**'d known** Lisa was there?

You wouldn't have lost your job if you hadn't been late every day.

- We normally use third conditional sentences to talk about how things could have been different in the past, i.e. for hypothetical / imaginary situations. Compare:
  Yesterday I got up late and missed my train. (= the real situation)
  If I hadn't got up late yesterday, I wouldn't have missed my train. (= the hypothetical or imaginary past situation)
- To make a third conditional, use *if* + past perfect and *would have* + past participle.
- The contraction of both *had* and *would* is *'d*.
- We can use *might* or *could* instead of *would* to make the result less certain.
  If she'd studied harder, she might have passed the exam.

a Match the phrases.

Billy wouldn't have injured his head	D	A if you'd gone to university?
1 If I'd driven any faster,	☐	B you wouldn't have been so cold.
2 Jon might have got the job	☐	C if I'd asked you?
3 She would have hurt herself badly	☐	D ~~if he had worn his helmet~~.
4 If Katy hadn't gone to the party,	☐	E she wouldn't have met her new boyfriend.
5 What would you have studied	☐	F if he'd been on time for his interview.
6 How would you have got to the airport	☐	G if they had come with us.
7 If you'd worn a warmer coat,	☐	H if she'd fallen down the stairs.
8 Your parents would have enjoyed the trip	☐	I I could have got a speeding fine.
9 Would you have helped me	☐	J if the trains had been on strike?

b Cover A–J. Look at 1–9 and try to remember the end of the sentence.

c Complete the third conditional sentences with the correct form of the verbs.

If Tom *hadn't gone* to university, he *wouldn't have met* Sarah. (not go, not meet)

1 If you _____ me to the airport, I _____ my flight. (not take, miss)
2 We _____ the match if the referee _____ us a penalty. (not win, not give)
3 You _____ the weekend if you _____ with us. (enjoy, come)
4 If I _____ the theatre tickets online, they _____ more expensive. (not buy, be)
5 Mike _____ his wife's birthday if she _____ him. (forget, not remind)
6 If the police _____ five minutes later, they _____ the thief. (arrive, not catch)
7 If you _____ me the money, I _____ to go away for the weekend. (not lend, not be able)
8 You _____ yourself if you _____ off the horse. (hurt, fall)
9 We _____ the hotel if we _____ the signpost. (not find, not seen)
10 If I _____ about the job, I _____ for it. (know, apply)

◀ *p.85*

quantifiers

large quantities

1 My uncle and aunt have **a lot of** money.   5 10))
  Nina has **lots of** clothes.
2 James eats **a lot**.
3 There aren't **many** cafés near here.
  Do you have **many** close friends?
  Do you watch **much** TV?
  I don't eat **much** chocolate.
4 Don't run. We have **plenty of** time.

1 Use *a lot of* or *lots of* in ⊞ sentences.
2 Use *a lot* when there is no noun, e.g. *He talks a lot*. NOT *He talks a lot of*.
3 *much | many* are normally used in ⊟ sentences and ⁇, but *a lot of* can also be used.
4 Use *plenty of* in ⊞ sentences. (= more than enough)

small quantities

1 **A** Do you want some more ice cream?   5 11))
  B Just **a little**.
  The town only has **a few cinemas**.
2 I'm so busy that I have **very little time** for myself.
  Sarah isn't popular and she has **very few friends**.

1 Use *little* + uncountable nouns, *few* + plural countable nouns.
  • *a little* and *a few* = some, but not a lot.
2 *very little* and *very few* = not much | many.

more or less than you need or want

1 I don't like this city. It's **too big** and it's **too noisy**.   5 12))
2 There's **too much traffic** and **too much noise**.
  There are **too many tourists** and **too many cars**.
3 There aren't **enough parks** and there aren't **enough trees**.
  The buses aren't **frequent enough**.
  The buses don't run **frequently enough**.

There's too much traffic and too much noise.

1 Use *too* + adjective.
2 Use *too much* + uncountable nouns and *too many* + plural countable nouns.
3 Use *enough* before a noun, e.g. *enough eggs*, and after an adjective, e.g. *It isn't big enough*, or an adverb, e.g. *You aren't walking fast enough*.

zero quantity

1 There **isn't any** room in the car.   5 13))
  We **don't have any** eggs.
2 There**'s no** room in the car.   We **have no** eggs.
3 **A** How many eggs do we have?
  B **None**. I've used them all.

1 Use *any* (+ noun) for zero quantity with a ⊟ verb.
2 Use *no* + noun with a ⊞ verb.
3 Use *none* (without a noun) in short answers.

---

a Circle the correct answer. Tick ✓ if both are possible.

  My husband has *too much |* (*too many*) electronic gadgets.

1 I just have to reply to *a few | a little* emails and then I've finished.
2 Do you spend *much | many* time on social networking sites?
3 My bedroom is a nice size. There's *enough room | plenty of room* for a desk.
4 I know *very few | very little* people who speak two foreign languages.
5 My brother has downloaded *a lot of | lots of* apps onto his new phone.
6 I have some cash on me, but not *a lot | a lot of*.
7 Their new TV is *too | too much* big. It hardly fits in the living room.
8 *There aren't any | There are no* potatoes. I forgot to buy some.
9 My niece isn't *old enough | enough old* to play with a games console.
10 I don't have *a lot of | many* friends on Facebook.

b Tick ✓ the correct sentences. Correct the mistakes in the **highlighted** phrases.

  My nephew got **lots of video games** for his birthday. ✓
  I don't post **much videos** on Facebook.   *many videos*

1 How many presents did you get? **A lot of**!
2 I buy **very few paper books** now because I have an e-reader.
3 I **don't use no social networks** because I don't like them.
4 Please turn that music down. It's **too much loud**!
5 There aren't **many good programmes** on TV tonight.
6 My internet connection **isn't enough fast** for me to download films.
7 I make **too much phone calls**. My phone bill is enormous!
8 **A** How much fruit do we have?
  B **Any**. Can you buy some?
9 There are only **a little websites** that I use regularly.
10 Karen has **plenty of money**, so she always has the latest gadgets.

◄ *p.88*

10A

relative clauses

defining relative clauses (giving essential information)

1 Julia's the woman **who** / **that** works in the   **5 29**))   office with me.
It's a self-help book **which** / **that** teaches you how to relax.
That's the house **where** I was born.
2 Is Frank the man **whose** brother plays for Manchester United?
It's a plant **whose** leaves change colour in spring.
3 I've just had a text from the girl (**who** / **that**) I met on the flight to Paris.
This is the new phone (**which** / **that**) I bought yesterday.

To give important information about a person, place, or thing use a relative clause (= a relative pronoun + subject) + verb.

1 Use the relative pronoun *who* for people, *which* for things / animals, and *where* for places.
  - You can use *that* instead of *who* or *which*.
  - You cannot omit *who* / *which* / *that* / *where* in this kind of clause. NOT ~~Julia's the woman works in the office with me.~~
2 Use *whose* to mean 'of who' or 'of which'.
3 *who*, *which*, and *that* can be omitted when the verbs in the main clause and the relative clause **have a different subject**, e.g. *She's the girl I met on the plane.*
  - *where* and *whose* can never be omitted, e.g. NOT ~~Is that the woman dog barks?~~

non-defining relative clauses (giving extra non-essential information)

This painting, **which** was painted in 1860, is worth millions   **5 30**))   of pounds.
Last week I visited my aunt, **who's** nearly 90 years old.
Burford, **where** my grandfather was born, is a beautiful little town.
My neighbour, **whose** son goes to my son's school, has just remarried.

- Non-defining relative clauses give extra (often non-essential information) in a sentence. If this clause is omitted, the sentence still makes sense.
  This painting, ~~which was painted in 1860~~, is worth millions of pounds.
- Non-defining relative clauses must go between commas (or a comma and a full stop).
- In these clauses, you <u>can't</u> leave out the relative pronoun (*who*, *which*, etc.)
- In these clauses, you <u>can't</u> use *that* instead of *who* / *which*. NOT ~~This painting, that was painted in 1860, is worth millions of pounds.~~

This painting, which was painted in 1860, is worth millions of pounds.

---

a Complete with *who*, *which*, *where*, or *whose*.

Mountain View is the area <u>where</u> Steve Jobs grew up.

1 Rob and Corinna, _____ have twins, often need a babysitter.
2 Downing Street, _____ the British Prime Minister lives, is in Central London.
3 The sandwich _____ you made me yesterday was delicious.
4 The woman _____ lived here before us was a writer.
5 Stieg Larsson, _____ books form the Millennium Trilogy, died in 2004.
6 My computer is a lot faster than the one _____ you bought.
7 The *Mona Lisa*, _____ has been damaged several times, is now displayed behind bulletproof glass.
8 Look! That's the woman _____ dog bit me last week.
9 On our last holiday we visited Stratford-Upon-Avon, _____ Shakespeare was born.
10 We all went to the match except Marianne, _____ doesn't like football.
11 That man _____ you saw at the party was my boyfriend!
12 That's the park _____ I learnt to ride a bike.

b Look at the sentences in **a**. Tick ✓ the sentences where you could use *that* instead of *who* / *which*. (Circle) the relative pronouns which could be left out.

c Add commas where necessary in the sentences.

Caroline, who lives next door to me, is beautiful.

1 This is the place where John crashed his car.
2 The castle that we visited yesterday was amazing.
3 Beijing which is one of the world's biggest cities hosted the 2008 Olympic Games.
4 Michael Jackson's *Thriller* which was released in 1982 was one of the best-selling albums of the 80s.
5 These are the shoes which I'm wearing to the party tonight.
6 Sally and Joe who got married last year are expecting their first baby.

◀ *p.95*

10B

question tags

question tags

positive verb, negative tag	negative verb, positive tag	(5) 38))
It's cold today, **isn't it?**	She **isn't** here today, **is she?**	
You're Polish, **aren't you?**	You **aren't** angry, **are you?**	
They live in Ankara, **don't they?**	They **don't** smoke, **do they?**	
The match **finishes** at 8.00, **doesn't it?**	Lucy **doesn't** eat meat, **does she?**	
Your sister **worked** in the USA, **didn't she?**	You **didn't** like the film, **did you?**	
We've met before, **haven't we?**	Mike **hasn't** been to Rome before, **has he?**	
You'll be OK, **won't you?**	You **won't** tell anyone, **will you?**	
You'd go on holiday with me, **wouldn't you?**	Sue **wouldn't** quit her job, **would she?**	

It's cold today,
isn't it?

- Question tags (*is he?, aren't they?, do you?, did we?*, etc.) are often used to check something you already think is true.
  Your name's Maria, isn't it?
- To form a question tag use:
  – the correct auxiliary verb, e.g. *do / does, be* for the present, *did* for the past, *will / won't* for the future, etc.
  – a pronoun, e.g. *he, it, they*, etc.
  – a negative auxiliary verb if the sentence is positive, and a positive auxiliary verb if the sentence is negative.

a Match the phrases.

	You know that man,	G	A	didn't you?
1	You're going out with him,	☐	B	will you?
2	You haven't told your family about him,	☐	C	did you?
3	You met him last month,	☐	D	won't you?
4	You were at the same party,	☐	E	have you?
5	You didn't know he was a criminal,	☐	F	weren't you?
6	You aren't happy in the relationship,	☐	G	don't you?
7	You don't want to see him again,	☐	H	are you?
8	You'll tell us the truth,	☐	I	aren't you?
9	You won't tell any lies,	☐	J	don't you?
10	You understand what I'm saying,	☐	K	do you?

b Complete with a question tag (*are you?, isn't it?*, etc.).

Your name's Jack, _isn't it_?

1 Your brother works at the petrol station, _____?

2 They don't have any proof, _____?

3 That man isn't the murderer, _____?

4 You were a witness to the crime, _____?

5 The police have arrested someone, _____?

6 The woman wasn't dead, _____?

7 That girl took your handbag, _____?

8 He won't go to prison, _____?

9 You haven't seen the suspect, _____?

10 They didn't have enough evidence, _____?

◄ p.99

Food and cooking

1 FOOD

a Match the words and pictures.

Fish and seafood

1 crab /kræb/

   mussels /ˈmʌslz/

   prawns /prɔːnz/

   salmon /ˈsæmən/

   squid /skwɪd/

   tuna /ˈtjuːnə/

Meat

   beef /biːf/

   chicken /ˈtʃɪkɪn/

   duck /dʌk/

   lamb /læm/

   pork /pɔːk/

Fruit and vegetables

   aubergine /ˈəʊbəʒiːn/
(*AmE* eggplant)

   beetroot /ˈbiːtruːt/

   cabbage /ˈkæbɪdʒ/

   cherries /ˈtʃeriz/

   courgette /kɔːˈʒet/
(*AmE* zucchini)

   cucumber /ˈkjuːkʌmbə/

   grapes /greɪps/

   green beans /griːn biːnz/

   lemon /ˈlemən/

   mango /ˈmæŋgəʊ/

   melon /ˈmelən/

   peach /piːtʃ/

   pear /peə/

   raspberries /ˈrɑːzbəriz/

   red pepper /red ˈpepə/

b 🔊 **1 2**))) Listen and check.

c Are there any things in the list that you…?

  a love

  b hate

  c have never tried

d Are there any other kinds of fish, meat, or fruit and vegetables that are very common in your country?

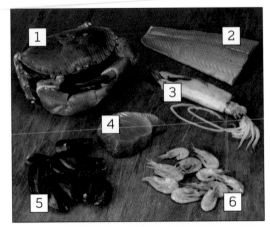

2 COOKING

a Match the words and pictures.

4 boiled /bɔɪld/	grilled /grɪld/
roast /rəʊst/	fried /fraɪd/
baked /beɪkt/	steamed /stiːmd/

b 🔊 **1 3**))) Listen and check.

c How do you prefer these things to be cooked?

eggs	chicken
potatoes	fish

🔍 **Phrasal verbs**

Learn these phrasal verbs connected with food and diet.

*I **eat out** a lot because I often don't have time to cook.*
(= eat in restaurants)

*I'm trying to **cut down on** coffee at the moment. I'm only having one cup at breakfast.* (= have less)

*The doctor told me I had very high cholesterol and that I should completely **cut out** all high-fat cheese and dairy products from my diet.*
(= eliminate)

◀ p.4

Personality

1 WHAT ARE THEY LIKE?

a Complete the definitions with the adjectives.

---
affectionate /əˈfekʃənət/   aggressive /əˈɡresɪv/
ambitious /æmˈbɪʃəs/   anxious /ˈæŋkʃəs/   bossy /ˈbɒsi/
charming /ˈtʃɑːmɪŋ/   competitive /kəmˈpetɪtɪv/
independent /ˌɪndɪˈpendənt/   jealous /ˈdʒeləs/
moody /ˈmuːdi/   rebellious /rɪˈbeliəs/   reliable /rɪˈlaɪəbl/
selfish /ˈselfɪʃ/   sensible /ˈsensəbl/   sensitive /ˈsensətɪv/
sociable /ˈsəʊʃəbl/   spoilt /spɔɪlt/   stubborn /ˈstʌbən/

---

1 _Selfish_ people think about themselves and not about other people.
2 A _____ person always wants to win.
3 _____ children behave badly because they are given everything they want.
4 An _____ person gets angry quickly and likes fighting and arguing.
5 _____ people have an attractive personality and make people like them.
6 A _____ person has common sense and is practical.
7 A _____ person is friendly and enjoys being with other people.
8 _____ people are often worried or stressed.
9 A _____ person is happy one minute and sad the next, and is often bad-tempered.
10 _____ people like doing things on their own, without help.
11 A _____ person likes giving orders to other people.
12 An _____ person shows that they love or like people very much.
13 A _____ person thinks that someone loves another person more than them, or wants what other people have.
14 A _____ person can be easily hurt or offended.
15 An _____ person wants to be successful in life.
16 A _____ person is someone who you can trust or depend on.
17 A _____ person doesn't like obeying rules.
18 A _____ person never changes his (or her) opinion or attitude about something.

b (**1** 23)》 Listen and check.

c Cover the definitions and look at the adjectives. Remember the definitions.

2 OPPOSITES

a Match the adjectives and their opposites.

---
hard-working /hɑːd ˈwɜːkɪŋ/   mean /miːn/
outgoing /aʊtˈɡəʊɪŋ/   self-confident /self ˈkɒnfɪdənt/
stupid /ˈstjuːpɪd/   talkative /ˈtɔːkətɪv/

	Opposite
clever	_____
generous	_____
insecure	_____
lazy	_____
quiet	_____
shy	_____

b (**1** 24)》 Listen and check. Then cover the opposites and test yourself.

c With a partner, look at the adjectives again in **1** and **2**. Do you think they are positive, negative, or neutral characteristics?

3 NEGATIVE PREFIXES

a Which prefix do you use with these adjectives? Put them in the correct column.

---
ambitious   friendly   honest   imaginative
kind   mature   organized   patient   reliable
responsible   selfish   sensitive   sociable   tidy

---

un- / dis-	im- / ir- / in-
unambitious	

b (**1** 25)》 Listen and check. Which of the new adjectives has a positive meaning?

c Cover the columns. Test yourself.

🔍 **False friends**

Some words in English are very similar to words in other languages, but have different meanings.

Sensible looks very similar to *sensible* in Spanish and French, but in fact in English it means someone who has common sense and is practical. The Spanish / French word *sensible* translates as **sensitive** in English (to describe a person who is easily hurt).

Sympathetic does not mean the same as *sympatyczny* in Polish or *sempatik* in Turkish (which mean **nice, friendly**). In English, **sympathetic** means a person who understands other people's feelings, e.g. *My best friend was very sympathetic when I failed my exam last week.*

◀ *p.11*

Money

1 VERBS

a Complete the sentences with a verb from the list.

be worth /bi wɜːθ/   borrow /ˈbɒrəʊ/   can't afford /kɑːnt əˈfɔːd/   charge /tʃɑːdʒ/   cost /kɒst/   earn /ɜːn/
inherit /ɪnˈherɪt/   invest /ɪnˈvest/   lend /lend/   owe /əʊ/   raise /reɪz/   save /seɪv/   waste /weɪst/

1	My uncle is going to leave me £2,000.	I'm going to _inherit_ £2,000.
2	I put some money aside every week for a holiday.	I _____ money every week.
3	My brother has promised to give me €50 until next week.	He has promised to _____ me €50.
4	I need to ask my mum to give me £20 until Friday.	I need to _____ £20 from my mum.
5	I often spend money on stupid things.	I often _____ money.
6	I don't have enough money to buy that car.	I _____ to buy that car.
7	I usually have to pay the mechanic £100 to service my car.	The mechanic _____ me £100.
8	These shoes are quite expensive. They are $200.	They _____ $200.
9	Jim gave me £100. I haven't paid it back yet.	I _____ Jim £100.
10	I want to put money in a bank account. They'll give me 5% interest.	I want to _____ some money.
11	I work in a supermarket. They pay me £1,000 a month.	I _____ £1,000 a month.
12	I could sell my house for about €200,000.	My house _____ about €200,000.
13	We need to get people to give money to build a new hospital.	We want to _____ money for the new hospital.

b ▶ 1 35))) Listen and check. Cover the sentences on the right. Try to remember them.

2 PREPOSITIONS

a Complete the **Preposition** column with a word from the list.

back   by   for (x2)   from   in (x2)   into   on   to

		Preposition
1	Would you like to pay ☐ cash or ☐ credit card?	in, by
2	I paid ☐ the dinner last night. It was my birthday.	
3	I spent £50 ☐ books yesterday.	
4	My uncle invested all his money ☐ property.	
5	I don't like lending money ☐ friends.	
6	I borrowed a lot of money ☐ the bank.	
7	They charged us €60 ☐ a bottle of wine.	
8	I can only lend you the money if you pay me ☐ next week.	
9	I never get ☐ debt. I hate owing people money.	

b ▶ 1 36))) Listen and check.

c Cover the **Preposition** column. Look at the sentences and remember the prepositions.

3 NOUNS

a Match the nouns and definitions.

bill /bɪl/   cash machine (AmE ATM) /kæʃ məˈʃiːn/
coin /kɔɪn/   loan /ləʊn/   mortgage /ˈmɔːgɪdʒ/
note /nəʊt/   salary /ˈsæləri/   tax /tæks/

1	_note_	a piece of paper money
2	_____	a piece of money made of metal
3	_____	a piece of paper which shows how much money you have to pay for something
4	_____	the money you get for the work you do
5	_____	money that you pay to the government
6	_____	money that somebody (or a bank) lends you
7	_____	money that a bank lends you to buy a house
8	_____	a machine where you can get money

b ▶ 1 37))) Listen and check. Cover the words and look at the definitions. Try to remember the words.

> 🔍 **Phrasal verbs**
>
> I **took out** €200 from a cash machine. (= took from my bank account)
>
> When can you **pay** me **back** the money I lent you? (= return)
>
> I have to **live off** my parents while I'm at university. (= depend on financially)
>
> It's difficult for me and my wife to **live on** only one salary. (= have enough money for basic things you need to live)

◀ p.14

Transport

1 PUBLIC TRANSPORT AND VEHICLES

a Match the words and pictures.

☐ carriage /'kærɪdʒ/
☐ coach /kəʊtʃ/
☐ lorry /'lɒri/ (AmE truck)
☐ motorway /'məʊtəweɪ/
☐ 1 platform /'plætfɔːm/
☐ scooter /'skuːtə/
☐ the underground /'ʌndəgraʊnd/ (AmE subway)
☐ tram /træm/
☐ van /væn/

b 2 2)) Listen and check.

c Cover the words and look at the pictures. Try to remember the words.

2 ON THE ROAD

> 🔍 **Compound nouns**
> Compound nouns are two nouns together where the first noun describes the second, e.g. *a child seat* = a seat for a child, *a bus stop* = a place for buses to stop, etc. In compound nouns the first noun is stressed more strongly than the second. There are many compound nouns related to road travel.

a Complete the compound nouns.

belt /belt/   camera /'kæmərə/   ~~crash~~ /kræʃ/   crossing /'krɒsɪŋ/   fine /faɪn/
hour /'aʊə/   jam /dʒæm/   lane /leɪn/   lights /laɪts/   limit /'lɪmɪt/   rank /ræŋk/
station /'steɪʃn/   works /wɜːks/   zone /zəʊn/

1 car *crash*   2 cycle _____   3 parking _____

4 pedestrian _____   5 petrol _____   6 road _____

7 rush _____   8 seat _____   9 speed _____   10 speed _____

11 taxi _____   12 traffic _____   13 traffic _____   14 zebra _____

b 2 3)) Listen and check. Then cover the compound nouns and look at the pictures. Remember the compound nouns.

3 HOW LONG DOES IT TAKE?

> 🔍 **How long does it take?**
> It **takes** about an hour to get from London to Oxford by train.
> It **took (me)** more than an hour to get to work yesterday.
> **How long does it take (you)** to get to school?
> Use *take* (+ person) + time (+ *to get to*) to talk about the duration of a journey, etc.

Read the information box above. Then ask and answer with a partner.

1 How do you get to work / school? How long does it take?

2 How long does it take to get from your house to the town centre?

> 🔍 **Phrasal verbs**
> **Learn these phrasal verbs connected with transport and travel.**
> We **set off** at 7.00 in the morning to try to avoid the traffic. (= leave on a journey)
> I arrive at 8.15. Do you think you could **pick** me **up** at the station? (= collect sb, in a car, etc.)
> I got on the wrong bus, and I **ended up** on the opposite side of town. (= find yourself in a place / situation that you did not expect)
> We're **running out of** petrol. Let's stop at the next petrol station. (= finish your supply of sth)
> **Watch out! / Look out!** You're going to crash! (= be careful or pay attention to sth dangerous)

◀ *p.24*

Dependent prepositions

1 AFTER VERBS

a Complete the **Preposition** column with a word from the list.

about   at   between   for   in   of   on   to   with

He apologized to the policeman for driving fast.

b ② **25** ⟩⟩ Listen and check.

c Cover the **Preposition** column. Say the sentences with the correct preposition.

	Preposition
1 He apologized ___ the policeman ___ driving fast.	_to_ , _for_
2 We're arriving ___ Milan on Sunday.	_____
3 We're arriving ___ Malpensa airport at 3.45.	_____
4 Who does this book belong ___ ?	_____
5 I never argue ___ my husband ___ money.	_____ , _____
6 Could you ask the waiter ___ the bill?	_____
7 Do you believe ___ ghosts?	_____
8 I can't choose ___ these two bags.	_____
9 We might go out. It depends ___ the weather.	_____
10 I dreamt ___ my childhood last night.	_____
11 Don't laugh ___ me! I'm doing my best!	_____
12 I'm really looking forward ___ the party.	_____
13 If I pay ___ the meal, can you get the drinks?	_____
14 This music reminds me ___ our honeymoon in Italy.	_____
15 I don't spend a lot of money ___ clothes.	_____

2 AFTER ADJECTIVES

a Complete the **Preposition** column with a word from the list.

about   at   for   from   in   of   on   to   with

My brother is afraid of* bats.

*also scared of and frightened of

b ② **26** ⟩⟩ Listen and check.

c Cover the **Preposition** column. Say the sentences with the correct preposition.

> 🔍 **Gerunds after prepositions**
> Remember that after a preposition we use a verb in the gerund (+ -ing).
> We're really excited **about going** to Brazil.
> I'm tired **of walking**.

◀ p.31

	Preposition
1 My brother is afraid* ___ bats.	_of_
2 She's really angry ___ her boyfriend ___ last night.	_____
3 I've never been good ___ sport.	_____
4 Eat your vegetables. They're good ___ you.	_____
5 I'm very close ___ my elder sister.	_____
6 This exercise isn't very different ___ the last one.	_____ (or _to_)
7 We're really excited ___ going to Brazil.	_____
8 I'm fed up ___ listening to you complaining.	_____
9 Krakow is famous ___ its main square.	_____
10 My sister is very interested ___ astrology.	_____
11 I'm very fond ___ my little nephew. He's adorable.	_____
12 She's very keen ___ cycling. She does about 50 kilometres every weekend.	_____
13 I don't like people who aren't kind ___ animals.	_____
14 She used to be married ___ a pop star.	_____
15 I'm really pleased ___ my new motorbike.	_____
16 My dad was very proud ___ learning to ski.	_____
17 Why are you always rude ___ waiters and shop assistants?	_____
18 Rachel is worried ___ losing her job.	_____
19 I'm tired ___ walking. Let's stop and have a rest.	_____

Sport

1 PEOPLE AND PLACES

a Match the words and pictures.

☐ captain /ˈkæptɪn/	☐ spectators /spekˈteɪtəz/ /
☐ coach /kəʊtʃ/	☐ the crowd /kraʊd/
1 fans /fænz/	☐ team /tiːm/
☐ players /ˈpleɪəz/	☐ stadium /ˈsteɪdiəm/
☐ referee /refəˈriː/ /	☐ sports hall /spɔːts hɔːl/ /
☐ umpire /ˈʌmpaɪə/	☐ arena /əˈriːnə/

b ③2)) Listen and check. Cover the words and look at the pictures. Test yourself.

c Match the places and sports.

circuit /ˈsɜːkɪt/   course /kɔːs/   ~~court~~ /kɔːt/   pitch /pɪtʃ/
pool /puːl/   slope /sləʊp/   track /træk/

1 tennis / basketball _court_
2 football / rugby / hockey _____
3 swimming / diving _____
4 athletics _____
5 Formula 1 / motorcycling _____
6 golf _____
7 ski _____

d ③3)) Listen and check. Then test a partner.

A (book open) say a sport, e.g. *tennis*.
B (book closed) say where you do it, e.g. *tennis court*.

2 VERBS

> 🔍 **win and beat**
> You *win* a match, competition, medal, or trophy.
> You *beat* another team or person NOT ~~Milan won Chelsea.~~

a Complete with the past tense and past participles.

beat	_beat_	_____
win	_____	_____
lose	_____	_____
draw	_____	_____

b Complete the **Verb** column with the past tense of a verb from **a**.

	Verb
1 Milan ☐ Chelsea 3–0.	_____
2 Milan ☐ the match 3–0.	_____
3 The Chicago Bulls ☐ 78–91 to the Boston Celtics.	_____
4 Spain ☐ with Brazil 2–2.	_____

c ③4)) Listen and check **a** and **b**.

d Complete the **Verb** column with a verb from the list.

do   get fit   get injured   go   kick   score   throw   ~~train~~

	Verb
1 Professional sportspeople have to ☐ every day.	_train_
2 Don't play tennis on a wet court. You might ☐.	_____
3 A footballer has to try to ☐ the ball into the goal.	_____
4 I've started going to the gym because I want to ☐.	_____
5 Our new striker is going to ☐ a lot of goals.	_____
6 Would you like to ☐ swimming this afternoon?	_____
7 My brothers ☐ yoga and tai-chi.	_____
8 In basketball, players ☐ the ball to each other.	_____

e ③5)) Listen and check. Cover the **Verb** columns in **b** and **d**. Test yourself.

> 🔍 **Phrasal verbs**
> It's important to **warm up** before you do any vigorous exercise. (= do light exercise to get ready, e.g. for a match)
> My daughter **works out** every afternoon. (= does exercise at a gym)
> The player got a red card and was **sent off** after committing a foul. (= told to leave the pitch / court, etc.)
> My team was **knocked out** in the semi-finals. (= eliminated)

◀ p.44

Relationships

1 PEOPLE

a Match the words and definitions.

classmate /ˈklɑːsmeɪt/
close friend /kləʊs frend/
colleague /ˈkɒliːg/ ~~couple~~ /ˈkʌpl/
ex /eks/   fiancé /fiˈɒnseɪ/ (*female* fiancée)
flatmate /ˈflætmeɪt/   partner /ˈpɑːtnə/

1	*couple*	two people who are married or in a romantic relationship
2	_____	your husband, wife, boyfriend, or girlfriend
3	_____	the person that you are engaged to be married to
4	_____	a person that you share a flat with
5	_____	a person that you work with
6	_____	(*colloquial*) a person that you used to have a relationship with
7	_____	a very good friend that you can talk to about anything
8	_____	a friend from school or college

b (3 19)) Listen and check. Cover the definitions and look at the words. Remember the definitions.

2 VERBS AND VERB PHRASES

a Complete the sentences with a verb or verb phrase in the past tense.

be together	become friends	break up	get in touch	get married	get on
get to know	go out together	have (sth) in common	lose touch	~~meet~~	propose

1 I *met* _____ Mark when I was studying at York University.
2 We _____ each other quickly because we went to the same classes.
3 We soon _____, and we discovered that we _____ a lot _____. For example, we both liked art and music.
4 We _____ in our second term and we fell in love.
5 We _____ for two years, but we argued a lot and in our last term at university we _____.
6 After we left university, we _____ because I moved to London and he stayed in York.
7 Five years later we _____ again on *Facebook*. We were both still single, and Mark had moved to London too.
8 This time we _____ better than before, maybe because we were older.
9 After two months Mark _____ and I accepted.
10 We _____ last summer. A lot of our old university friends came to the wedding!

b (3 20)) Listen and check.

c Look at the pictures. Try to remember the story.

> 🔍 **Colloquial language**
> I went out last night with some **mates**. (= friends)
> I really **fancy** a girl I met in class last week. (= I'm attracted to her)
> Jane **dumped** her boyfriend last night! (= told him that their relationship was over)
> My younger sister **has a crush on** Justin Bieber! (= be madly in love with when you are young)
>
> **Phrasal verbs**
> My sister and her boyfriend **broke up / split up** last month. (= ended their relationship)
> My daughter has **fallen out with** her best friend. They aren't speaking to each other at the moment. (= had an argument with and stopped being friends)

◀ *p.50*

Cinema

1 KINDS OF FILM

a Match the photos with the kinds of films.

	an <u>ac</u>tion film /'ækʃn fɪlm/
	an ani<u>ma</u>tion /ænɪ'meɪʃn/
	a <u>co</u>medy /'kɒmədi/
1	a <u>dra</u>ma /'drɑːmə/
	a his<u>to</u>rical film /hɪ'stɒrɪkl fɪlm/
	a <u>ho</u>rror film /'hɒrə fɪlm/
	a <u>mu</u>sical /'mjuːzɪkl/
	a <u>rom</u>-com /'rɒm kɒm/
	a science <u>fic</u>tion film /'saɪəns 'fɪkʃn fɪlm/
	a <u>thri</u>ller /'θrɪlə/
	a war film /wɔː fɪlm/
	a <u>wes</u>tern /'westən/

b (3 33)) Listen and check.

c Think of a famous film for each kind.

d What kind of film is often…?

<u>fu</u>nny   <u>vio</u>lent   ex<u>ci</u>ting   <u>sca</u>ry   <u>mo</u>ving

e What kind of films do you / don't you like? Why?

> 🔍 **film and movie**
> Film and movie mean the same, but movie is more common in American English.

2 PEOPLE AND THINGS

a Match the nouns and definitions.

<u>au</u>dience /'ɔːdiəns/   ~~cast~~ /kɑːst/   <u>ex</u>tra /'ekstrə/   plot /plɒt/
re<u>view</u> /rɪ'vjuː/   scene /siːn/   script /skrɪpt/   <u>se</u>quel /'siːkwəl/
<u>sound</u>track /'saʊndtræk/   special ef<u>fects</u> /'speʃl ɪ'fekts/
star /stɑː/   <u>sub</u>titles /'sʌbtaɪtlz/

1	_cast_	all the people who act in a film
2	_____	(also *verb*) the most important actor or actress in a film
3	_____	the music of a film
4	_____	the story of a film
5	_____	a part of a film happening in one place
6	_____	the people who watch a film in a cinema
7	_____	a film which continues the story of an earlier film
8	_____	images often created by a computer
9	_____	the words of the film
10	_____	a person in a film who has a small unimportant part, e.g. in a crowd scene
11	_____	the translation of the dialogue into another language
12	_____	an article which gives an opinion on a new film, book, etc.

b (3 34)) Listen and check. Cover the definitions and look at the words. Remember the definitions.

3 VERBS AND PHRASES

a Match sentences 1–6 with sentences A–F.

1 | It **was directed** by Tate Taylor.
2 | It **was dubbed** into other languages.
3 | Viola Davis **played the part of** Aibileen Clark.
4 | The film **is set** in Mississippi in the USA during the 1960s.
5 | It **is based on** the novel of the same name by Kathryn Stockett.
6 | It **was shot (filmed) on location** in Greenwood, Mississippi.

A It was situated in that place at that time.
B He was the director.
C This was her role in the film.
D The voices of foreign actors were used.
E It was an adaptation of the book.
F It was filmed in the real place, not in a studio.

> 🔍 **be on**
> be on = being shown on TV or at the cinema
> What's **on** TV tonight?
> What's **on** at the cinema at the moment?

b (3 35)) Listen and check. Cover 1–6 and look at A–F. Remember 1–6.

◄ p.56

The body

1 PARTS OF THE BODY

a Match the words and pictures.

- arms /ɑːmz/
- back /bæk/
- ears /ɪəz/
- eyes /aɪz/
- face /feɪs/
- feet /fiːt/ (*singular* foot /fʊt/)
- <u>fingers</u> /ˈfɪŋɡəz/
- hands /hændz/
- head /hed/
- knees /niːz/
- legs /leɡz/
- lips /lɪps/
- *1* mouth /maʊθ/
- neck /nek/
- nose /nəʊz/
- <u>shoulders</u> /ˈʃəʊldəz/
- <u>stomach</u> /ˈstʌmək/
- teeth /tiːθ/ (*singular* tooth /tuːθ/)
- toes /təʊz/
- tongue /tʌŋ/

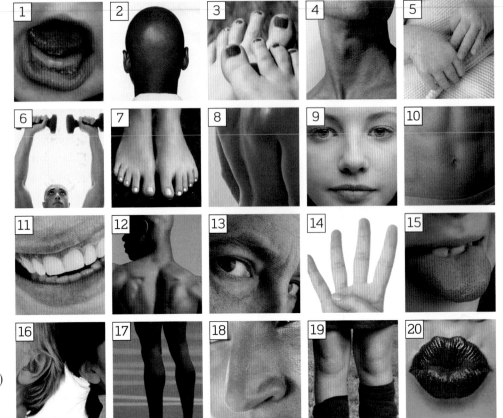

b (3 39)) Listen and check.

c Cover the words and test yourself or a partner. Point to a part of the body for your partner to say the word.

> 🔍 **Possessive pronouns with parts of the body**
> In English we use possessive pronouns (*my, your,* etc.) with parts of the body, not *the*.
> *Give me **your** hand.* NOT ~~*Give me the hand.*~~

2 VERBS RELATED TO THE BODY

a Complete the sentences with a verb from the list in the correct tense. Which three verbs are irregular in the past tense?

~~bite~~ /baɪt/   clap /klæp/   kick /kɪk/   nod /nɒd/
point /pɔɪnt/   smell /smel/   smile /smaɪl/
stare /steə/   taste /teɪst/   throw /θrəʊ/
touch /tʌtʃ/   <u>whistle</u> /ˈwɪsl/
---

b (3 40)) Listen and check. Which parts of the body do you use to do all these things?

◀ *p.59*

1 Don't be frightened of the dog. He won't _bite_ .
2 Jason _____ the ball too hard and it went over the wall into the next garden.
3 Don't _____ stones – you might hit somebody.
4 Mmm! Something _____ delicious! Are you making a cake?
5 The stranger _____ at me for a long time, but he didn't say anything.
6 Can you _____ the rice? I'm not sure if it's cooked yet.
7 Some builders _____ when the girl walked past.
8 Don't _____ the oven door! It's really hot.
9 The audience _____ when I finished singing.
10 The teacher suddenly _____ at me and said 'What's the answer?' I hadn't even heard the question!
11 In Russia if you _____ at strangers, people think you're mad!
12 Everybody _____ in agreement when I explained my idea.

Education

1 THE SCHOOL SYSTEM IN THE UK AND THE US

a Complete the text about the UK with words from the list.

> boarding /ˈbɔːdɪŋ/   graduate /ˈgrædʒuət/
> head /hed/   nursery /ˈnɜːsəri/   primary /ˈpraɪməri/
> private /ˈpraɪvɪt/   pupils /ˈpjuːplz/   religious /rɪˈlɪdʒəs/
> secondary /ˈsekəndri/   state /steɪt/   terms /tɜːmz/

b (4 3)) Listen and check.

c Complete the text about the US with words from the list.

> college /ˈkɒlɪdʒ/   elementary /elɪˈmentəri/
> grades /greɪdz/   high /haɪ/   kindergarten /ˈkɪndəgɑːtn/
> semesters /sɪˈmestəz/   twelfth grade /twelfθ greɪd/

d (4 4)) Listen and check.

e Cover both texts. With a partner, try to remember the different types of school (starting from the lowest level) in both countries.

In the UK

Children start ¹*primary* school when they are five. Before that, many children go to ²_____ school, e.g. between the ages of two and four, but this is not compulsory. From 11–18, children go to ³_____ school. The majority of schools in the UK (about 90%) are ⁴_____ schools, which means that they are paid for by the government, and education is free. The other 10% are ⁵_____ schools, where parents have to pay. A few of these are ⁶_____ schools, where children study, eat, and sleep. There are also some ⁷_____ schools, where the teachers may be priests or nuns. Schoolchildren are usually called ⁸_____ (not 'students' which only refers to people who are at university), and the person who is in charge of a school is called the ⁹_____ teacher. The school year is divided into three ¹⁰_____.

If you want to go to university, you have to take exams in your last year, and if your results are good enough, you get a place. A person who has finished university and has a degree is called a ¹¹_____.

In the US

The school system is divided into three levels, ¹*elementary* school, middle school (sometimes called junior high school), and ²_____ school. In almost all schools at these levels, children are divided by age groups into ³_____. The youngest children begin with ⁴_____ (followed by first grade) and continue until ⁵_____, the final year of high school. The school year is divided into two ⁶_____. Higher education is often called ⁷_____ in the US.

2 VERBS

a Complete the texts with a verb from the list.

> be expelled /bi ɪkˈspeld/   behave /bɪˈheɪv/   be punished /bi ˈpʌnɪʃt/
> cheat /tʃiːt/   fail /feɪl/   pass /pɑːs/   revise /rɪˈvaɪz/   take /teɪk/ (or do)

1 Discipline is very strict in our school. If children *behave* badly, for example if they _____ in an exam, they will probably _____, and might even _____.

2 Marc has to _____ an important English exam next week. He hopes he'll _____, but he hasn't had much time to _____, so he's worried that he might _____.

b (4 5)) Listen and check. Cover the texts and look at the pictures. Remember the texts.

> 🔍 **educate or bring up?**
> **educate** = to teach sb at school / university
> *Luke was **educated** at a private school and Manchester University.*
>
> **bring up** = to look after a child and teach him / her how to behave. This is usually done by parents or a family member at home.
> *Lily was **brought** up by her mother in a small village.*
>
> **learn or study?**
> **learn** = to get knowledge or a skill (from sb)
> *I'm **learning** to drive at the moment. How long have you been **learning** Russian?*
>
> **study** = to spend time learning about something
> *Liam is **studying** Economics at university.*

◀ *p.64*

Houses

1 WHERE PEOPLE LIVE

a Complete the **Preposition** column with *in* or *on*.

	Preposition
1 I live ⬜ **the country**, surrounded by fields.	*in*
2 I live ⬜ **the outskirts** of Oxford, about 5 miles from the centre.	
3 I live ⬜ **a village** (a town / a city).	
4 I live in Aldeburgh, a small town ⬜ **the east coast**.	
5 I live ⬜ **the second floor** of a large block of flats.	
6 I live ⬜ Croydon, **a suburb** of London about 10 miles from the city centre.	

🔍 **suburbs or outskirts?**
The *suburbs* is a residential area outside the centre of a large city.
*Croydon is **a suburb of** London.*
The *outskirts* is the area around a city which is the furthest from the centre.
*They live **on the outskirts of** Milan.*

b ④ **19** 》 Listen and check.

c Cover the **Preposition** column. Say the sentences with the correct preposition.

d Describe where you live to your partner.

2 PARTS OF A HOUSE OR BLOCK OF FLATS

a Match the words and pictures.

A flat

⬜ balcony /ˈbælkəni/
⬜ basement /ˈbeɪsmənt/
⬜ entrance /ˈentrəns/
⬜ ground floor /ɡraʊnd flɔː/ (AmE first floor)
1 top floor /tɒp flɔː/

A house

1 chimney /ˈtʃɪmni/
⬜ gate /ɡeɪt/
⬜ path /pɑːθ/
⬜ roof /ruːf/
⬜ steps /steps/
⬜ terrace /ˈterəs/ / patio /ˈpætɪəʊ/
⬜ wall /wɔːl/

b ④ **20** 》 Listen and check. Cover the words and look at the pictures. Test yourself.

3 DESCRIBING A HOUSE OR FLAT

a Match the descriptions and photos.

⬜ I live in a cottage in the country. It's old and made of stone, and the rooms have very low ceilings. There's an open fire in the living room and it's very cosy in the winter.

⬜ I live in a modern flat in the city centre. It's spacious and very light, with wooden floors and big windows.

b ④ **21** 》 Listen and check. Focus on how the highlighted phrases are pronounced.

c Cover the descriptions and look at the photos. Describe the rooms.

🔍 **chimney or fireplace?**
In English *chimney* only refers to the structure on the roof of the house.
Fireplace is the place where you burn wood or coal. For some nationalities *chimney* is a 'false friend'.

roof or ceiling?
Roof is the top part of a house. *Ceiling* is the top part of a room.

◀ p.69

Word building

1 MAKING NOUNS FROM VERBS

a Make nouns from the verbs in the list and write them in the correct column.

achieve /ə'tʃiːv/   agree /ə'griː/   argue /'ɑːgjuː/
attach /ə'tætʃ/   choose /tʃuːz/   compensate /'kɒmpənseɪt/
complain /kəm'pleɪn/   deliver /dɪ'lɪvə/
demonstrate /'demənstreɪt/   explain /ɪk'spleɪn/   lose /luːz/
pay /peɪ/   respond /rɪ'spɒnd/   sell /sel/   succeed /sək'siːd/

1 + ation	2 + ment	3 new word
		choice

b (4 38)》 Listen and check. Underline the stressed syllable in the nouns.

c Test a partner. Then swap roles.

A (book open) say the verb.
B (book closed) say the noun.

d Complete the questions with a noun from **a** in the singular or plural.

1 Have you ever opened an _attachment_ on an email that contained a virus?
2 Do you often have _____ with your family? What about?
3 Do you prefer reading grammar _____ in your own language, or do you think it's better to read them in English?
4 Have you ever made a _____ to a company and got _____?
5 Do you think that there's too much _____ when you're shopping, e.g. for a new phone?
6 Have you ever been on a _____? What were you protesting about?

e (4 39)》 Listen and check. Then ask and answer the questions with partner.

◀ p.77

2 MAKING ADJECTIVES AND ADVERBS

a Look at the adjectives and adverbs that can be made from the noun *luck* in the chart below. Then in pairs complete the chart.

noun	adjectives		adverbs	
	+	–	+	–
luck	lucky	unlucky	luckily	unluckily
fortune	fortunate	unfortunate		
comfort				
patience				
care				

b (5 7)》 Listen and check.

c Complete the sentences with the correct form of the **bold** noun.

1 The beach was beautiful, but _unfortunately_ it rained almost every day.   **fortune**
2 My new shoes are very _____. I wore them for the first time yesterday and they didn't hurt at all.   **comfort**
3 He did the exam quickly and _____, and so he made lots of mistakes.   **care**
4 We were really _____. We missed the flight by just five minutes.   **luck**
5 Jack is a very _____ driver! He can't stand being behind someone who is driving slowly.   **patience**
6 It was a bad accident, but _____ nobody was seriously hurt.   **luck**
7 It was raining, but fans waited _____ in the queue to buy tickets for tomorrow's concert.   **patience**
8 The roads will be very icy tonight, so drive _____.   **care**
9 The temperature dropped to minus 10 degrees, but _____ we were all wearing warm coats and jackets.   **fortune**
10 The bed in the hotel was incredibly _____. I hardly slept at all.   **comfort**

d (5 8)》 Listen and check.

◀ p.87

Work

1 VERB PHRASES

a Complete the verb phrases with a word or phrase from the list.

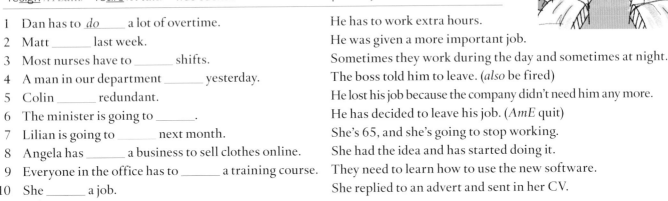

applied for /əˈplaɪd fɔː/   do (x2) /duː/   was made /wəz ˈmeɪd/   got promoted /gɒt prəˈməʊtɪd/
resign /rɪˈzaɪn/   retire /rɪˈtaɪə/   was sacked /wəz sækt/   set up /set ʌp/   work /wɜːk/

1 Dan has to _do_ a lot of overtime.   He has to work extra hours.
2 Matt _____ last week.   He was given a more important job.
3 Most nurses have to _____ shifts.   Sometimes they work during the day and sometimes at night.
4 A man in our department _____ yesterday.   The boss told him to leave. (*also* be fired)
5 Colin _____ redundant.   He lost his job because the company didn't need him any more.
6 The minister is going to _____.   He has decided to leave his job. (*AmE* quit)
7 Lilian is going to _____ next month.   She's 65, and she's going to stop working.
8 Angela has _____ a business to sell clothes online.   She had the idea and has started doing it.
9 Everyone in the office has to _____ a training course.   They need to learn how to use the new software.
10 She _____ a job.   She replied to an advert and sent in her CV.

b (4 42)) Listen and check. Cover the first sentence and look at the second. Can you remember the verb?

2 SAYING WHAT YOU DO

a Match the adjectives and definitions.

part-time /pɑːt ˈtaɪm/   self-employed /self ɪmˈplɔɪd/
temporary /ˈtempərəri/   unemployed /ʌnɪmˈplɔɪd/
well qualified /wel ˈkwɒlɪfaɪd/

for people
1 I'm _____.   without a job
2 He's _____.   working for himself
3 She's _____.   with, e.g. a university degree or with a lot of experience

for a job or work
4 It's a _____ job.   (opposite *permanent*) with only a short contract, e.g. for six months
5 It's a _____ job.   (opposite *full-time*) only working a few hours a day

b Complete the sentences with the correct prepositions.
1 I **work** _in (for)_ a multinational company.
2 I'm _____ **charge** _____ the Marketing Department.
3 I'm **responsible** _____ customer loans.
4 I'm _____ school (university).
5 I'm _____ my third year.

c (4 43)) Listen and check **a** and **b**.

3 WORD BUILDING

a Make nouns from the following verbs by adding -*ment*, -*ion*, or -*ation*, and making any other necessary changes.

1	promote	promotion	4	employ	
2	apply		5	qualify	
3	retire		6	resign	

b Make nouns for the people who do the jobs by adding -*er*, -*or*, -*ian*, or -*ist*, and making any other necessary changes.

1	science		4	pharmacy	
2	law		5	farm	
3	music		6	translate	

c (4 44)) Listen and check **a** and **b**. Underline the stressed syllable in the new words.

d Cover the nouns and look at 1–6 in **a** and **b**. Say the nouns. Think of two more jobs for each ending.

> 🔍 **job** or **work**?
> I'm looking for **work**.   I'm looking for a **job**.
> *Work* is an uncountable noun and has no plural.
> NOT ~~I'm looking for a work.~~
> *Job* is a countable noun.
> *There are several jobs available in this company.*

◀ p.78

Irregular verbs

Infinitive	Past simple	Past participle
be /bi/	was /wɒz/ were /wɜː/	been /biːn/
beat /biːt/	beat	beaten /'biːtn/
become /bɪ'kʌm/	became /bɪ'keɪm/	become
begin /bɪ'gɪn/	began /bɪ'gæn/	begun /bɪ'gʌn/
bite /baɪt/	bit /bɪt/	bitten /'bɪtn/
break /breɪk/	broke /brəʊk/	broken /'brəʊkən/
bring /brɪŋ/	brought /brɔːt/	brought
build /bɪld/	built /bɪlt/	built
buy /baɪ/	bought /bɔːt/	bought
can /kæn/	could /kʊd/	–
catch /kætʃ/	caught /kɔːt/	caught
choose /tʃuːz/	chose /tʃəʊz/	chosen /'tʃəʊzn/
come /kʌm/	came /keɪm/	come
cost /kɒst/	cost	cost
cut /kʌt/	cut	cut
do /duː/	did /dɪd/	done /dʌn/
draw /drɔː/	drew /druː/	drawn /drɔːn/
dream /driːm/	dreamt /dremt/ (dreamed /driːmd/)	dreamt (dreamed)
drink /drɪŋk/	drank /dræŋk/	drunk /drʌŋk/
drive /draɪv/	drove /drəʊv/	driven /'drɪvn/
eat /iːt/	ate /eɪt/	eaten /'iːtn/
fall /fɔːl/	fell /fel/	fallen /'fɔːlən/
feel /fiːl/	felt /felt/	felt
find /faɪnd/	found /faʊnd/	found
fly /flaɪ/	flew /fluː/	flown /fləʊn/
forget /fə'get/	forgot /fə'gɒt/	forgotten /fə'gɒtn/
get /get/	got /gɒt/	got
give /gɪv/	gave /geɪv/	given /'gɪvn/
go /gəʊ/	went /went/	gone /gɒn/
grow /grəʊ/	grew /gruː/	grown /grəʊn/
hang /hæŋ/	hung /hʌŋ/	hung
have /hæv/	had /hæd/	had
hear /hɪə/	heard /hɜːd/	heard
hit /hɪt/	hit	hit
hurt /hɜːt/	hurt	hurt
keep /kiːp/	kept /kept/	kept
know /nəʊ/	knew /njuː/	known /nəʊn/

Infinitive	Past simple	Past participle
learn /lɜːn/	learnt /lɜːnt/	learnt
leave /liːv/	left /left/	left
lend /lend/	lent /lent/	lent
let /let/	let	let
lie /laɪ/	lay /leɪ/	lain /leɪn/
lose /luːz/	lost /lɒst/	lost
make /meɪk/	made /meɪd/	made
mean /miːn/	meant /ment/	meant
meet /miːt/	met /met/	met
pay /peɪ/	paid /peɪd/	paid
put /pʊt/	put	put
read /riːd/	read /red/	read /red/
ride /raɪd/	rode /rəʊd/	ridden /'rɪdn/
ring /rɪŋ/	rang /ræŋ/	rung /rʌŋ/
run /rʌn/	ran /ræn/	run
say /seɪ/	said /sed/	said
see /siː/	saw /sɔː/	seen /siːn/
sell /sel/	sold /səʊld/	sold
send /send/	sent /sent/	sent
set /set/	set	set
shine /ʃaɪn/	shone /ʃɒn/	shone
shut /ʃʌt/	shut	shut
sing /sɪŋ/	sang /sæŋ/	sung /sʌŋ/
sit /sɪt/	sat /sæt/	sat
sleep /sliːp/	slept /slept/	slept
speak /spiːk/	spoke /spəʊk/	spoken /'spəʊkən/
spend /spend/	spent /spent/	spent
stand /stænd/	stood /stʊd/	stood
steal /stiːl/	stole /stəʊl/	stolen /'stəʊlən/
swim /swɪm/	swam /swæm/	swum /swʌm/
take /teɪk/	took /tʊk/	taken /'teɪkən/
teach /tiːtʃ/	taught /tɔːt/	taught
tell /tel/	told /təʊld/	told
think /θɪŋk/	thought /θɔːt/	thought
throw /θrəʊ/	threw /θruː/	thrown /θrəʊn/
understand /ʌndə'stænd/	understood /ʌndə'stʊd/	understood
wake /weɪk/	woke /wəʊk/	woken /'wəʊkən/
wear /weə/	wore /wɔː/	worn /wɔːn/
win /wɪn/	won /wʌn/	won
write /raɪt/	wrote /rəʊt/	written /'rɪtn/

Vowel sounds

	usual spelling	! but also

fish	**i** dish bill
	    pitch fit
	    ticket since
		pretty women
		 busy decided
		 village physics

tree	**ee** beef speed **ea** peach team **e** refund medium	people magazine key niece receipt

cat	**a** mango tram
	    crash tax
	    carry bank	

car	**ar** garden charge
	     starter
	 a pass drama
	    cast
		heart

clock	**o** lorry cost
	    plot bossy
	    off on
		watch want
		 sausage because

horse	**(o)or** score floor **al** bald wall **aw** prawns draw	warm course thought caught audience board
bull	**u** full put **oo** cook foot look good	could should would woman
boot	**oo** moody food **u*** argue rude **ew** few flew	suitcase juice shoe move soup through queue
computer	Many different spellings. /ə/ is always unstressed. <u>o</u>ther <u>ner</u>vous <u>a</u>bout com<u>pl</u>ain infor<u>ma</u>tion <u>ca</u>mera	
bird	**er** term prefer **ir** dirty circuit **ur** nursery turn	learn work world worse journey

egg	**e** lemon lend
	    text spend
	    plenty cent
		friendly already
		 healthy jealous many
		 said

	usual spelling	! but also

up	**u** public subject
	    ugly duck
	    hurry rush
		money tongue
		 someone enough
		 touch couple

train	**a*** save gate **ai** fail train **ay** may say	break steak great weight they grey
phone	**o*** broke stone frozen slope **oa** roast coach	owe elbow although aubergine shoulders
bike	**i*** bite retire **y** shy cycle **igh** flight lights	buy eyes height
owl	**ou** hour mouth proud ground **ow** town brown	
boy	**oi** boiled noisy spoilt coin **oy** enjoy employer	
ear	**eer** beer engineer **ere** here we're **ear** beard appearance	really idea serious
chair	**air** airport upstairs fair hair **are** stare careful	their there wear pear area
tourist	A very unusual sound. euro furious sure plural	
/i/	A sound between /ɪ/ and /iː/. Consonant + *y* at the end of words is pronounced /i/. happy angry thirsty	
/u/	An unusual sound between /ʊ/ and /uː/. education usually situation	

* especially before consonant + *e*

○ short vowels   ◐ **long** vowels   ○ diphthongs

Consonant sounds

		usual spelling	! but also
parrot	**p** / **pp**	plate pupil / transport trip / shopping apply	
bag	**b** / **bb**	beans bill / probably crab / stubborn dubbed	
key	**c** / **k** / **ck**	court script / kind kick / track lucky	chemist's school / stomach squid / account
girl	**g** / **gg**	golf grilled / colleague forget / aggressive luggage	
flower	**f** / **ph** / **ff**	food roof / pharmacy nephew / traffic affectionate	enough laugh
vase	**v**	van vegetables / travel invest / private believe	of
tie	**t** / **tt**	taste tidy / stadium strict / attractive cottage	worked passed
dog	**d** / **dd**	director afford / comedy graduate / address middle	failed bored
snake	**s** / **ss** / **ce/ci**	steps likes / boss assistant / ceiling cinema	science scene / cycle
zebra	**z** / **s**	lazy freezing / nose cosy / loves toes	
shower	**sh** / **ti (+ vowel)** / **ci (+ vowel)**	show dishwasher / selfish cash / ambitious explanation / spacious sociable	sugar sure / machine chef
television	An unusual sound. revision decision confusion usually courgette		

		usual spelling	! but also
thumb	**th**	throw thriller / healthy path / maths teeth	
mother	**th**	the that / with / further together	
chess	**ch** / **tch** / **t (+ure)**	change cheat / pitch match / picture future	
jazz	**j** / **g** / **dge**	jealous just / generous manager / fridge judge	
leg	**l** / **ll**	limit salary / until reliable / sell rebellious	
right	**r** / **rr**	result referee / primary fried / borrow carriage	written wrong
witch	**w** / **wh**	war waste / western motorway / whistle which	one once
yacht	**y** / **before u**	yet year / yoghurt yourself / university argue	
monkey	**m** / **mm**	mean arm / romantic charming / summer swimming	lamb
nose	**n** / **nn**	neck honest / none chimney / tennis thinner	knee knew
singer	**ng** / **before g / k**	cooking going / spring bring / think tongue	
house	**h**	handsome helmet / behave inherit / unhappy perhaps	who whose / whole

◯ voiced   ◯ unvoiced

OXFORD
UNIVERSITY PRESS

Great Clarendon Street, Oxford, OX2 6DP,
United Kingdom

Oxford University Press is a department of the University of
Oxford. It furthers the University's objective of excellence in
research, scholarship, and education by publishing worldwide.
Oxford is a registered trade mark of Oxford University Press in
the UK and in certain other countries

© Oxford University Press 2013

The moral rights of the author have been asserted

First published in 2013

2017 2016 2015

10 9 8 7 6

No unauthorized photocopying

ISBN: 978 0 19 451975 5
ISBN: 978 0 19 452035 5 (with Online Skills)

Printed in China

This book is printed on paper from certified and well-managed
sources.

ACKNOWLEDGEMENTS

The authors would like to thank all the teachers and students round the world whose feedback has helped us to shape English File.

The authors would also like to thank: all those at Oxford University Press (both in Oxford and around the world) and the design team who have contributed their skills and ideas to producing this course.

Finally very special thanks from Clive to Maria Angeles, Lucia, and Eric, and from Christina to Cristina, for all their support and encouragement. Christina would also like to thank her children Joaquin, Marco, and Krysia for their constant inspiration.

The publisher and authors would also like to thank the following for their invaluable feedback on the materials: Uğur Akpur, Robert Anderson, Kinga Belley, Brian Brennan, Isabel Gonzalez Bueno, Rachel Buttery-Graciani, Thelma Eloisa Félix de Oliveira, Maria Antonietta Di Palma, Maria Lorena Urquiza Droffa, Erika Feszl, Banu Ozer Griffin, Gill Hamilton, Maria Belen Saez Hernaez, Jane Hudson, Deborah Keeping, Edit Liegner, Beatriz Martín, Sandy Millin, Magdalena Miszczak-Berbec, Magdalena Muszyńska, María Florencia Nuñez, Mónica Gómez Ruiz, Melis Senol, Rachel Smith, Emilie Řezníčková, Wayne Rimmer, Graham Rumbelow, Joanna Sosnowska, Ágnes Urbán, Pavlina Zoss.

The Publisher and Authors are very grateful to the following who have provided information, personal stories, and/or photographs: Steve Anderson, p.6 (interview and photos); Rena Latham-Koenig, p.9 (photo); Jane Cadwallader, p.18 (interview and photos); Beatriz Martín, Sean Gibson, and Joaquin Cogollos, pp.34-35 (texts and photos); Juan Antonio Fernandez Marin, p.46 (interview); Dagmara Walkowicz, p.57 (interview and photos). The authors would also like to thank Krysia Cogollos for invaluable research assistance, and to all the friends, colleagues, and family who have answered our endless questions.

The authors and publisher are grateful to those who have given permission to reproduce the following extracts and adaptations of copyright material: p.10 Extract from 'He claims we used to play Cowboys and Indians. I recall him trying to suffocate me' by Tim Lott, The Times, 20 November 2010. Reproduced by permission of NI Syndication. p.10 Extract from 'The seven ages of an only child' by Joanna Moorhead, The Guardian, 4 March 2006. Copyright Guardian News & Media Ltd 2006. Reproduced by permission. p.17 Extract from 'The millionaire who couldn't write his name' by Karen Bartlett, The Times, 4 February 2011. Reproduced by permission of NI Syndication. p.20 Extract from 'Blue Peter presenter Helen Skelton begins epic Amazon kayaking adventure' by Cassandra Jardine, Telegraph Online, 23 January 2010. © Telegraph Media Group Limited 2010. Reproduced by permission. p.20 Extract from 'Blue Peter presenter Helen Skelton's Amazon diaries: week one', Telegraph Online, 31 January 2010. © Telegraph Media Group Limited 2010. Reproduced by permission. p.20 Extract from 'Blue Peter presenter Helen Skelton's Amazon diaries: week two', Telegraph Online, 8 February 2010. © Telegraph Media Group Limited 2010. Reproduced by permission. p.28 Extract from 'Gossip with the girls but men only have four subjects' by Peter Markham, The Daily Mail, 18 October 2001. Reproduced by permission of Solo Syndication. p.30 Extract from 'New baby? No problem for Commando Dad' by Neil Sinclair, The Times, 7 May 2012. Reproduced by permission of NI Syndication. p.36 Extract from 'Alex Rawlings most multi-lingual student in UK' by Hannah White-Steele, Cherwell.org, 24 February 2012. Reproduced by permission. p.38 Extract from 'Debrett's guide to mobile phone etiquette', Telegraph Online, 5 August 2011. © Telegraph Media Group Limited 2011. Reproduced by permission. p.40 Extract from 'Mother-in-law from hell sends harsh lesson in manners to 'uncouth' bride-to-be in email that becomes worldwide sensation', The Daily Mail, 29 June 2011. Reproduced by permission of Solo Syndication. p.45 Extract from 'Very superstitions' Andy Murray, Wimbledon and sport stars everywhere' by Matthew Syed, The Times, 1 July 2009. Reproduced by permission of NI Syndication. p.48 Extract from 'Sealed with a kiss and 35¢: how a singer and a toll booth operator set out on the road to love' by Will Pavia, The Times, 14 February 2012. Reproduced by permission of NI Syndication. p.58 Extract from 'What does your profile picture say about you?' by Una Mullally, The Irish Times, 29 October 2011. Article Courtesy of the Irish Times. p.61 Extract from 'Yes, Looks do Matter' by Pam Belluck, The New York Times, 26 April 2009 © 2009 The New York Times. All rights reserved. Used by permission and protected by the Copyright Laws of the United States. The printing, copying, redistribution, or retransmission of this Content without express written permission is prohibited. p.66 Extract from 'The Chinese way of bringing up children' by Alexandra Frean, The Times, 10 January 2011. Reproduced by permission of NI Syndication. p.76 Extract from 'Don't shout. Don't swear. And use pink envelopes drenched in aftershave: How to complain successfully to the King of the complainers' by Julia Lawrence, The Daily Mail, 15 October 2011. Reproduced by permission of Solo Syndication. p.84 Extract from 'A real Good Samaritan' from BBC News at bbc.co.uk/news, 24 December 2010. Reproduced by permission. p.84 Extract from 'Your Good Samaritan stories' from BBC News at bbc.co.uk/news, 7 January 2011. Reproduced by permission. p.23 Extract from 'Not exactly life-changing, is it…' by Matt Rudd, The Sunday Times, 9 October 2011. Reproduced by permission of NI Syndication. p.43 Extract from 'A Maestro Sets the Tone' by David Masello, The New York Times, 18 January 2012 © 2012 The New York Times. All rights reserved. Used by permission and protected by the Copyright Laws of the United States. The printing, copying, redistribution, or retransmission of this Content without express written permission is prohibited. p.83 Extract from 'The Importance of Doing What You Love' by Stephanie Lewis, www.workawesome.com, 31 March 2012. Reproduced by permission. p.103 Extract from 'How Bob Dylan changed my life' by Anonymous, The Times, 24 June 2011. Reproduced by permission of NI Syndication. p..14 "Girls & Boys" Words and Music by Benji Madden and Joel Madden © 2002, Reproduced by permission of EMI Music Publishing Ltd, London W8 5. Source: p.3–4 The Times

The publisher would like to thank the following for their kind permission to reproduce photographs: Adelante Africa pp.18, 19 (logo); Annabel Acton p.74; Alamy Images pp.7 (Garlic prawns/Yiap Creative), 7 (Dish of snails/Miscellaneoustock), 7 (fancy food/Davide Piras), 10 (Girl in school uniform/Loop Images Ltd), 11 (girl in garden/ableimages), 14 (Ferrari/Oleksiy Maksymenko Photography), 15 (1 dollar bill/Steve Stock), 20 (Iguana/Martin Harvey), 21 (Mosquito/Redmond Durrell), 23 (Oxfam shop/Shangara Singh), 24 (Aerial view of Fulham Football Club/Andrew Holt), 24 (Eros Piccadilly/Neil Matthews), 25 (Plane landing/Robert Stainforth), 38 (old telephone/Ninette Maumus), 44 (helmet/Noe Kafer Cutouts), 44 (skateboard/Urban Zone), 44 (baseball mitt/Corbis Flint), 44 (black belt/Richard Watkins), 54 (Highclere Castle/Dov Makabaw), 55 (Staircase, Christ Church College, Oxford/Peter de Clercq), 55 (Christ Church dining room/Ben Nicholson), 58 (man in sea/PhotoAlto), 58 (iPhone/Cyberstock), 63 (King Kong 1933/AF Archive), 66 (Student with A-level results/Mark Bassett), 70 (Pyotr Tchaikovsky museum/RIA Novosti), 70 (Study living room of Tchaikovsky), 70 (Tchaikovsky's desk/RIA Novosti), 74 (Wedding day outfit/Ivor Toms), 80 (Reggae Reggae sauce/whiteboxmedia limited), 83 (Trinity College, Dublin/AA World Travel Library), 86 (Perch/Quagga Media), 86 (White clover/Quagga Media), 87 (Ice hockey team/Stefan Sollfors), 94 (Mac classic computer/Oliver Leedham), 96 (Vintage union jack flag/Sean Gladwell), 97 (Andres Iniesta/ALLSTAR Picture Library), 97 (Ikea entrance/David Pearson), 97 (Toaster/Niall McDiarmid), 97 (Rolex watch/John Henshall), 99 (Prince Albert Victor/Chris Hellier), 103 (Peter Cushing as Sherlock Holmes), 115 (London Underground Station/Alex Segre), 115 (Double decker bus/Steve Vidler), 115 (Cyclist on double white line/format4), 115 (London taxi/David R. Frazier Photolibrary, Inc), 118 (Villa with pool/MARKA), 121 (Winter car breakdown/CandyBox Photography), 121 (Mark Zuckerberg's facebook page/Erkan Mehmet), 152 (Cooking an egg/Gastromedia), 152 (Boiled egg/studiomode), 152 (Steamed sugar snap peas/Food and Drink Photos), 154 (1 euro coin/artpartner-images.com), 154 (Close-up of coin/PjrStudio), 154 (Ten Piece coin/incamerastock), 155 (Train station/David Cole), 155 (Tour bus/Peter Titmuss), 155 (M4 motorway/mkTransport), 155 (Underground station/Greg Balfour Evans), 155 (Post office van at Buckingham Palace/David Gee), 155 (The American Orient Express train/Robert Harding Picture Library Ltd), 155 (DHL lorry/Justin Kase ztwoz), 155 (Couple on motor scooter/imagebroke), 155 (Tram/Alex Segre), 155 (Penalty charge notice on car/DBURKE), 155 (Pedestrian area in inner city/Michael Runkel), 155 (Petrol station/Ian Dagnall), 155 (Gas main repairs/AKP Photos), 155 (Buckling car seat belt/Tetra Images), 155 (Speed camera/AKP Photo), 155 (50mph speed limit sign/Jack Sullivan), 155 (Yellow taxi cabs/Kumar Sriskandan), 155 (Traffic jam/JTB Media Creation, Inc.), 155 (Pedestrian crossing/Oote Boe 2), 157 (Football match/Jonathan Larsen/Diadem Images), 157 (Football referee/imagebroker), 157 (Emirates Stadium/Stadium Bank), 157 (Soccer team/Corbis Super RF), 157 (Brazilian soccer fans/Caro), 157 (The Copper Box arena/Mark Davidson), 160 (back & shoulders/Karen Spencer), 160 (eyes/Silas Manhood), 160 (toddler/PBWPIX), 160 (baby hands/D.Hurst), 160 (hands/Lusoimages), 160 (mature couple/PhotoAlto), 160 (runners legs/Aflo Foto Agency), 161 (Primary school classroom/Keith Morris); BBC pp.20 (Helen Skelton), 21(Helen in Canoe); Corbis p.6 (food market/Alessandro Della Valle/Keystone), 11 (kids/Inti St.Clair, Inc./SuperStock), 21 (Dolphin/Kevin Schafer), 25 (2006 Mercedes-Benz ML500/David Freers/Transtock), 25 (Cyclist in city/Image Source), 25 (Speedboat/Rainbow/amanaimages), 37 (Young woman smiling/Westend61), 37 (Woman wearing knitted hat/Brüderchen & Schwesterchen GmbH), 39 (Man using phone in theatre/John Lund/Paula Zacharias/Blend Images), 69 (Woman wearing headscarf/Tetra Images), 71 (Lily of the Valley/Radius Images), 79 (Taking patient's blood pressure/Ragnar Schmuck), 79 (Drawing a Minnesota Cicada at a Scriptorium/Michael Freeman), 85 (Nara, Japan/Sven Hagolani/fstop), 160 (mans neck/13/Ocean), 160 (tongue/William Radcliffe/Science Faction), 162 (Cozy living room/Brian Harrison/Kudos; Elizabeth Whiting & Associates); Dagmara Walkowicz p.57; Shannon DeCelle p.48 (tool booth); Stephen Lance Dennee p.48 (couple); Getty Images pp.7 (chicken casserole/Iain Bagwell/Photolibrary), 8 (family picnic/Gerard Fritz/Photographer's Choice), 14 (party girl/Luis Alvarez/Stockbyte), 20 (Butterfly/Stockbyte), 20 (California Condor/John Cancalosi), 20 (Butterfly/Nation Wong), 24 (Business people rushing/Maciej Noskowski), 24 (Trafalgar Square/Slow Images), 25 (Richard Hammond/Stuart Wilson), 25 (Commuters on the London Underground/Dan Kitwood), 25 (The Stig/Steve Haag/Gallo Images), 25 (James Clarkson and James May/Mike Flokis), 25 (London Tower Bridge/Medioimages/Photodisc), 29 (rooftop party/Tim Klein/Taxi), 36 (Theatre audience/Michael Cogliantry), 37 (Young woman smiling/Carlo A), 37 (Casually dressed man/Lilly Roadstones), 37 (Young man portrait/Tara Moore), 37 (Smiling woman/Radius Images), 43 (music director Alan Gilbert/Charles Eshelman/FilmMagic), 43 (London bicycle sharing scheme/Peter Macdiarmid), 44 (shuttlecock/Richard Drury/Digital Vision), 44 (rugby ball/Thomas Northcut/Lifesize), 44 (ice hockey stick/David Madison/Photographer's Choice RF), 44 (skates/Kathy Quirk-Syvertsen/Photodisc), 44 (rhythmic gymnastics equipment/Ray Moller/Dorling Kindersley), 44 (table tennis/Sami Sarkis/Photographer's Choice RF), 45 (Serena Williams/Simon Bruty/Sports Illustrated), 45 (Tiger Woods/Jamie Squire), 45 (Fabien Barthez & Laurent Blanc/Patrick Hertzog/AFP), 45 (Arsenal footballer Kolo Toure/Adrian Dennis/AFP), 45 (Lines on tennis court/Marc Debnam), 45 (Alexander Wurz/Rick Dole), 46 (Football referee/Graham Chadwick/Allsport), 46 (Rosie Ruiz/David Madison), 47 (Diego Maradona/Bob Thomas), 54 (Cortlandt Alley/Oleg Korshakov/Flickr), 58 (young girl/Mark Roberts/Flickr), 58 (couple/Guido Mieth/Flickr), 58 (three friends/Paper Boat Creative/Digital Vision), 60 (Mira Sorvino/Suzanne Kreiter/The Boston Globe), 60 (Olga Rutterschmidt/Allen J. Schaben), 61 (Michael Foot/Evening Standard), 61 (Susan Boyle/Charlie Gray/Contour by Getty Images), 63 (theatre/Bob O'Connor/Photonica), 68 (Kitchen/Carolyn Barber), 69 (Man smiling/Tim Kitchen), 69 (Smiling young woman/Echo), 69 (Portrait of man/Burke/Triolo Productions), 69 (Living room/David Papazian), 69 (Kitchen/Kim Sayer), 69 (Bedroom/Ryan McVay), 80 (Levi Roots/Caitlin Mogridge/Redferns), 81 (Mystery box/Jorg Greuel), 84 (Train departing station/Ekaterina Nosenko), 85 (Man repairing bike in field/Smith Collection), 85 (Electricity pylons/Stephen Smith), 86 (The Beatles, 1964/Popperfoto), 86 (Bill Gates, 1986/Joe McNally), 86 (Golf ball on tee/Antar Dayal), 86 (Handshake/Antar Dayal), 94 (Steve Jobs/Diana Walker/SJ/Contour by Getty Images), 94 (Steve Jobs and Steve Wozniak/Tony Avelar/Bloomberg via Getty Images), 94 (Mountain View sign/Visions of America/UIG via Getty Images), 94 (Mona Simpson/Jay L. Clendenin/Los Angeles Times/Contour by Getty Images), 94 (Steve Jobs Apple logo/Laurent Fievet/AFP), 96 (London Eye/Laurie Noble), 97 (Flatiron building/Andrea Sperling), 97 (Stop watch/artpartner-images), 98 (London at sunset/Simone Becchetti), 98 (Man in Dracula costume/Dod Miller), 99 (James Maybrick/Hulton Archive), 99 (Walter Sickert/George C. Beresford/Beresford), 100 (English writer Graham Greene/Popperfoto), 100 (Sony e-reader/David Paul Morris/Bloomberg via Getty Images), 103 (Bob Dylan/Popperfoto), 106 (Tiger Woods/Jonathan Ferrey), 106 (Kolo Toure/Hamish Blair), 106 (Mira Sorvino/Suzanne Kreiter/The Boston Globe), 106 (Olga Rutterschmidt/Allen J. Schaben), 110 (Laurent Blanc and goalkeeper Fabien Barthez/Philippe Huguen/AFP), 110 (Alexander Wurz of Austria poses with his Colour coded slippers/Mark Thompson/Allsport), 113 (Portrait of young woman/Westend61), 114 (Woman hugging children/moodboard), 115 (Regent Street, London/Alan Copson/JAIs), 118 (Modern condo interior/Stuart Dee), 119 (Coffee machine/Creative Crop), 121 (Businessman on mobile phone/Anna Peisl), 152 (Jacket potato/Dave King), 152 (Roast chicken/Jon Whitaker), 152 (Grilled salmon/2011 Annabelle Breakey), 155 (Car crash/Chris Ryan), 155 (Cycle lane/Tom and Steve), 155 (Commuters on London Bridge/Travelpix Ltd), 155 (Traffic lights/Alan Schein), 157 (Coach Slaven Bilic/Dmitry Korotayev/Epsilon), 157 (Tiger Woods/Kevin C. Cox), 157 (Football captain armband/Matthew Ashton/AMA), 157 (Umpire at Wimbledon/VisitBritain/Andrew Orchard), 160 (Man with bare chest/Win Initiative), 160 (lips/Juan Silva/The Image Bank), 160 (feet/altrendo images), 160 (footballers legs/Kris Timken/Digital Vision), 160 (male back/Philipp Nemenz/Lifesize), 160 (toenails/Jenna Woodward Photography/Flickr Open), 161 (Student in school hallway/Will & Deni McIntyre), 162 (Modern living room/Fotosearch), 163 (Protestors/AFP Photo/Bruno Fahy), 163 (Person standing in sea with umbrella/John Short/Design Pics); Kirsty Henshaw p.81 (Freedom Food); iStockphoto p.30 (camouflage/CollinsChin); Kobal Collection pp.56 (War Horse 2011/Dreamworks SKG), 56 (Indiana Jones & the Temple of Doom 1984/Lucasfilm Ltd/Paramount), 56 (ET The Extra-Terrestrial 1982/Universal), 56 (Minority Report 2002/Twentieth Century Fox/Dreamworks), 56 (Catch Me if You Can 2002/Dreamworks/Andrew Cooper), 97 (Vertigo/Paramount/Bass, Saul), 117 (The Godfather/Paramount), 159 (Blood Diamond 2006/Warner Bros./Jaap Buitendijk), 159 (Shrek 2001/Dreamworks LLC), 159 (I/Morgan Creek International/J Farmer), 159 (Birth 2004/New Line/James Bridges), 159 (Elizabeth: The Golden Age 2007/Universal/Studio Canal/Working Title/Laurie Sparham), 159 (Dracula Has Risen From the Grave 1968/Hammer), 159 (The Sound of Music 1965/Twentieth Century Fox), 159 (Star Wars Episode V: The Empire Strikes Back 1980/Lucasfilm/Twentieth Century Fox), 159 (Flightplan 2005/Touchstone), 159 (Apocalypse Now 1979/Zoetrope/United Artists), 159 (Pale Rider 1985/Warner Bros.), 159 (The Proposal 2009/Touchstone Pictures), 159 (The Help.2011/Dreamworks Pictures); Lostandtaken.com pp.14 (Gold texture background), 80 (Black texture background); Nature Picture Library p.21 (Marbled hatchetfish/Reinhard/ARCO); Christina Latham-koenig pp.6 (waiter), 7(mussels), 9(grandmother with child); Rob Law p.80 (Trunki); Tim Lott p.10 (two brothers); Oxford University Press pp.45 (Tennis ball/Photodisc), 79 (Office workers/zefa RF), 79 (Scientist/Deco), 113 (Businesswoman/Blend Images), 160 (close up of face/Masterfile), 160 (woman/BananaStock), 160 (smiling woman/BananaStock); Erin Patrice p.66 (Amy Chua); Jeff Pearce p.17; Piatkus p.11 (Birth Order book cover); Profile Books p.91; Alex Rawlings p.37; Rex Features pp.60 (Dominic McVey), 61 (Susan Boyle/Ken McKay), 80 (Duncan Bannatyne), 80 (Peter Jones/Justin Williams), 80 (Deborah Meaden/Ken McKay), 96 (Underground map/Bournemouth News), 97 (Audrey Hepburn in Breakfast at Tiffany's/Courtesy Everett Collection), 98 (Jack the Ripper letter), 106 (Dominic McVey); Shed-Media p.65; Shutterstock p.80 (Dragon silhouettes/Elena Kazanskaya); Paul Simpson p.80 (coffee table); Solo Syndication p.40 (Heidi Withers) 105 (Heidi Withers wedding); South West News Service p.40 (Carolyn Bourne/James Dadzitis/SWNS.com); Summersdale Publishers p.31; SuperStock pp.8 (couple arguing/PhotoAlto), 14 (celeb/Image Source), 28 (office gossip/Westend61), 160 (weightlifting/Somos), 160 (Bald head/Fancy); Trevor Marriott p.99 (Jack the Ripper photo-fit); Howard Walker p.84 (Bernard hare).

Pronunciation chart artwork by: Ellis Nadler

Commissioned photography by: Gareth Boden pp.26, 27, 30 (two dads in park), 38 (mobile phone) 68, 75 (Macbook pro, Tiffany heart necklace). Ryder Haske: pp.12, 13, 32, 33, 52, 53, 72, 73, 92, 93. MM studios pp.96 (Beatles album, Penguin books), p.152 (meat, fish and vegetable groups).

Illustrations by: Peter Bull: pp.20, 24, 116; Alex Green/Folio Art: p.100/101; Olivier Latyk/Good Illustration Ltd: pp.34, 35, 90, 138, 162; Lyndon Hayes/Dutch Uncle: pp.16, 19, 59, 76, 77; Atsushi Hara/Dutch Uncle: pp.49, 78, 120, 133, 134, 135, 137, 138, 142, 143,144, 145, 148, 149, 150, 151, 156, 158, 161, 164; Sophie Joyce: p.47; Jonathan Krause: p.64; Tim Marrs: pp.50/51, 88/89; Joe McLaren: p.4; Matt Smith: pp.30/31.

Although every effort has been made to trace and contact copyright holders before publication, this has not been possible in some cases. We apologize for any apparent infringement of copyright and if notified, the publisher will be pleased to rectify any errors or omissions at the earliest opportunity.